Apperception and Self-Consciousness in Kant and German Idealism

Also available from Bloomsbury

The Bloomsbury Companion to Kant, ed. Gary Banham,
Dennis Schulting, Nigel Hems
The German Idealism Reader, ed. Marina F. Bykova
The Schelling Reader, ed. Benjamin Berger, Daniel Whistler
Hegel on Possibility, Nahum Brown
Hegel, Logic and Speculation, ed. Paolo Diego Bubbio, Alessandro De Cesaris,
Maurizio Pagano, Hager Weslati

Apperception and Self-Consciousness in Kant and German Idealism

Dennis Schulting

BLOOMSBURY ACADEMIC
LONDON • NEW YORK • OXFORD • NEW DELHI • SYDNEY

BLOOMSBURY ACADEMIC
Bloomsbury Publishing Plc
50 Bedford Square, London, WC1B 3DP, UK
1385 Broadway, New York, NY 10018, USA
29 Earlsfort Terrace, Dublin 2, Ireland

BLOOMSBURY, BLOOMSBURY ACADEMIC and the Diana logo are trademarks
of Bloomsbury Publishing Plc

First published in Great Britain 2021
This paperback edition published in 2022

Copyright © Dennis Schulting, 2021

Dennis Schulting has asserted his right under the Copyright, Designs and
Patents Act, 1988, to be identified as Author of this work.

Cover design by Charlotte Daniels
Cover image: *Titus in a Monk's Habit*, Rembrandt Harmensz. van Rijn, (1660)
reproduced by permission of the Rijksmuseum, Amsterdam

All rights reserved. No part of this publication may be reproduced or transmitted in
any form or by any means, electronic or mechanical, including photocopying,
recording, or any information storage or retrieval system, without prior permission
in writing from the publishers.

Bloomsbury Publishing Plc does not have any control over, or responsibility for, any
third-party websites referred to or in this book. All internet addresses given in
this book were correct at the time of going to press. The author and publisher
regret any inconvenience caused if addresses have changed or sites have
ceased to exist, but can accept no responsibility for any such changes.

A catalogue record for this book is available from the British Library.

Library of Congress Cataloging-in-Publication Data

Names: Schulting, Dennis, author.
Title: Apperception and self-consciousness in Kant and German idealism /
Dennis Schulting.
Description: London ; New York : Bloomsbury Academic, 2021. |
Includes bibliographical references and index.
Identifiers: LCCN 2020023056 (print) | LCCN 2020023057 (ebook) |
ISBN 9781350151390 (hardback) | ISBN 9781350151413 (epub) |
ISBN 9781350151406 (ebook)
Subjects: LCSH: Kant, Immanuel, 1724–1804. | Apperception. | Idealism, German. |
Philosophy, German—18th century.
Classification: LCC B2798 .S326 2021 (print) | LCC B2798 (ebook) | DDC 126.0943—dc23
LC record available at https://lccn.loc.gov/2020023056
LC ebook record available at https://lccn.loc.gov/2020023057

ISBN: HB: 978-1-3501-5139-0
PB: 978-1-3502-1340-1
ePDF: 978-1-3501-5140-6
eBook: 978-1-3501-5141-3

Typeset by RefineCatch Limited, Bungay, Suffolk

To find out more about our authors and books visit www.bloomsbury.com
and sign up for our newsletters.

Per Cristiana, per sempre

Contents

Preface		viii
Key to Abbreviations of Cited Primary Works		x
1	Introduction: Ineliminably Reflexive Human Experience	1
2	The 'Self-Knowledge' of Reason: Kant's Copernican Hypothesis	15
3	'A representation of my representations': Apperception and the Leibnizian-Wolffian Background	47
4	Apperception, Self-Consciousness, and Self-Knowledge in Kant	71
5	Reflexivity, Intentionality, and Animal Perception	93
6	Disciple or Renegade? On Reinhold's Representationalism, the Principle of Consciousness, and the Thing in Itself	115
7	Apperception and Representational Content: Fichte, Hegel, and Pippin	141
8	On the Kinship of Kant's and Hegel's Metaphysical Logics	165
9	Hegel, Transcendental Philosophy, and the Myth of Realism	187
Notes		201
Bibliography		229
Index		237

Preface

In my previous two monographs, *Kant's Deduction From Apperception. An Essay on the Transcendental Deduction* (second edition, De Gruyter, 2018) and *Kant's Radical Subjectivism. Perspectives on the Transcendental Deduction* (Palgrave Macmillan, 2017), I wrote in detail about the arguments Kant puts forward in the Transcendental Deduction of the Categories. In the present book I look more specifically, both systematically and historically, at one central element of Kant's reasoning in the Deduction in particular, and in the *Critique of Pure Reason* in general. This concerns transcendental apperception or transcendental consciousness, and the relation apperception has to self-consciousness more commonly understood. This aspect is a common thread in Kant's philosophy and the thought of his successors in German Idealism; it also links Kant to a neglected aspect of his rationalist predecessors' thought, that of Leibniz and Wolff in particular. Some of the arguments discussed here have been covered, in a different manner, in the two earlier aforementioned books, but there are additional new discussions of especially figures like Reinhold and Fichte as well as Leibniz and Wolff, and more in particular Hegel. The theme of this book is however a unitary one: the centrality of transcendental apperception and self-consciousness both in Kant's philosophy and for the project of German Idealism.

Some of the material presented here is rehearsed from papers published earlier elsewhere. I am grateful to editors for permission to retain copyright for the articles involved. The subject matter in Chapter 2 goes back to an article first published in Dutch, under the title, 'Wat is eigenlijk copernicaans aan Kants copernicaanse revolutie?', in *Algemeen Nederlands Tijdschrift voor Wijsbegeerte* 100(1) (2008): 41–66. An earlier version of Chapter 3 was published under the title 'Transcendental Apperception and Consciousness in Kant's Lectures on Metaphysics' in Robert Clewis (ed.), *Reading Kant's Lectures* (De Gruyter, 2015), pp. 89–113. Material in Chapters 4 and 7 is based on papers that appeared in *The Palgrave Kant Handbook* (Palgrave Macmillan 2017), ch. 7, and the edited volume *Kantian Nonconceptualism* (Palgrave Macmillan 2016), ch. 10, respectively. An earlier version of Chapter 6 was published in *Kant Yearbook* 8 (2016): 87–116.

I am grateful yet again to Christian Onof for his invaluable comments on the penultimate draft of the book. Thanks are also due to Sacha Golob, who critically engaged, with his usual rigour, with my previous book *Kant's Radical Subjectivism*, and to whom I respond in Chapter 5; and to Paul Giladi, who critiqued my earlier reading of Hegel's critique of Kant (see for a response Chapter 9). I further thank Kees Jan Brons, who read an earlier version of Chapter 8. I am certain our approaches have now reached a point of convergence when it comes to understanding Hegel's intimate relation to Kant.

Key to Abbreviations of Cited Primary Works

I. Kant

All English language quotations from Kant's works in this book are from *The Cambridge Edition of the Works of Immanuel Kant*, ed. P. Guyer & A. Wood (Cambridge: Cambridge University Press, 1992ff.), except for the following: The *Prolegomena* is used in the Ellington/Carus edition (see details in the bibliography), but sometimes I make use of the Cambridge translation. Occasionally, I make use of Kemp Smith's translation of the *Critique of Pure Reason* (Bastingstoke: Palgrave Macmillan, 2003 [1929]). Where a translation was not available I provided my own. The following abbreviations are used for Kant's works:

AA	*Kants gesammelte Schriften*, ed. Königlich Preußische (später: Deutsche) Akademie der Wissenschaften (Berlin, 1900–) [=*Akademische Ausgabe*]
A/B	*Critique of Pure Reason*, first (1781) and second (1787) edition (AA 4; AA 3)
Anth	*Anthropology from a Pragmatic Point of View* (AA 7)
Br	*Correspondence* (AA 10–11)
De medicina corporis	*On the Philosophers' Medicine of the Body* (AA 15)
DfS	*The False Subtlety of the Four Syllogistic Figures* (AA 2)
FM	*What Real Progress Has Metaphysics Made in Germany Since the Time of Leibniz and Wolff?* (Prize Essay) (AA 20)
GMS	*Groundwork of the Metaphysics of Morals* (AA 4)
GSE	*Observations of the Feeling of the Beautiful and Sublime* (AA 2)
KpV	*Critique of Practical Reason* (AA 5)
KU	*Critique of the Power of Judgement* (AA 5)
Log	*Jäsche Logic* (AA 9)
MAN	*Metaphysical Foundations of Natural Science* (AA 4)
NG	*Negative Magnitudes* (AA 2)
NTH	*Universal Natural History and Theory of the Heavens* (AA 1)
OP	*Opus postumum* (AA 21–2)

PG	*Physical Geography* (AA 9)
PhilEnz	*Philosophical Encyclopædia* (AA 29)
PND	*Principiorum primorum cognitionis metaphysicae nova dilucidatio* (AA 1) [*A New Elucidation*]
Prol	*Prolegomena to Any Future Metaphysics* (AA 4)
Refl	*Reflexionen* (AA 14–19)
SF	*The Conflict of the Faculties* (AA 7)
TG	*Dreams of a Spirit-Seer* (AA 2)
UD	*Inquiry Concerning the Distinctness of the Principles of Natural Theology and Morality* (AA 2)
ÜE	*On a Discovery Whereby Any New Critique of Pure Reason is to be Made Superfluous by an Older One* (AA 8)
V-Anth/Collins	Collins Anthropology Lectures (AA 25)
V-Anth/Fried	Friedländer Anthropology Lectures (AA 25)
V-Anth/Mron	Mrongovius Anthropology Lectures (AA 25)
V-Anth/Pillau	Pillau Anthropology Lectures (AA 25)
V-Lo/Blomberg	Blomberg Logic Lectures (AA 24)
V-Lo/Dohna	Dohna Logic Lectures (AA 24)
V-Lo/Philippi	Philippi Logic Lectures (AA 24)
V-Lo/Pölitz	Pölitz Logic Lectures (AA 24)
V-Lo/Wiener	Vienna Logic Lectures (AA 24)
V-Met/Dohna	Dohna Metaphysics Lectures (AA 28)
V-Met/Herder	Herder Metaphysics Lectures (AA 28)
V-Met-K2/Heinze	Heinze/Schlapp Metaphysics Lectures (AA 28)
V-Met-L1/Pölitz	Pölitz Metaphysics Lectures I (AA 28)
V-Met-L2/Pölitz	Pölitz Metaphysics Lectures II (AA 28)
V-Met/Mron	Mrongovius Metaphysics Lectures (AA 29)
V-Met/Schön	Von Schön Metaphysics Lectures (AA 28)
V-Met/Vigil	Vigilantius Metaphysics Lectures (AA 29)
V-Met/Volckmann	Volckmann Metaphysics Lectures (AA 28)
VT	*On A Recently Prominent Tone of Superiority in Philosophy* (AA 8)

Other Works

All translations are my own except where indicated between square brackets after the respective edition mentioned here below (see for details the bibliography). In the case of Reinhold's *Versuch*, all translations are equally my own, though I have consulted, and sometimes adopted without comment, the recent translation by Mehigan & Empson (Reinhold 2011). The following abbreviations are used:

R. Descartes

AT   *Œuvres de Descartes*, ed. C. Adam & P. Tannery (Paris: Vrin, 1996)

J.G. Fichte

GA   *Gesamtausgabe der Bayerischen Akademie der Wissenschaften*, volume IV: *Kollegnachschriften 1796–1804*, Bd. 2, ed. R. Lauth & H. Gliwitzky (Stuttgart Bad-Canstatt: Frommann-Holzboog, 1978)

GWL   *Grundlage der gesamten Wissenschaftslehre* (1794), ed. F. Medicus & W. Jacobs (Hamburg: Meiner, 1997)

G.W.F. Hegel

Enz   *Enzyklopädie der philosophischen Wissenschaften* I, in: *Werke*, ed. E. Moldenhauer & K. Michel (Frankfurt a.M.: Suhrkamp, 1986), vol. 8

GuW   *Glauben und Wissen* (GW, vol. 4)

GW   *Gesammelte Werke*, ed. Nordrhein-Westfällische Akademie der Wissenschaften und der Künste (Hamburg: Meiner, 1968–)

W   *Werke*, ed. E. Moldenhauer & K. Michel (Frankfurt a.M.: Suhrkamp, 1986)

WL   *Wissenschaft der Logik. Zweiter Band. Die subjektive Logik* (GW, vol. 12)

G.W. Leibniz

G   *Die philosophische Schriften*, ed. C. I. Gerhardt (Berlin: Weidmann, 1875–90)

New Essays	*New Essays on the Human Understanding,* trans. and ed. J. Bennett & P. Remnant (Cambridge: Cambridge University Press, 1996)

J. Locke

Essay	*An Essay Concerning Human Understanding*, ed. P. Nidditch (Oxford: Clarendon Press, 1975)

K.L. Reinhold

Versuch	*Versuch einer neuen Theorie des menschlichen Vorstellungsvermögens*, 2 vols, ed. E.-O. Onnasch (Hamburg, 2010, 2012)

C. Wolff

PE	*Psychologia empirica* (Frankfurt/Leipzig, 1738)
PR	*Psychologia rationalis* (Frankfurt a.M., 1737)
VG	*Vernünfftige Gedancken von Gott, der Welt und der Seele des Menschen, auch allen Dingen überhaupt* (Frankfurt/Leipzig, 1733)

1

Introduction: Ineliminably Reflexive Human Experience

When I experience a particular object that is in front of me, the screen of the laptop on which I am currently typing these words, say, I can justifiably assert that *I* am the one experiencing the screen, or more precisely, the window in which I type those words. I need not be explicitly aware of my typing words on the keyboard and seeing them appear on the screen—it would be impractical if I were constantly aware of my typing and the letters appearing in the window as I type. But I must at least be able to be explicitly aware of my so typing and seeing the words appear on the screen. That is, I must be able to think of myself as being engaged in the activity of typing and reading. This reminds us of the well-known and oft-cited phrase at the start of the actual argument for the deduction of the categories of experience in the B-Deduction of Kant's *Critique of Pure Reason*, namely that 'the *I think* must *be able* to accompany all my representations' (B131). This phrase has often been misinterpreted as to its scope[1] but what is at any rate clear is that it expresses Kant's principle of transcendental apperception, which basically says that

> all my representations ... must stand under the condition under which alone I can ascribe them to the identical self as *my* representations, and thus can grasp them together, as synthetically combined in an apperception, through the general expression *I think*.
>
> B138

This is a trivially true, 'analytical proposition' (B135): it does not say that I must grasp all representations that are had (those which occur in someone's mind) as *my* representations, but rather it says that I can say of those representations occurring in someone's mind that they are mine only under a certain condition under which these representations share an identical element which makes them mine in the strict sense (of being all together *my* representations). To put this differently, any set of representations that I have, such as a representation of the keyboard of my laptop, a representation of the white window or interface of my word processor, or a representation of the various words that appear in the window as I type, is not just a set of consecutive representations occurring during a specific time interval, but they are representations that I *take* to be mine just in case I apprehend them together to indicate the activity of typewriting that I am undertaking. What is conspicuous about this way of looking at representing is that a kind of self-awareness of one's representing is always in principle involved in the first-order representing that is going on. Note that I say 'in principle'. Representations *need* not be apprehended in such a way that I always apprehend them together by 'ascrib[ing] them to the identical self as *my* representations'; representations could just be varyingly prompted over time without myself noticing that they constitute a unitary representation of 'all *my* representations' together. For example, I could just, while looking up from my screen, find myself staring into the distance, momentarily lost for words; that is, more precisely, I could just *be* staring. In that case, various representational goings-on—catching a glimpse of the clear sky outside, detecting the smell of the coffee I had made earlier etc.—occur in my mind without them having a unitary focal point, that is, without them sharing the mark of an identical self to which I would necessarily ascribe them if they were to have that unitary focal point. This implies that representations being represented would not constitute a necessary unitary representation of 'all my representations' together if I didn't notice it: the noticing and the necessary unity among my representations hang together.

What is important here is to realize that Kant is not making a simple claim as to the fact that all representations necessarily share an identical representing 'I', an identical self, just in virtue of *being* representations. Nor, even, does he claim that, while not all representations need *actually* share the same self, they nonetheless necessarily *entail* sharing the same self; in other words, that representations *could not fail* to be accompanied by a same self at least at some point in time, or that they have a necessary disposition to being accompanied by a same self. The principle of apperception is not a psychological principle that stipulates the necessary conditions under which one can have representations *simpliciter*. The relevance of Kant's point lies rather in the fact that in order to have a unitary representation of some object or objective event, a representation that is *objectively* valid, for it to be something for one, the representations that make up this unitary representation must stand under a condition of them belonging together necessarily, and this condition is precisely the condition of ascribing them to an identical self that takes these representations together.

Kant's argument operates at a very general level, of course, but it is clear that self-consciousness in some form is, at least potentially, involved in our representing of objects. More precisely, whenever we represent something as an object or objective event, self-consciousness is at least involved as an awareness of our so representing. We could call this, in Robert Pippin's words (1997a:39), the 'ineliminably reflexive' aspect of human representing or experience. Every possible instance of human experience of some object or event is accompanied by an element of reflection or self-awareness. The self-awareness here does not concern a specific consciousness of oneself as oneself, a numerically stable self-substance or person, but rather a consciousness of oneself as an agent of doing something, namely thinking or representing something. This reflexive aspect is not entirely unique or original to Kant's thought, since already his predecessors Leibniz and Wolff entertained a view of consciousness as having in some sense to do with the second-order accompanying of one's first-order perceptions of objects. Kant's term for the self-reflexiveness of representing, 'apperception', is also directly inherited from Leibniz, who first coined it (though it appears already in Descartes). But unlike his predecessors, Kant made self-consciousness into the central pillar of his system. It is even present in the very title of his *chef d'œuvre*: the *Critique of Pure Reason*. The genitive in the title can and must be read as a subjective as well as an objective genitive. In the preface to the first edition, Kant also speaks strikingly of the 'self-knowledge' of reason (Axi), by which he means that the critique of dogmatic metaphysics, which is the central project of the *Critique*, is not just an objective account of what is wrong with the metaphysics of his predecessors, including Hume and Locke, but also a subjective reflection on reason itself, a self-reflection *by* reason itself, or a reflection on the origin and bounds of metaphysical claims in reason itself. The critique of metaphysics is thus first and foremost an inner reflection on the question of what reason itself is and, importantly, what it can and cannot accomplish in terms of the acquisition of knowledge.

Self-consciousness thus lies at the centre of Kant's Critical project of examining the objective validity of metaphysical claims to knowledge about the world. The centrality of the self is first presented in the B-preface by means of a thought experiment: Kant asks whether we could not make greater advance in metaphysics just as in science and mathematics if we assumed that rather than our thinking conforming to objects, objects conformed to our mindedness, that is, to the forms of our sensibility and our understanding. Our mindedness, not objects or things, becomes the measure by which the validity of metaphysics is established. The motivation behind this thought experiment is the lack of a pure universal criterion, in metaphysical studies up until Kant's times, in virtue of which the objective validity or truth of metaphysical claims can be assessed. Philosophers have erected whole systems of thought dealing with the conceptual analysis of all kinds of metaphysical issues and beliefs, but they failed first to properly analyse the very capacity to understand by means of which such claims are being made (A65/B90). Only through such an analysis can a pure criterion of understanding be found in virtue of which the validity of metaphysical claims can be appraised.

By instead bringing the capacity to understand itself into the focus of philosophical analysis, Kant moves metaphysics away from a direct preoccupation with the standard metaphysical topics towards a more formal approach. The result of this is an abandonment of a realist ontology, for which the concepts analysed map being itself, in favour of what Kant comes to call transcendental idealism—but in the *Prolegomena*, after being unfavourably compared to Berkeleyan idealism, he prefers to call it a 'formal' idealism (Prol, AA 4:375). Though it is often denied by commentators, there is a direct connection between, on the one hand, Kant's formal concerns with the objective validity of knowledge claims, as a whole and not just those aspects that concern our human sensibility—that is, his *epistemology*—and, on the other hand, his doctrine of idealism, namely the doctrine that the objects of our knowledge are in fact nothing but representations, and not things outside these representations, namely, not things in themselves—that is, his *metaphysics* strictly speaking. *The Copernican hypothesis thus directly entails transcendental idealism.* This is because Kant's Critical theory of knowledge is not a standard theory of knowledge but a theory of knowledge that is as much a metaphysical investigation into the very categories that determine objects *as* objects. Kant aims to show that the categories are constitutive of the very objectivity of objects, but since the categories are in fact nothing but the functions of our representations, more specifically, the functions of our judging, objects are therefore nothing but functions of our judging too, that is, insofar as their objectivity is concerned. These objects Kant calls appearances. Inasmuch as the objects are functions of our judging, the objects of our knowledge or cognition are limited to the appearances of things in themselves. Transcendental idealism is *both* an epistemology and a metaphysics, but at the same time it is not a theory about how things are in themselves, that is, an old-style ontology.

The central theme of this book is the inseparable connection between representation, idealism, objectivity and self-consciousness, whereby the latter, the representing *self*, is the pivot around which everything else turns. This arguably holds even more so for the post-Kantians—but, I argue, this is not despite Kant, but rather because of their Kantian heritage. Apperception, as developed by Kant, fundamentally and centrally informs not just Kant's thought but *mutatis mutandis* also that of his followers Reinhold, Fichte, Schelling, and Hegel. The central thesis of this book is that all of them should be seen as Kantians in the systematic sense of being centred on the principle of transcendental apperception, and that absent an understanding of the centrality of apperception their philosophical systems cannot be really understood.

Karl Leonard Reinhold (1757–1823) argues that what we represent of things is only the representeds as the direct objects of the representing consciousness, literally nothing about how the things are in themselves. Of all the post-Kantians, Reinhold remains closest to the spirit if not the letter of Kant, but unlike Kant he seems to base what in the Kant literature has been called the restriction thesis on a self-standing pure principle of representation. I believe Reinhold is absolutely right to emphasize the representationalism in Kant, but by seemingly basing his system on a self-standing principle of representation, rather than on an analysis of the capacity to understand, as does Kant, Reinhold thus might seem to risk making it impossible to utter true analytic statements about things in themselves such as God and the soul.

At first blush, for Johann Gottlieb Fichte (1762–1814) and G.W.F. Hegel (1770–1831) the idealism becomes much more radical, one that dispenses entirely with the thing in itself. For Fichte and even more for Hegel, the identity that lies in the activity of the judging subject becomes an absolute identity that is no longer constrained by pure forms of sensibility that, in Kant's view, alone gives our concepts real possibility. Transcendental idealism has turned, with Hegel, into an absolute idealism that has no use for independently given intuitions (or things in themselves) as markers of real possibility. The self's knowledge of its own thinking activity is no longer bound by constraints from outside, and maps onto being itself *simpliciter*—there is an identity of sorts between the thinking self and its apperceptive activity, on the one hand, and the world of objects insofar as it can be known, on the other hand; and there is no restriction that says that we can have knowledge of appearances only, but not of things in themselves. This has often been considered a ground for dismissing absolute idealism, for while Kant's restriction thesis modestly refrains from making unwarranted existence claims, absolute idealism apparently makes intemperate metaphysical claims that it cannot prove. But I think (and shall argue in Chapters 7–9) that especially Hegel's conception of absolute idealism is much closer to Kant's formal idealism than most so-called metaphysical interpretations make it out to be. Hegel, in other words, builds on Kant's transcendental turn, rather than turning his back on it by returning in some way to a pre-Critical metaphysics, that is, by advancing an old-style metaphysics or some sort of conceptual realism in pseudo-critical form. My view is closer to Pippin's so-called a-metaphysical or non-metaphysical reading of absolute idealism than to most other current interpretations, which tend to read it in a more ontologically committed way much less beholden to a Kantian, transcendental approach.[2]

First, in Chapter 2, I examine the central element of Kant's metaphysics which he himself highlighted in the already mentioned preface to the second edition of the *Critique*, namely its Copernican nature. The pivotal role of the subject in Kant's thought can be traced back to his so-called Copernican Turn. Kant's analogy with Copernicus's revolution in astronomy is of course often cited and discussed, but it is also often misunderstood. I claim that there are clear systemic parallels between Kant's revolution in metaphysics and the Copernican revolution in astronomy. It is commonly thought that Kant makes the Copernican analogy solely in order to point out the fact as such of a paradigm shift in philosophy. The reference to Copernican is then merely a *façon de parler*, in the sense that one should not read it as if a *systematic* parallel should be drawn between Copernicus's thoughts and Kant's. I argue that this is too historical an interpretation of the analogy. It leaves unexplained both Kant's and Copernicus's *reasons* for advancing their respective hypotheses, which brought about major changes in the conceptual schemes of philosophy and astronomy. My contention is that something much more specific, systematic is at issue, which contrary to the received understanding makes Kant's analogy in fact particularly apt. Understanding the basic facets of the Copernican revolution in general as well as the Copernican 'revolution in the way of thinking', as Kant called it (Bxii), will greatly help grasp the centrality of the subject in Kant's philosophy, and why the subject as agent of thought is an ineliminable, constitutive feature of human cognition. It will also help in comprehending the specific nature of *transcendental* idealism.

In Chapters 3 to 5, I focus on the theme of transcendental apperception in Kant and his predecessors. Although the notion of transcendental apperception as such is original to Kant, the term 'apperception' itself is, as I said earlier, of course owed to Leibniz, and there are parallels especially with Wolff's idea of consciousness of self as derivative of object consciousness, as a kind of reflexive consciousness that accompanies the consciousness of objects.[3] For Wolff a central aspect of consciousness is that it expresses a two-way relation to objects: consciousness is not just consciousness of things but also, *and at the same time*, a consciousness of self. There is thus always a reflexive element involved in the perception of an object, and this element is consciousness or apperception (*apperceptio*), which points to the subject of representation or perception. Apperception is the consciousness of the self's own activity present *in perceiving objects outside of herself*. This idea of apperception is based on Wolff's definition of consciousness as the capacity to distinguish. In being conscious of things, one differentiates things from one another, but also thereby from *oneself* as the agent of differentiation. So the subject is differentiated from objects precisely in her being conscious of those various objects through differentiation.

This fundamental and specifically non-psychological concept of self-consciousness as reflexivity, which has its roots in Wolff, is to become central to Kant's thought and that of the later German Idealists, not least Hegel's. Kant's view of self-consciousness is similar to Wolff's in that the 'derivative' model of consciousness that Wolff adopts (Thiel 2011:308) is *mutatis mutandis* applicable to Kant's view of transcendental consciousness as constitutive of the objective unity of representations as defining an object. While Kant's view is much less overtly characterized in terms of explicit subject–object oppositions, as are later, presumably, Fichte's and Hegel's, transcendental apperception must not be seen as prior to, and somehow independent of, the perception of objects, but—to put it in terms proposed by Pippin (1997a)—as 'adverbial' to it. Transcendental consciousness and consciousness of objects are, in some sense, equiprimordial. As Kant puts it at A108,

> the original and necessary consciousness of the identity of oneself is <u>at the same time</u> a consciousness of an equally necessary unity of the synthesis of all appearances in accordance with concepts ... for the mind could not possibly think of the identity of itself in the manifoldness of its representations, and indeed think this *a priori*, if it did not have before its eyes the identity of its action, which subjects all synthesis of apprehension (which is empirical) to a transcendental unity, and first makes possible their connection in accordance with *a priori* rules.
>
> my underlining

The 'necessary unity of the synthesis of all appearances' is—as explained in this section of the A-Deduction—what first constitutes a possible object of experience. However, this necessary unity is nothing but the necessary unity that results from the act of synthesis of representations that also, simultaneously, first constitutes one's identity as self-consciousness. There is no discrepancy between the application of a priori rules that bring unity to one's representations of an *object* and the a priori rules that unify one's very representations *as one's own*.

They are the same set of rules. Both the representation of an object and self-consciousness rest on the very same act of synthesis, i.e. transcendental apperception. Transcendental apperception could then be said—similarly to Wolff's reflexive understanding of consciousness—to be that which lies at the origin of the differentiation between subject and object,[4] and is, in a sense, 'derivative' of, or adverbial to, the consciousness of objects, since it does not exist other than in the act of synthesis that enables the perception of objects. The equiprimordiality of the synthesis that enables object perception and the consciousness of one's identity *in* this very act explains Kant's phrase 'at the same time' in the above-quoted passage at A108 in the A-Deduction.

In Chapter 3, I first approach apperception historically, through a discussion of its appearance chiefly in the metaphysics lectures that are contemporaneous with the Critical phase of Kant's work. The lectures give a good idea of how apperception is rooted in Kant's reading of the works of his predecessors, chiefly Wolff and Baumgarten. I explore to what extent, and in which context, transcendental apperception and consciousness are featured in the lectures and what changes (or not) in the conception of these notions from the pre-Critical to the Critical phase of Kant's lecturing activity. After introducing the theme of apperception and consciousness in Kant and addressing some terminological issues, I look first at the Leibnizian and Wolffian background of Kant's theory of apperception, and the usage and occurrence of the term 'consciousness' in the lectures notes and in Kant's pre-Critical published work. I also address aspects of Leibniz's theory of obscure representations in order to clarify Kant's differentiation of apperception from mere consciousness. Subsequently, I examine how Kant's conception of 'consciousness' develops from the pre-Critical *Herder* and *Pölitz* metaphysics lectures to the lectures of the Critical period, specifically the *Metaphysik von Schön* and *Metaphysik Mrongovius*, where the notion of 'apperception' first crops up and which show that Kant departs from the Leibnizian-Wolffian conflation of apperception and consciousness, although there appear to remain some carry-overs from the pre-Critical lectures. I then briefly consider a lingering ambiguity about the relation between inner sense and transcendental apperception in the *Mrongovius* notes and conclude that, in line with Leibniz's gradual theory of perceptions and his law of continuity, Kant espouses a gradual theory of consciousness. The central argument of the chapter is that Kant's principle of apperception should not be conflated with a putative principle of consciousness *simpliciter*.

In Chapter 4, in a systematic account of Kant's theory of self-consciousness I concentrate on two connected elements: the transcendental conditions for establishing the identity of self-consciousness, which first enable the awareness thereof, namely self-consciousness strictly speaking, and the relation between self-consciousness and self-knowledge. I contend that two mistaken assumptions underlie the critique of Kant's 'derivative' or so-called 'reflection-theoretical' view of self-consciousness, namely the belief that it does not accommodate a *sui generis* theory of self-consciousness: (1) that the identity of self is somehow a priori given, and presumably any act of transcendental apperception, which is interpreted as an act of reflection, always already presupposes this a priori self-identity, and (2) that the awareness of the identity of self-consciousness *ipso facto* amounts to self-knowledge. Concerning assumption (1), often it is thought that Kant's so-called reflective 'I think', which accompanies my representations, is only secondary to, or derivative[5] of, the transcendental unity of self-consciousness, or indeed, secondary to the identity of self-consciousness.

In Section 4.2, I address some more general, systematic issues, which directly bear on the aforementioned topics. In particular, I address criticisms of putatively Kantian type forms of self-consciousness as grounds of cognitive knowledge ('epistemic consciousness'), which, presumably, lack the means to account for a *sui generis* self-consciousness. The general criticism, which goes back to Fichte, is that if the identity of self is first established in the *reflection on* oneself (a turning back into oneself), then the self-identity and the knowledge thereof is not immediate, but secondary to the reflection. But at the same time, it is argued, the reflection *presupposes* the identity of the self in order to be able to carry out the reflection, for the reflection is of course done by the same person or self whose identity is reflected upon. Such a cognitive model of self-consciousness *ipso facto* cannot attain determination of self-identity per se, or indeed self-consciousness, because it fundamentally misconstrues the nature of self-consciousness or the 'I' as a function of thought or cognition. I point out that Kant's view of transcendental consciousness is not vulnerable to this charge of circularity.

In Section 4.3, I approach assumption (1) from an interpretative point of view, by looking more closely at Kant's argument in §16 of the B-Deduction (B131-6). This will show that Kant's view of self-consciousness is in fact not derivative (in the 'reflection-theoretical' sense of unoriginal), and that instead it shows how any account of self-consciousness and the identity of self is first made possible by transcendental consciousness or transcendental apperception, which is nothing but the act itself of accompanying, through the 'I think', one's representations as one's own. Transcendental consciousness is an original consciousness, which a priori grounds any form of self-consciousness or self-knowledge, and is 'the consciousness of myself, as original apperception' (A117n).

In Section 4.4, I consider (*ad* assumption 2) why, for Kant, awareness of the identity of self-consciousness does not *ipso facto* amount to self-knowledge, and explain that, in addition to transcendental self-consciousness, what Kant calls the 'affection' of inner sense is needed for self-knowledge to be possible.

Chapter 5 addresses a topic that concerns the possibility of animal perception in relation to Kant's conception of objectivity, and the question whether Kant allows animal intentionality in the same vein as human discursive objective intentionality. This relates centrally to Kant's concept of object and the necessary form of reflexivity that is part and parcel of that concept. Kant observes that the principle of apperception is uniquely characteristic for beings that have a representation of themselves as subjects: as an 'I' that thinks and is thereby aware of herself as existing as thinker ('I am'). This implies that non-human animals do not apperceive the representations that they have. In early work and in the lectures, Kant clearly sided with his rationalist predecessors in denying animals inner sense, that is, a consciousness of self, identified with inner sense (V-Met/Herder, AA 28:901). But commentators have read this as saying that animals have no consciousness *simpliciter*. That belief appears to be informed by the standard interpretation of the principle of apperception as a principle of mere consciousness. If animals do not have apperception, then by implication they do not have consciousness. But this reading of apperception is mistaken on purely interpretative grounds, as I have argued in detail elsewhere. Transcendental apperception is not a necessary nor a sufficient condition of consciousness. Scientific evidence moreover supports the view that most vertebrates do arguably have at least creature consciousness and some mammals such as dolphins and elephants have shown evidence even of some form of bodily self-awareness. Another implication of the claim that animals do not have the capacity for apperception is that, because apperception grounds objective cognition, animals also do not have awareness of, or represent, objects. But this seems a rather unwelcome consequence of Kant's claim about the intimacy between self-consciousness (apperception) and the experience of objects. Animals are as much part of phenomenal nature as we are, one should think. In this chapter I argue that Kant's concept of object and what it means to be reflexively aware of an object excludes the idea that animals can have objective intentionality, but also that it does not exclude complex animal interaction with determinate spatial objects nor that animals have creature consciousness.

Chapter 6 is dedicated entirely to Reinhold, who must be considered the first major post-Kantian, but, at least in his early work, also the most consistently *Kantian* post-Kantian, despite his reputation as being the first to have distorted the original Kantian message. Like Kant, Reinhold wants to base his theory of knowledge on a firm a priori, transcendental footing, which for him is the principle of consciousness. With this principle in hand, we can further analyse the diverse elements of cognition as well as the transcendental constraints of knowledge. One of the most significant outcomes of Reinhold's account is the idea that the concept of representation itself provides the ground of cognition. Reinhold denies that in our representations we represent anything of the thing itself that we represent because we represent the thing only *as* represent*ed*, not *as* it is in itself. So nothing *of* the thing itself qua thing in itself is represented in our representation of it as represent*ed*. We still need the thing as it is in itself, metaphysically, though. So, unlike Fichte and in some sense Hegel, Reinhold does not give up on the thing in itself. In this chapter, I want to zero in on the Kantian idea that Reinhold elaborates on in his first major work *Versuch einer neuen Theorie des menschlichen Vorstellungsvermögens*, published in 1789, namely that, whilst things in themselves must logically be presupposed as the ground underlying appearances and things are not reducible to their representations, (1) objects as appearances are not properties *of* things in themselves, and (2) things in themselves or the thing in itself cannot properly be represented or even thought—though the *notion* of a thing in itself must of course be able to be conceived, and things in themselves must be taken to exist independently. I am here interested neither in the extent to which Reinhold's interpretation of Kant is correct or even adequately represents Kant's thought in all of its aspects, nor whether Reinhold's attempt to present a systematic philosophy based on a rigorous deduction from a single principle (his strong foundationalism) stands up to scrutiny. I am here solely interested in some of Reinhold's positive insights, in the *Versuch*, concerning elements of his representationalism that may shed light on Kant's idealism, specifically, the relation between appearances (as objects of knowledge) and things in themselves, i.e. points (1) and (2) described above. I read the early Reinhold of the *Versuch* as confirming the Kantian view that objects as appearances are not properties of things in themselves and that we are radically ignorant of things in themselves, in the sense that we can neither know things in themselves (through the senses) nor even intellectually grasp things in themselves through the understanding alone. Reinhold's representationalism, which is based on what he calls the principle of consciousness, is not a tautological representationalism. It is not based on the trivial idea that whatever is not a representation cannot be represented. By comparing his views to Sellars' view on representationalism in his *Science and Metaphysics* (1992 [1968]) I show that Reinhold's representationalism provides useful insights as to why Kant rightfully restricts possible knowledge to appearances and prohibits knowledge of things in themselves.

In Chapter 7, I am particularly interested in pursuing the question of how, following Hegel's critique of Kant, Hegelians have recently interpreted, under the influence of a Fichtean reading, Kant's theory of apperception and the cognitive role of self-consciousness, as chiefly elaborated in the Transcendental Deduction. Hegelians such as Pippin think that in the Deduction Kant effectively compromises or wavers on the strict separability between concepts and intuitions he stipulates at A51/B75. For if the argument of the Deduction, in particular in its B-version, is that the categories are not only the necessary conditions under which I think objects, by virtue of applying concepts, but also the necessary conditions under which anything is first given in sensibility, the fixed separation of concepts and intuitions seems incompatible with the very aim and conclusion of the Deduction. I want to examine these charges by looking more closely at Pippin's reading of the Deduction and his more general approach to Kant's strategy, in particular by looking at Pippin's reading of the scope of the principle of apperception as the principle of representational content. Pippin believes the orthodox Kant cannot be retained if we want to extract something of philosophical value from the Deduction. He defends a Kantian conceptualism shorn of the remaining nonconceptualist tendencies, which are in his view antithetical to the spirit of Kant's Critical revolution. I believe, however, that we must retain the orthodox Kant, including its nonconceptualist tendencies, in order not to succumb to an intemperate conceptualism. This means, as I argue, that the principle of apperception must be read in a modally less strong sense than Fichte and following him Hegel and Pippin do. Not all representations that are occurrent in one's head need be accompanied by an 'I think', even if it is of course true to say that representations must be so accompanied for them to have epistemic relevance, that is, objective validity.

In Chapter 8, I consider the relation between Kant and Hegel from a different, more overtly Hegelian angle, while expanding on the central theme of Chapter 7. This will be done in a somewhat more programmatic or speculative vein than before. The rationale for this and the following chapter is to show that there is a direct connection between Kant's theory of apperception to Hegel's idea of a metaphysical logic, and that Hegel's metaphysics is wholly continuous with Kant's. I want to look at some aspects of Pippin's compelling arguments, in his recent essay 'Logik und Metaphysik: Hegels "Reich der Schatten"' (Pippin 2016), for seeing Hegel's logic as a metaphysics, which takes objects, in some sense, to be a product and content of thought. Pippin's general conceptualist approach to

Hegel's metaphysical logic is, it seems to me, the only viable one, interpretatively as well as philosophically, though other recent readings that are more ontologically inclined, such as Martin (2012), and Kreines (2015), and in particular Houlgate (e.g. 2006, 2015, 2018), merit closer attention (I have only space to look at some of Houlgate's arguments). I beg to differ however with respect to some of the details of Pippin's reading in relation to Kant, which I shall be focusing on in this chapter. Pippin rightly emphasizes the subjective, reflexive element of Hegel's metaphysics. As Pippin says, it is noteworthy that Hegel connects the 'universal' (*Allgemeine*) with 'activity' (*Tätigkeit*). Concepts themselves do not make assertions. Rather, it is *self-consciousness*, thinking, which 'drives' the logic of concepts. But equally, Pippin is keen to point out that Hegel is not a mere category theorist. The logic of concepts is not merely a logic of the intelligibility of our conceptual claims, but it is a metaphysical logic that concerns Being itself. Hegel's absolute idealism is therefore not a form of subjective idealism that reduces reality to how things are merely for us; rather, it is an idealism that demonstrates the conceptual conditions under which reality itself can and must be understood without there being a gap between a putative conceptual scheme and its objective application conditions.

However, as Pippin argues, Hegel wants the identity that exists between the two set of conditions that govern the 'making sense of our understanding' and the 'making sense of things', of how things are, to go deeper than Kant's putatively 'excessively subjectivist approach' (2016:172). The identity between thought and being is a real one, and not restricted to *human* spatiotemporal experience. Pippin argues that Kant did not go far enough in affirming the identity between the forms of thought and the categories of objective experience, reasoning that the relation between general logic and transcendental logic is far closer than Kant acknowledges. This brings me back to the theme of the previous chapter: For Hegel, there simply is no gap that needs bridging, given his denial of a sharp distinction between the pure concepts and pure intuitions, and given the systematic and consistently immanent deduction of the pure concepts, which does not require any application, schematization, or demonstration of the instantiation, of concepts in objects or intuitions of objects. But I argue that, appearances to the contrary, Kant is much closer here to Hegel than Pippin and Hegel make it out to be, despite the fact that Hegel insists more overtly on the intrinsic intelligibility of Being itself, more so than Kant would appear to allow.

In the last chapter of the book, Chapter 9, I elaborate on the arguments broached in the previous two chapters by addressing two broadly naturalist readings of Hegel's criticism of Kant's transcendental logic and idealism. Such a reading espouses the idea that nature or reality is not reducible to what subjects make of nature or reality, but is rather that into which the cognitive agent or subject is herself integrated. The subject is, on such an account, as much *part* of nature as it has *knowledge of* nature, and as such it is constrained and determined by it. Hegel is often read as if he abandoned the transcendental perspective that Kant inaugurated in philosophy, whereby nature or reality, insofar as the physical realm of spatiotemporal objects is concerned, depends for its objectivity wholly on the transcendental subject. Hegel, it is thought, rejects such a subjective, transcendental idealism in favour of an idealism that is actually a fully-fledged realism in all but name, a realism *sans phrase* which makes substantial claims about the fundamental structure of reality itself and that encompasses knowledge about how things in themselves are constituted. Unlike Kant, Hegel is often considered a thoroughbred naturalist. There are a couple of assumptions here that persist among Hegelians discussing Kant's philosophy and Hegel's relation to it, and that create the continuing misunderstanding of the core of Kant's Copernican thought. Unlike what Hegelians—but not Pippin, it seems—continue to believe, Kant's category theory is not at all subjective in the bad sense ('bad' as opposed to my 'radically' subjectivist reading as espoused in Schulting 2017a), and so least of all 'solipsist' in whatever sense, and it does not entail scepticism or epistemological relativism. On the other hand, Hegel should not be read as if he were returning to a pre-Kantian metaphysics, which sees our forms of thought as conforming to the objects, rather than the objects as a priori conforming to our thought forms as it is on the Copernican hypothesis. In my view, Hegel's absolute idealism is informed by a *transcendental* logic that is thoroughly Kantian in spirit, which excludes the possibility of reading absolute idealism as a naturalism or realism *sans phrase* which is seen to replace transcendental logic. The main difference with Kant is that Hegel sees no reason to restrict this idealism to *empirical* objects. The idealism in absolute idealism is, if anything, not less but more idealist than transcendental idealism.

2

The 'Self-Knowledge' of Reason: Kant's Copernican Hypothesis

2.1 Introduction: Kant's Copernican Analogy

In the preface to the second edition (hereafter: B-preface) of the *Critique of Pure Reason* Kant invokes the well-known Copernican image that is often associated with the subjective turn that the so-called Critical philosophy inaugurated in metaphysics. The passage where Kant makes the analogy with Copernicus reads:

> This would be just like the first thoughts of Copernicus, who, when he did not make good progress in the explanation of the celestial motions [*Himmelsbewegungen*] if he assumed that the entire celestial host [*das ganze Sternheer*] revolves around the observer, tried to see if he might not have greater success if he made the observer revolve and left the stars at rest. Now in metaphysics we can try in a similar way regarding the intuition of objects.
>
> Bxvi–xvii

In the past, some interpreters (e.g. Hanson 1959) contended that there is some ambiguity as to whether (i) Kant actually speaks of an *analogy* with Copernicus here and (ii) he indeed herewith refers to the Copernican *revolution*, more in particular the postulation of the heliocentric universe, which some have deemed irrelevant to Kant's analogy.[1] As regards point (i), it should be observed that plainly Kant does not use the literal words 'Copernican analogy', neither here nor anywhere else in the *Critique* nor in his other works for that matter. (Notice that he does use the word 'analogy' with reference to the sciences a few lines prior to the quoted passage.) However, that in the above passage Kant does effectively make an analogy is, to my mind, evident from his use of the phrases '[t]his would be just like …'—Kant refers to his hypothesis concerning the possibility of a priori knowledge—and 'in a similar way'. Also, in a note close to the above-cited passage (Bxxii note) Kant explicitly speaks of an 'analogical' relation between the hypothesis of a reversal of thought in metaphysics and Copernicus's hypothesis of a moving earth.[2]

Concerning point (ii), it has been the subject of some debate in the earlier Anglophone Kant literature (Hanson 1959)[3] as to what extent the analogy with Copernicus should be linked with the Copernican *revolution*, suggesting that there is significant disparity between what Kant had in mind in making the analogy and the particular nature of Copernicus's revolution in planetary astronomy. Hanson even goes so far as to claim that Kant's reference to a revolution 'has *nothing whatever* to do with Copernicus' (1959:276, original emphasis) but merely refers to the success of the sciences of which Kant speaks in the paragraphs preceding the Copernicus passage. As Hanson (1959:276, 278) noted correctly, neither in the preface nor anywhere else in the Kantian *corpus* does Kant himself employ the phrase 'Copernican revolution'. He does speak however, in general terms, of a revolution in the sciences[4] and a revolution in metaphysics modelled after it (Bxxii), which is clearly an allusion to his own philosophy that he advances in the *Critique*. I believe that the reference to Copernicus must be seen in that context.[5] I also believe that in the above-quoted passage Kant implicitly refers to the Copernican revolution by explicitly asserting that the acceptance of the hypothesis of earth rotation yielded an improvement in the calculation of planetary cycles (Kant speaks, less accurately, of 'the celestial motions' [*Himmelsbewegungen*]).[6] It is precisely this acceptance that kick-started the Copernican revolution. Consequently, given that in the above-quoted passage to my mind Kant indeed makes an analogy with Copernicus, a *prima facie* connection is thereby made between Copernicus's revolution and Kant's own revolution in metaphysics.

In light of these remarks, I fully concur with the observation made by Murray Miles in regard to the question apropos of the above-quoted passage as to whether it is justified to speak of an analogy, and if so whether the analogy must be seen as linked to the Copernican *revolution*:

> [T]he philosophical point made with such fanfare by the commentators [such as Hanson, D.S.] may be philosophically moot after all.
>
> Miles 2006:1, 6

The *communis opinio* among Kant interpreters now is that, in the passage at Bxvi, (a) Kant *de facto* makes an analogy with Copernicus, which (b) by implication refers, in some way, to the Copernican revolution, and that consequently (c) it is justified to speak of Kant's own Copernican revolution (in some sense). Today, Kant commentators freely use the Copernican image in accounts of, or references to, Kant's thought without having much concern for the earlier controversies concerning the very appropriateness of Kant's reference to Copernicus or the Copernican revolution. I follow this practice and shall henceforth simply assume the connection between the Copernican analogy and the Copernican revolution. (Hereafter, I shall equally refer to Kant's or the Copernican analogy, Kant's or the analogy with Copernicus, and Kant's analogy for short.) I shall also speak of Kant's Copernicanism, by which I mean his own Copernican revolution in metaphysics, though it should be noted that Kant never labels his philosophy in this way. Having clarified what Kant did or did not say, the question regarding the *meaning* or *sense* of Kant's Copernicanism and *how* the analogy with Copernicus should be read, and also the question as *to the extent* in which there is a parallel between Kant and Copernicus are of course still in need of answering. This then is the subject of my exposition here. My central contention is that no commentator up until now, including Miles, has been able to cash out Kant's reference to Copernicus so as to explain the key aspect of his proposed 'alteration in our way of thinking' (Bxix) in metaphysics.

It has become virtually a commonplace in both Kant commentaries and more general references to his thought[7] that the essence of the analogy that Kant makes with Copernicus's breakthrough in astronomy lies in a change of perspective that Kant introduces in the way we relate to the world of objects. Many, if not the majority of, Kant commentators (see e.g. Allison 2004:36, Guyer 2006:49–50)[8] assume that the meaning of the Copernican analogy must primarily be sought in the simple fact that Kant has in mind a change in standpoint or view, or stipulates a choice between either a realist or an idealist—Kant's own alternative—view of the world. This suggests that one should attach no deeper meaning to the analogy with Copernicus. The analogy would merely allude to the *fact* of a change from an object oriented ontological metaphysics to a subject-centred de-ontologised epistemology, analogous to the way in which Copernicus's investigations brought about a change from a geocentric to a heliocentric worldview. Kant's Copernicanism would on this view merely consist in the notion of his new philosophy being as revolutionary in effect as Copernicus's explorations were in astronomy. But then one must ask: apart from its revolutionary character, what is actually *Copernican* about Kant's Copernican revolution?

Hanson (1959:278) suggests that 'Kant's reference to Copernicus in Bxvii [*sic*] may not stand in any primary relation to the main thrust of his [i.e. Copernicus's] arguments'. Hanson believes—and Allison (2004:456n36), Guyer and a host of others, appear to follow him in this respect—that

> Kant openly asserts a similarity between himself and Copernicus *in but one respect*; each of them made trial of an alternative hypothesis when existent theories proved unsatisfactory,

whereby it is emphasized that

> [t]he revolutions in thought with which Kant explicitly compares his own revolution have nothing *specifically* to do with Copernicus's.
>
> Hanson 1959:278, emphasis added

Let us call this minimal, *non-specific* reading of Kant's Copernican analogy the 'alternative hypothesis' reading (AH). AH asserts that the analogy simply lies in the fact that both Kant and Copernicus propose a change in respective position or perspective.

AH is related to a commonly held view of Kant's Copernicanism. This view sees Kant's Copernicanism in terms of perspectivism, whereby perspectivism is defined as the epistemological theory that all knowledge or experience of any object x is necessarily constrained by the context in which, or the viewpoint from which, that knowledge is claimed or the experience occurs. Perspectivism implies context dependence and a certain extent of subjectivism, partiality and/or prejudice. *Perspectivism* (italicized) is the abbreviation I use henceforth for the reading of Kant's Copernicanism in terms of perspectivism as defined. *Perspectivism* itself is not strictly speaking an identifiable interpretation of the Copernican analogy with which any one commentator or school of interpretation could be associated. It rather refers to a certain widespread tendency in interpreting Kant's revolution in metaphysics, his Copernicanism so to speak. This tendency concerns an insistence on the subjective or epistemic aspect as the primary characteristic of Kant's Copernicanism (see below, Section 2.2).[9] As will become clear in due course, AH is a compromise solution, a concession in response to the failure of *perspectivism* as an adequate interpretation of Kant's Copernicanism. However, whilst avoiding the patent faults of *perspectivism*, AH is not capable of explaining how the mere *fact* of a putative turn in perspective relates to what that turn substantially typifies and makes it necessary, viz. to answer the question what the epistemic relevance of subjectivity is. Consequently, AH is not a viable replacement candidate for interpreting Kant's analogy.

As I shall argue, the deeper meaning behind Kant's analogy has nothing to do with perspectivism as such. Nor is the analogy to do with the simple historical fact of a change in perspective, as AH implies. For if the analogy were indeed merely to be about perspectivism, or concern the generalization of a paradigm shift, then it would be clear, as has been pointed out many times by other commentators, that the analogy is not particularly apt. At first blush, Kant's change in perspective appears to be the inverse of Copernicus's cosmological revolution (cf. Guyer 2006:50). Whereas in Kant's epistemological revolution the subject becomes the centre of the cognitive framework, Copernicus's astronomy would appear to highlight precisely the move away from any anthropocentrically centred worldview. In the literature, this conspicuous discrepancy is sometimes referred to as Kant's 'anthropocentric fallacy'.[10] It is considered characteristic of Kant's so-called Critical philosophy to regard the human being as the measure of all things, whereas in a real Copernican paradigm it would exactly *not* be the human observer, casting her eyes onto the heavens above her, who provided the standard with which to determine the laws of the cosmos. Thus, if we were to read the analogy simply in terms of a change in perspective or *perspectivism tout court*, then we would better agree with Russell's snide remark[11] that Kant's revolution resembles a Ptolemaic reaction or counter-revolution more than a Copernican revolution. To avoid unnecessary confusion it would in that case be recommendable no longer to link Kant's revolutionary thought to the Copernican revolution.

However, if, for some important reason, we do not want to give up characterizing Kant's thought as Copernican—and the practice in Kant interpretation indicates we do not—then, I contend, *perspectivism* must be abandoned; and lest the term 'Copernican' be meaningless, AH must equally be given up. This is what I shall argue. The core of my argument consists in pointing out that Kant's Copernican analogy should not be read in terms of a mere allusion to the trial of an alternative hypothesis (AH), but shows up a *systematic* connection between Kant's and Copernicus's explorations. For if the analogy is to be taken seriously at all, that is, taken as indicating a likeness of sorts between Kant's and Copernicus's systems of thought, then the connection between them must be more substantial than the non-specific link that AH suggests and, given Russell's criticism, different in nature from *perspectivism*. To shore up my argument concerning AH I first want to assess *perspectivism*, the view that is in some way related to it.

In Section 2.2, I examine *perspectivism*. I give reasons why I think that that approach to Kant's Copernicanism is mistaken and why AH fails to provide an adequate alternative interpretation of the analogy. In Section 2.3, I spell out some general features of Kant's novel strategy in the *Critique*, which suggest a different interpretation of Kant's reference to Copernicus. In that context, I briefly address the meaning of the so-called 'transcendental turn'. Next I expound, very broadly, the general characteristics of Copernicus's revolution in light of its importance for the progress in planetary astronomy (Section 2.4). In Section 2.5, I show the extent to which Kant's revolution in metaphysics is typically Copernican and why, therefore, Kant's analogy should be considered apt. I conclude with a short note on the broadly hypothetico-experimental conception that is behind Kant's idea of rationality, which reinforces the aptness of the Copernican analogy.

2.2 Perspectivism and the Copernican Analogy

Before jettisoning *perspectivism*, let us consider some of the aspects that might seem to commend it as an appropriate take on Kant's Copernicanism. Although many have faulted *perspectivism* for its misleading picture of Kant's thought, some of its assumptions still hold sway considering the popularity of AH. It is important to expose them.

The first impression one has when reading the above-quoted passage from the B-preface, where Kant makes the analogy with Copernicus, suggests that Kant alludes to the ostensible fact that Copernicus, making no headway in his calculations of the planetary orbits, had a flash of insight: instead of supposing that the observer is the centre around which the galaxy, and in particular the sun, revolves we suppose that the cosmos is the stationary centre within which the observer takes her place. In the common picture, the sun moves across the horizon plane from east to west. There is nothing illusory about what the observer sees. But—and this is what, according to *perspectivism*, we imagine Copernicus thinking—the observer is not justified, based on her observations, to conclude that the earth and, therefore, her own geographical location is the stationary centre of the universe and that the sun in fact revolves in a sphere of which the earth is the centre.

One ostensible reason for Copernicus to deny the, philosophically speaking, 'objective validity' of our perception of the apparent movement of the sun lies in the fact that, if it were the case that the earth orbited a (relatively) stationary sun (as we now, post-Copernicus, take for granted), then the observed phenomena would be exactly the same as in the converse Ptolemaic scenario of a stationary earth around which the sun circles. Put differently, the differences in the angular distance between the sun and the horizon, which can be determined during a solar day, can be caused by either the movement of the horizon or the apparent movement of the sun. This is in fact what Kant says in *Physical Geography*:

> The motion of the heavens is only apparent since, as we do not perceive the motion of the earth on which we are situated, we have an apparent motion of the

heavens, but we do not know whether it is the heavens or the earth that moves. . . .
We do not know whether we or the stars are changing position. The proof that
the earth does not stand still, but that it is actually the earth that moves, has to be
argued with great subtlety.

PG §9, AA 9:170 [Kant 2012b:457]

In other words, the observer, from the vantage point of her observation, that is, purely on the basis of the data delivered through perception, does not have at her disposal the adequate criteria for objectively establishing the truth of either perspective.

This situation suggests that the perspective that the observer adopts or finds herself in determines, or more appropriately put, *constrains* her knowledge of reality. The constraint concerns a necessary dispositional condition of her perception of reality. Consequently, the straightforward reading of Kant's Copernicanism, viz. *perspectivism*, insists on the necessarily *perspectival* nature of our relation to objective reality: objects must be explained in terms of our perceptual point of view; in other words, they must be taken in a point-of-viewish way. This is taken to explain the subjective turn of Kant's philosophy, for all experience of reality rests on the necessary subjective condition, a transcendental condition, under which experience is first possible (with respect to the meaning of the term 'transcendental' see further below, Section 2.3).[12] To be sure, Kant himself seems to suggest such a perspectivist reading in another passage where he makes an analogy with Copernicus, who according to Kant hypothesized that we 'seek for the observed movements not in the objects of the heavens, *but in their observer*' (Bxxii note, emphasis added).[13]

One could argue that notwithstanding the fact that we now take for granted that it is not the case that the earth is the centre of the cosmos, we do hold on, as if *per habitum infusum*, to the picture of a sun that moves from east to west across the horizon plane. Of course, this is not because of a habit we cannot give up. That we cling to this picture rather issues from the incontrovertible contingent fact that our perceptive abilities are constrained by our characteristic space-time perception (and therefore by our location in space and time) and from certain optical considerations.[14] The scientific determination that the resulting representation of the sun's motion across the horizon plane is merely an appearance does nothing to detract from that fact. In other words, the scientific worldview is not simply a substitute for the manifest worldview.

For one thing, our perceptual constitution is such that it *eo ipso* constrains the number of stars that in any arbitrary observation, at some point during the night, can be observed. At a particular moment on any given night two fifths of the number of stars in the galaxy are located below the horizon beyond which they would be observable. Furthermore, the possibility of observing a particular star is determined by the particular point in time at which the observation takes place. These are both *empirical* constraints that have to do with the observer's perceptual constitution and geographical position vis-à-vis the constellation of the stars (cf. Copernicus 1992:8ff.). *Perspectivism* refers to these unmistakable features of our human perceptual capacity.

However, *perspectivism* is problematic as a reading of Kant's Copernicanism. On this reading, important aspects of both Copernicus's 'invention' and Kant's reasons for referring to it by way of analogy remain unexplained or are entirely neglected. I list five reasons why I believe that *perspectivism* is misguided or at least inadequate for explaining the Copernican nature of Kant's philosophical revolution (some aspects already passed in review):

1. It would be scarcely original if Kant's intention with the analogy (merely) concerned the necessary subjective nature of a description of reality, that is, the thought that we necessarily relate to the world in a point-of-viewish way, say. Strictly speaking, it is Descartes, not Kant, who should be credited for introducing the original subjective viewpoint in philosophy,[15] first made manifest in the publication of his *Discours de la méthode* in 1637. Taken at face value, the subjective turn in philosophy took place some 150 years prior to Kant's *Critique*. Kant's Copernicanism therefore cannot consist *merely* in a certain necessary subjectivism.
2. *Perspectivism* (and a fortiori AH; see below) does not explain the *reasons* both Copernicus and Kant had for bringing about their respective paradigm shifts through their 'altered method[s] of [our] way of thinking' (Bxviii, Bxix).[16] The changes in cosmology, in Copernicus's case, and in epistemology, in Kant's, are not the result of a trivial claim concerning the conceptual necessity of adopting a perspective. Nor is it the case that those changes refer simply to the *historical fact that* another perspective has been adopted (this is all too often the association that one has with the notion of a paradigm shift). The respective changes are motivated by what they can accomplish in terms of solving a lingering problem in a related field of research, that is, a problem in mathematical astronomy for Copernicus and a problem of metaphysics for Kant. *Perspectivism* cannot accommodate this two-tier feature of Copernicanism.

3. Whereas *perspectivism* might at first sight seem appropriate as an interpretation of the Kantian story (that is, on a certain phenomenalistic reading of it; see point [4] below), it quite clearly does not sit well with Copernicus's intentions, for perspectivism could not explain *why* we should substitute a heliocentric worldview for a geocentric one (this hangs together with what was said under point [2] and earlier on in this section).[17] There must be another reason for Copernicus to stipulate heliocentrism other than the simple idea of perspectivism. *Perspectivism* as such does not differentiate between the geocentric view and the heliocentric one; in both cases the celestial host is observed empirically in the same way, given spatiotemporal conditions, so that from a purely conceptual point of view both perspectives are equally possible and equally valid. Put differently, at a time when the geocentric worldview was in force, in 150 AD say, one observed exactly the same phenomenon—viz. the sun moving across the horizon plane—as we do in our post-1543 heliocentric worldview. Worldviews do not in any way change the physio-psychological structure of our mode of perception. They have the function of giving coherence to our observations against the backdrop of the whole of our opinions and views. Thus, if *perspectivism* seems to fit Kant's story, but at any rate not Copernicus's, then at least *perspectivism* cannot claim on account of the theory of perspectivism that there is any significant analogy between Kant and Copernicus; and so, even generally, *perspectivism* fails as a relevant approach to Copernicanism.

4. *Perspectivism* falsely suggests a psychologistic reading of Kant's representationalism and of his notorious thesis of the ideal nature of objects, as if the most important result of Kant's revolution in metaphysics lie in an acknowledgement of the limitations of our cognition of things. Inevitably, *perspectivism* issues in cognitive relativism. This is conveyed by the strongly phenomenalist (read: Berkeleyan) interpretation of Kant's idealism.[18] The standard phenomenalistic reading of Kant comes down to an empirical construal of the 'appearances', Kant's technical term for the objects of perception, as mere mental states.[19] Although I cannot address here the ongoing controversies surrounding Kant's idealism and the specific meaning of Kant's theory of the phenomenality of material bodies,[20] I should like to note that there appears to be an internal relation between *perspectivism* and the strongly phenomenalistic interpretation of Kant's idealism. This is not to

say that Van Cleve is a perspectivist in his reading of Kant's Copernican turn or that phenomenalist readings of Kant are *eo ipso* perspectivist.
5. It would be reasonable to conclude that, if *perspectivism* (with its aforementioned phenomenalistic connotations) were right, Copernicus's revolution in astronomy and Kant's rather Ptolemaic approach would be at radical variance, a criticism already made by Russell (1948) and earlier by Kemp Smith (1913). That *perspectivism* is still, explicitly or implicitly, a popular strategy for reading Kant's Copernicanism is odd to say the least, for Russell's critique should have made clear that the analogy must be read differently, lest the term 'Copernican' be vacuous.[21]

Here, I want to concentrate on what I indicated under (2), i.e. the thought that both Copernicus and Kant would have had *specific* reasons for bringing about their respective revolutions. This implies that we should take the analogy in a more systematic fashion and not just as a broad indication of the historical fact of a paradigm shift (AH); and that accordingly Kant's Copernicanism cannot be interpreted in the merely conceptual sense of the necessity of adopting a perspective (*perspectivism*). As said earlier, the historical reading of Kant's analogy in terms of a proposal to change paradigm (AH) is a compromise solution meant to deflate Russell's misplaced criticism against Kant's alleged Ptolemaicism (in the vein of: 'since there indeed seems to be a fundamental dissimilarity between Copernicus's heliocentric perspective and Kant's anthropocentrism, the analogy should be taken in a loose sense only'). AH seems still determined by *perspectivism*. Instead of acceding to Russell's critique by pointing out, as Allison and others do, that Kant's reference to Copernicus is meant purely figuratively, as merely a *façon de parler* (cf. Miles 2006:7n.18), we would do better to reject *perspectivism* altogether and seek another explanation of Kant's Copernicanism.

I contend that Kant's Copernican analogy (and, equally, his references to Galileo, Bacon, Torricelli and, less felicitously, Stahl, and his references to mathematics, logic and physics in general; cf. Bxv–xvi) has a more than figurative, historical function. I argue that the analogy points to a rational-reconstructive strategy for solving a lingering problem, an approach that Kant copies from the experimental, hypothetico-deductive method that since the days of Bacon is the prototypical method of the empirical sciences. What is at issue here is what Kant characterizes as 'the *essential* element in the change in the ways of thinking that has been so advantageous to [the sciences]' (Bxvi, emphasis added); and so, by implication, the analogy that Kant makes points to the essential element of the Copernican revolution.

An important additional advantage of my proposal is that alleged problems concerning Kant's idealism can thus be avoided. If it becomes clear that Kant's Copernicanism has nothing to do with perspectivism or perspectival change per se, but instead concerns a methodological approach comparable to that of Copernicus, which charts our knowledge in a more 'scientifically' cogent and rational manner, then worries about Kant's alleged Berkeleyan idealism, which I noted are inherently related to *perspectivism*, rest on premises that are foreign to Kant's Copernicanism—though we should bear in mind this does not rule out a benignly phenomenalist reading of his idealism.[22]

It should be noted that the analogy with the experimental method of the empirical exact sciences holds only insofar as the typical *form* of the experiment is concerned, not its specific content, for, as Kant himself asserts, reason does not work with empirical facts, but with her own abstract forms, i.e. 'concepts and principles' (Bxviii note). It is thus inappropriate to criticize Kant, as Karl Popper (2002:268, 271) seems to do, for his failure to adopt the falsification model of science. Unlike in a scientific experiment, Kant's philosophical experiment, and philosophy in general, do not concern falsifiable empirical laws but logical principles for experience in general, which can (and must) be apodictically demonstrated (at least from a Kantian, transcendental perspective). One may well ask whether Kant is capable of proving the universal, apodictic validity of such principles; but criticisms against this do not rest on falsification. Falsification—in the sense that Popper has in mind for the sciences—cannot be an appropriate criterion for philosophy, for in philosophy there are no *facts* that contradict theory. Philosophical critique consists in the scrutiny of a certain form of reasoning as to its inner rational coherence (cf. Miles 2006:19ff; see 2006:20n.44 for a reference to a very crude reading of Kant's appeal to the experimental method). It is also important to note that although Kant's method bears an intimate relation to the method of science, clearly the systematicity that Kant has in mind for metaphysics is of a different kind than that which science aims for; the method of philosophy can therefore not be the *same* method that science employs in regard to its object, which for philosophy is not empirical and a posteriori but formal and a priori. Although I believe that for the purposes of introducing a new kind of philosophy Kant adopts a style of reasoning that is a close analogue of the hypothetico-deductive procedure of science, it would be mistaken straightforwardly to label the philosophical method, as conceived of by Kant and adopted throughout the *Critique*, hypothetico-deductive, much less to consider the outcome of his proper philosophical arguments merely hypothetical. This explains the fact that Kant was adamant not to regard the proofs provided in the body of the *Critique* as anything less than apodictic (see e.g. the note to Bxxii).[23]

2.3 Transcendental Reflection, 'How Possible'-Questions and Kant's 'Alteration in Our Way of Thinking'

Before I discuss, in Section 2.5, that which characterizes Kant's revolution in metaphysics as typically Copernican, I want to provide a broad outline of some general, basic features of Kant's new way of thinking. This will be somewhat sketchy.[24] These features concern Kant's view of what a critical metaphysics, which will be able to come forward as a rigorous science that proves to be the equal of the exact sciences, should be like.

To state it very sweepingly, a central feature of Kant's thought is a certain amount of self-reflexiveness. This is already made manifest by the very title of Kant's *Critique of Pure Reason*. The title indicates a subjective as well as an objective genitive declension, which implies that it concerns both a critique of pure reasoning insofar as reason threatens to become speculative and a critique that is self-reflexively performed by reason itself. It is in this context that in the preface to the first edition of the *Critique* Kant speaks strikingly of the 'self-knowledge' of reason (Axi).[25] Two aspects of one and the same act of reasoning are here at issue: explication of the conditions for possible knowledge and self-explication or a self-awareness of sorts.

The second, related element that I want to stress might strike one as obvious, which though it is not: Kant's Critical project concerns both a theory of experience or knowledge and a metaphysics. A theory of knowledge deals with the conditions of the cognition of things or events in the world. Metaphysics is traditionally concerned with the most fundamental determinations of beings in reality, of the grounds of the things or their properties and events themselves (the *ratio essendi*) independently of their being known (the *ratio cognoscendi*)—although for the rationalists of the School metaphysics these two *ratios* correspond strongly. Very broadly speaking, Kant's Copernican turn has repercussions for the way reality or beings themselves are to be viewed and how the *ratio cognoscendi* and the *ratio essendi* are related, which involves Kant's notorious doctrine of idealism. In Kant's view, it is not the case that the object itself, as it is *presented in reality*, comes apart from the way we represent it, notwithstanding the fact that, for Kant, we do not produce the object qua its existence; there is still, notoriously, the thing in itself that remains independent of our knowledge. Nor is it the case that, purely epistemically speaking, the manner in which we talk about the object is separable from the way the object, *qua object*, is itself characterizable. The thought of an object is reflected in the object itself, while the object is first made manifest in thought. The object is always an object *for* thought. In other words, the *objectivity* of an object is a characteristic attributed to it by thought. In this way, one discerns a certain conceptual reciprocity, in a one-to-one mapping of sorts, between thought and object *to the extent that the object is an object for thought.*

It should be stressed though that Kant opposes the straightforward conflation, in the School metaphysics, of the *nexus rationis*, the way things and their relations are conceived of in thought, and the way really existing things would have to be seen to be related in the realm of being; in Kant's view, the realm of thought and the realm of being *as such* no longer correspond in a strong sense (see further below on *adæquatio*), precisely as a result of his stronger sense of the bond between the object *as represented* and our representation of the object. The mutual aspect of both thought and object as the two relata of a reciprocal conceptual relation reflects two sides of the same function that reason or thought operates by means of a kind of self-reflection. This actuality necessarily arises from the notion that the thought itself about the relation between thought and the world of things, the very business of metaphysics, logically assumes the privileged position in that relation, which therefore is a three-place relation: *mind* thinks about how *mind* relates to *world*.

In the same vein should we understand Kant's oft-cited remark that 'the proud name of an ontology, which presumes to offer synthetic *a priori* cognitions of things in general in a systematic doctrine (e.g. the principle of causality), must give way to the modest one of a mere analytic of the pure understanding' (B303/A247). In the late, unpublished text *Real Progress*, Kant uses the term 'ontology' or also *Wesenlehre* for what in the *Critique* he calls analytic of experience, which is often conveniently interpreted as Kant's description for theory of knowledge. That is to say, it is not entirely the case, as many interpreters believe, that Kant's transcendental philosophy—the label for his particular critical reflection of reason—has discarded ontology once and for all. Kant's transcendental philosophy rather focuses on a different outlook on what is traditionally covered by ontology, viz. the fundamental predicates of being.[26] Transcendental philosophy is certainly no longer an ontology in the old style of the School metaphysics, viz. a doctrine of the essence of things which aims at an account of objects *omnimode determinata* (cf. Baumgarten, *Metaphysica* §4, §148). Kant's version of ontology concerns an account of the fundamental predicates of things insofar as they are real, that is, given in sensible intuition. More precisely, it concerns the necessary forms under which things can be known as objects of experience, where the existence of such objects is not just a complement to their possibility, as the rationalists of the School metaphysics thought. Transcendental philosophy is thus an ontology of sorts. In a *Reflexion*, likely from the period 1780–84, Kant writes for example:

> Ontology is the science of things in general, i.e., of the possibility of our cognition of things *a priori*, i.e., independently from experience. It can teach us nothing of things in themselves, but only of the *a priori* conditions under which we can cognize things in experience in general, i.e., principles of the possibility of experience.
>
> Refl 5936, AA 18:394 [Kant 2005:311]

In a letter dated 20 January 1792 to J.S. Beck, Kant seems to suggest that he 'made plans for a system of metaphysics', which would deal with 'a whole science of Ontology as *immanent* thinking, i.e., a science of things the objective reality of whose concepts can be securely established', on the basis of an exposition of each single category and 'all predicables included under it' (Br, AA 11:313–14 [Kant 1999:398]).[27]

It should be noted that in the Metaphysics lectures contemporaneous with the Critical period (e.g. V-Met/Mron, AA 29:752 [1782–83]), Kant might be taken to strictly separate the Critical transcendental philosophy and ontology, and he even says that 'it is wrong to call [transcendental philosophy] ontology' (AA 29:756 [Kant 2001:116]). Transcendental philosophy is a transcendental logic, which, unlike ontology where 'we consider things already according to their general properties', 'abstracts from all that; it is a kind of self-cognition'. But he also refers to ontology-old-style as '[a]n ontology that was not a transcendental philosophy' (AA 29:785 [Kant 2001:140]), suggesting that the 'critique of pure reason', of which he speaks just before this passage, is an ontology that *is* a transcendental philosophy. Nevertheless, as the Mrongovius notes further report, 'the science of all basic concepts and basic propositions upon which all of our pure cognitions of reason rest', that is, formerly ontology, 'will not be properly called ontology', '[f]or to have a thing in general as an object is as much as to have no object and to treat only of a cognition, as in logic' and '[t]he name, however, sounds as if it had a determinate object'. In other words, 'the most fitting name would be transcendental philosophy' (AA 29:786 [Kant 2001:141]).[28]

Whatever the case may be as to whether the new Critical, transcendental philosophy can in fact be titled an ontology, more generally, the new philosophy argues that any theory of knowledge presupposes a certain metaphysical outlook, and no metaphysics is meaningful without incorporating a theory of knowledge. This last aspect concerns the requirement of a reflexive stance towards one's own assumptions or basic beliefs, of a reflection on the capacity for cognition as such, which is always in the background while putting forward any arbitrary metaphysical postulate or principle or adopting any view apropos of the fundamental makeup of the world. Particularly in metaphysics, which according to Kant suffers from a grave lack of scientific standard—no guaranteed continuity and consolidation of success, no general, uniform criteria for evaluation, and so on (see further below)—such self-reflection on its speculative pretensions and its ways of cognizing is called for.

By highlighting the need for a self-reflection of reason Kant aims to delimit the boundaries of metaphysical speculation, for in virtue of reason's continuous self-examination one is always reminded of the necessary conditions under which claims about reality are justifiable, lawful (cf. Aix–xii). Kant directly associates a 'safeguard against the aberrations into which reason falls when it mistakes its destination', and illusorily holds 'the subjective ground of our judgments to be objective', with 'a self-knowledge of pure reason' (Prol §40, AA 4:328 [Kant 1977:70]). Already early on, in a letter from 1771 to one of his most valued students, Marcus Herz, Kant referred to his new project, which ten years later was to become the *Critique of Pure Reason*, as 'The bounds of sensibility and of reason' (Br, AA 10:123). For the greater part, the reflection of metaphysics consists, according to Kant, in delimiting the domain within which its a priori concepts are applicable, that is, delimiting them to what is capable of being sensibly perceived. This delimitation of the applicability of a priori concepts is congruent with determining the legitimacy of their *de facto* employment. This is in essence what constitutes the Critical project of a deduction of the pure concepts of the understanding or the categories.[29]

In the section 'On the amphiboly of the concepts of reflection' in the *Critique of Pure Reason*, where he accuses Leibniz of an ambiguous use of the concepts of reflection, Kant calls the self-reflection he is aiming at with the delimitation of reason a 'transcendental reflection' (A261/B317). A transcendental reflection is a reflection on the determination whether the representations one has belong to either the pure intellect or to sensible intuition. Without elaborating on the particularities of Kant's critique of Leibniz's rationalism, it may be argued that Kant's Critical project as a whole is such an exercise in transcendental reflection, a reflection namely on the relation of concepts and representations to their respective cognitive faculties, intuition and the understanding, between which

Kant famously makes an irreducible distinction but which he also claims are inextricably related.[30] This reflection takes place, not from within a putatively untainted, innate faculty of thought wholly in abstraction from experience. Rather, transcendental reflection concerns a dynamical process of thought, which thought or reason, by way of the understanding, executes in its very relation to objective reality, thus in some way *in* experience itself, although still a process conducted wholly a priori, that is, *independently of* experience. In other words, the critique that this reflection enacts is a mode of reasoning which consistently examines or explicates itself critically in its relation to its object, to the extent that while 'experiencing' empirically real objects, that is to say, being aware of its relation to such objects, self-critical thought is a process whereby one is aware of the concern of metaphysics, viz. explicating the fundamental predicates of being, of the very things that are being experienced. Metaphysics is no longer a discipline wholly separable from experience, but must be conducted in constant, critical relation to it.

The question that now arises is: what is exactly understood by the adjective 'transcendental' in transcendental reflection? Kant himself says that all cognition is transcendental 'that is occupied not so much with objects but rather with our mode of cognition of objects insofar as this is to be possible *a priori*' (B25). From this one might be inclined to infer that Kant keeps a certain distance from the objects, from reality as such. This would appear to present a different perspective than one gains from the above observation regarding the intimate relation of metaphysics to experience. Kant's remark at B25 would suggest that an epistemological preference is articulated, at the cost of metaphysical interests. In this respect one often speaks of Kant's transcendental turn, a turn away, as it were, from metaphysics and ontology (cf. again the dictum from B303), as was discussed above. But such talk reveals unexplained assumptions about the Kantian position more than that it clarifies it. Notice that in the Strawsonian school of Kantianism the term 'transcendental' underwent a transformation in the debate on 'transcendental arguments'. There, 'transcendental' no longer has the specific meaning that Kant lends it—cognition insofar as it is *a priori*—but becomes a kind of marker for a type of argument that, by virtue of conceptual analysis, stipulates a necessary condition *y* for some object or event *x*, that is, something that must be presupposed for something else to be possible. This type of argument concerns strictly *epistemological* questions of the 'how possible' kind, and shies away from metaphysical issues.[31]

Kant's transcendental philosophy can undoubtedly be characterized in terms of a 'how possible'-question if only because Kant himself couches the central concern of the Critical project in these terms—see for example the very chapter titles of the *Prolegomena* and in the section 'The general problem of pure reason' at B19–23. It concerns indeed the inquiry into the conditions of possibility of having experience or cognition of objects, of knowledge, and thus the very possibility of metaphysics as the science of the a priori concepts of the objects of experience. This question hangs together with the issue of which I spoke above, viz. the question of delineating the domain of possible cognition and establishing the legitimacy of a priori concepts (such as 'cause') and the principles in which these concepts find expression (e.g. the causality principle). So the 'how possible'-question addresses the legitimacy or objective validity of the categories as much as objective experience (A93–4/B126, A128, A130).

But more is at stake than merely a question concerning the conditions of possibility of experience or knowledge or providing a justification of the categories as those very conditions. Kant's strategy in the *Critique* resides precisely in proposing an 'alteration in our *way of thinking*' (Bxix, emphasis added), that is, an alternative *method* to explain truth and the possibility of knowledge—which, to be sure, is more than explaining what justifies *particular claims* to knowledge, the prerogative of standard epistemology. The novelty of Kant's thought is not just that it is about a new kind of *argument* for a known problem, which can be added to the arsenal of arguments, speculative or not, in the textbooks of metaphysics. Nor is it about a problem hitherto undiscovered. Kant's transcendental thinking rather introduces a new *approach* to an age-old question. That is why the transcendental concerns not just the object of inquiry, but also the manner in which the inquiry is launched and conducted. This introduces a particularly self-reflexive element in the account about the possibility of knowledge. That which is specifically transcendental about Kant's investigation does not merely boil down to what is characterizable as a 'how possible'-question, such as in the debate on transcendental arguments. Transcendental philosophy is just as well about how the 'how possible'-question is itself framed and how that question leads to newer, better results in philosophical inquiry. The manner in which this question must be posed relates to the fact that the 'transcendental' regards the possibility of *a priori* cognition of objects, namely, *insofar as thought from within itself* (thus a priori), through 'self-knowledge', provides the foundation for the possibility of knowledge in general. This is the self-reflexiveness of transcendental philosophy.

What is new about Kant's transcendental approach in metaphysics is that the analysis of the conditions of the ground of truth and knowledge must, in some sense, be able to explain *itself*, that is, *self*-explain its procedure. The analysis is 'self-explanatory', in the sense of self-explicatory or self-clarificatory, and as such self-reflexive. Put differently: given that analysis is the way of thinking, in the analysis of knowledge thought itself relates to itself in order to account for its manner of analysing or explicating. There is a lot here that needs elaboration and exegetical back-up, but this I believe is at any rate the general idea behind Kant's talk about the *Critique* being 'a treatise of method' (Bxxii). More in particular, the *Critique* is a treatise on how the method of explication must be made explicit in the exposition of the matter at hand. The explication of the conditions of possibility of knowledge or experience thus has a double, reflexive aspect, parallel to the dual aspect of the very title of the *Critique of Pure Reason*, which I indicated at the outset of this section. The explication is an explanation of the conditions of experience or knowledge, certainly, but equally it is an explanation, an exposition, of the method of such an explanation. In a word, it is 'the understanding knowing itself [*der sich selbst kennende Verstand*]' (Refl 4284, AA 17:495 [Kant 2005:125]).

A genuinely philosophical exposition of knowledge cannot simply rely on a pre-given method, which it subsequently applies axiomatically. Why not? In order for a philosophical argument to have probative force, the correlation between the method of reasoning and that for which it serves as such—viz. for the explication or analysis of knowledge or experience—must be demonstrated in the explication itself. In other words, the method must be accounted for in the explication itself. Philosophical analysis is a gradual process in which the elements of knowledge are shown in their interrelatedness, literally 'on the way' (*meta hodos*). Hence, the methodical procedure of philosophical analysis must be ostensive, a step-by-step procedure that *shows* why such and such is the case (cf. A789/B817).

An axiomatic approach in philosophy, on the other hand, would rely on the assumption of principles (or external grounds) for which it does not account or give legitimate internal grounds. This can only lead to an infinite regress—the methodical foundation calls forth a further ground and so on *ad infinitum*. With an axiomatic approach no account is given of the *relation between* the method or principles adopted and the exposition itself. To what extent is, on the axiomatic approach, the particular method adopted appropriate for the kind of analysis that is being provided? Could other methods (and what kind) do an equally good job? If applied to the particular case of Kant's epistemology, one discerns that an axiomatic approach would leave doubtful the question as to whether the stipulated necessary conditions of possibility for knowledge are indeed as necessary and a priori as Kant claims. Such a doubtful outcome is always the result of apagogic proof, for such a proof does 'never [produce] comprehensibility of the truth in regard to its connection with the grounds of its possibility', that is, it does not give 'insight into [the] sources [of truth]' (A789/B817). To avoid doubt, therefore, philosophical proofs cannot be apagogic (abductive) nor epagogic (inductive), as in the empirical sciences, but must be ostensive (deductive).[32]

2.4 Copernicus's Hypothesis

Before I relate Kant's general methodical approach to his Copernicanism, let us look at Copernicus's hypothesis, which led to the now standard astronomy that bears his name. The reasoning underlying Copernicus's basic proposition concerning a heliocentric universe, which he formulated in book I of his seminal *On the Revolutions*,[33] can be schematized as follows:[34]

(A) Astronomy calculates the planetary cycles in accordance with a standard calculative model.

(B) All sorts of modifications are added to the standard model, which should clarify or explain away observed irregularities in the circular motion of celestial bodies.[35]

(C) The sun circles around the observer. (*geocentric paradigm*)

Taking (A) and (B) as indications of the initial *de facto* situation in standard Ptolemaic astronomy and accepting (C) as the paradigmatic basic background assumption, which gives rise to (B), results in

(D) No uniform explanation can be found for the irregularities in planetary cycles.

But suppose we deny (C) and instead put forward the hypothesis that

(E) The observer (and the planet earth on which she is positioned) circles around the sun. (*hypothesis of earth rotation/heliocentric universe*)

Now if we accept (E), it appears that (D) does not result, for on (E) we get

(F) A more coherent, uniform calculative model provides a better, more precise explanation of planetary cycles, and also clarifies the apparent irregularities of their orbits.

Since (F) means that (B) no longer applies, and thus (C) is disconfirmed by implication, the hypothesis (E) is to be preferred on the grounds of it yielding a more parsimonious and coherent theory showing greater explanatory power than on (C).

What is significant here is that the thesis of a heliocentric perspective or earth rotation is not even the primary goal of Copernicus's revolution, but merely a means to an end. Copernicus's aim was an increase in the coherence of astronomical computation, so that the orbits of the planets could be calculated more precisely. The underlying premise of Copernicus's reasoning concerned mainly a lack of coherence in the existing mathematical models of astronomy. Thomas Kuhn observes that the Copernican revolution must primarily be considered a revolution in that it constituted an improvement upon the techniques employed by astronomers in order to determine the position of celestial bodies. Copernicus was concerned with astronomical reform more than with cosmological change. The notion of a heliocentric universe, more specifically the cosmological thesis of the earth's being in orbit around the sun, was in the first instance, as Kuhn (1985:137) avers, 'an anomalous by-product of a proficient and devoted astronomer's attempt to reform the techniques employed in computing planetary position'. In fact, the postulate itself of a rotating earth—the hypothesis actually concerned a threefold postulate: the earth's diurnal rotation, conical-axial rotation and orbital revolution, the last two annually[36]—was, as Kuhn (1985:144) remarks, not without precedent, for long before Copernicus, in the third century BC, the Greek mathematician Aristarchus of Samos had already advanced the notion of a heliocentric universe.[37]

In general, one may say that, as Kuhn writes, 'probably the single most prevalent claim advanced by the proponents of a new paradigm is that they can solve the problems that have led the old one to a crisis. . . . When it can legitimately be made, this claim is often the most effective one possible' (1996:153). Paradigm shifts are correlative with the need to solve persistent problems in a particular field of inquiry in the most economic way possible (though of course economy is not the only reason). As Kuhn (1996:67ff.) says, paradigm shifts characteristically result from an awareness of an anomaly. What caused the change in *cosmological* perspective (from geocentric to heliocentric) was Copernicus's growing discontent, being a technically proficient astronomer, with the increase in mathematical imprecision in the fundamental concepts of traditional *planetary astronomy*, which in essence was Ptolemaic (Copernicus 1992:8), which is comparable to Kant's displeasure with the many competing metaphysically speculative theories in the schools of rationalist philosophy, as on a 'battlefield of endless controversies' (Aviii). Kuhn refers to Copernicus's 'professional awareness of technical fallacy'. As Kuhn pithily notes, a 'felt necessity was the mother of Copernicus's invention' (1985:139).

It was thus a technical fallacy of mathematical astronomy that gave rise to a change in cosmology. For in the course of centuries a raft of modifications had been added to the original Ptolemaic system by means of the introduction of various astronomical techniques (e.g. eccentrics, epicycles, deferents, etc.) so as to account for the many observed irregularities in the astronomical computational system. As a consequence, there was effectively not just one Ptolemaic system, but many different versions of it. (Notice the parallel here with the German school metaphysics prior to Kant, in which various schools advanced often only minutely different versions of an essentially identical rationalist outlook on reality.) Kuhn (1985:139) speaks metaphorically of an astronomical 'monster'. The Ptolemaic system had lost its inner coherence and mathematical precision. Copernicus's central problem with the Ptolemaic astronomy related to the diffuse nature of all its various computational models and the different techniques invented to amend it, which effectively yielded great inaccuracy insofar as the determination of planetary cycles was concerned. Kuhn writes in this respect:

> The astronomical tradition had become diffuse; it no longer fully specified the techniques that an astronomer might employ in computing planetary position, and it could not therefore specify the results that he would obtain from his computations.
>
> 1985:140

Now the revolutionary nature of Copernicus's invention lies in the *use* he made of the postulate of earth rotation for the benefit of refining mathematical computation of the planetary orbital system. Copernicus became aware of the possibility that the hypothesis of a rotating earth could well solve a lingering astronomical problem. How? Kuhn writes, paraphrasing a passage from Copernicus's *On the Revolutions*:

> If the earth moves in an orbital circle around the centre as well as spinning on its axis, then, at least qualitatively, the retrograde motions and the different times required for a planet's successive journeys around the ecliptic can be explained without the use of epicycles.
>
> 1985:149ff.[38]

Copernicus's hypothesis proved useful because, whereas previously the addition of epicycles in the computations of the orbits of the planets—especially the sun bound planets Mercury and Venus—was an extra device, an *ad hoc addendum* to the geometry of geocentric astronomy, such an arbitrary addition was found to be unnecessary on the hypothesis of a rotating earth. In contrast to the scenario of an immobile earth, the orbital rotation of the earth in the heliocentric model *eo ipso* explains the irregularity of the retrograde planetary cycles without having to rely on too many epicycles (the scientific principle of parsimony!). Kuhn writes:

> Retrograde motion and the variation of the time required to circle the ecliptic are the two gross planetary irregularities which in antiquity had led astronomers to employ epicycles and deferents in treating the problem of the planets. Copernicus's system explains these same gross irregularities, and it does so without resorting to epicycles, or at least to major epicycles.
>
> 1985:168

The reason, therefore, for the correctness or at least the plausibility of Copernicus's hypothesis of a rotating earth lies in the fact that it is capable of explaining planetary orbits without the use of (too many) epicycles and deferents, whilst on that hypothesis it also becomes clear that observed irregularities only *seem* to be that as a consequence of earth rotation. As Kuhn indicates, the new astronomy exhibited a certain 'naturalness and coherence that were lacking in the older earth-centered version' (1985:177). No extra devices or external assumptions were required in order to acquire such coherence and an 'admirable symmetry', a 'clear bond of harmony in the motion and magnitude of the Spheres', as Copernicus himself describes it in the introduction to *On the Revolutions*.[39] Harmony, coherence and naturalness were clearly central to the Copernican revolution.

Mutatis mutandis, Kant's revolution in the ways of thinking in metaphysics suggests an alternative approach to an existing problem in a way very similar to Copernicus's innovation. Kant's particular problem concerns the question: How can our knowledge be justified, that is, when can we be sure that our claims to knowledge are legitimate? And, concomitant with that question, how is metaphysics itself possible as a science? This approach, however, is not just the fairly novel thought that everything that we experience is subject to certain necessary constraints or so-called transcendental conditions that relate to our subjective point of view (a question of the 'how possible' sort). It lies rather in the idea that the analysis that purports to explain these transcendental conditions must itself be capable of being clarified, in an a priori manner, *as the more coherent explanation*, comparable to the way in which the hypothesis of earth rotation enabled Copernicus to do away with the ad hoc revisions of the standard model and put forward a more coherent and stable explanatory model for planetary astronomy. In Kant's own case the increased coherence concerns a self-explanation, a self-reflection or, as he himself calls it, the 'self-knowledge' of reason with regard to its own analysis of the necessary conditions of knowledge. And it is this thought that is Kant's unique 'invention', which ushered in an entirely new way of doing philosophy. In the next section, the specific connection between this invention of Kant's and his Copernicanism will be explored further.

2.5 Kant's Veritable Copernicanism

What now has what was of inestimable importance for the development of modern astronomy, the Copernican revolution, got to do with Kant's 'alteration in our way of thinking'? What makes Kant's revolution in metaphysics typically *Copernican*? Can one consider Kant's analogy with Copernicus an apt one?

Kant's Copernicanism turns out to concern his view of science and its model function for philosophy. This does not mean that what is at issue in the B-preface in general and in the Analytic of the *Critique* more in particular concerns Kant's putative foundation of the sciences, specifically physical science. This is a view of Kant's theoretical philosophy made popular by the Marburg branch of the neo-Kantian school of thought. Kant's interest in science, in the B-preface and in the *Critique* (and also in the *Prolegomena*, for that matter), relates to the exemplary function it may have for metaphysics. The central question thus concerns the extent to which metaphysics amounts to science, not the metaphysical foundation of science. It is important to recognize that Kant's putative philosophy of science, articulated in his *Metaphysical Foundations of Natural Science* (1786), *presupposes, as a separate prior investigation*, a formal metaphysics of nature, that is, his transcendental philosophy, for which he argued in the *Critique* (and in capsule form in the *Prolegomena*). However, it is important to notice also that it is not the case that Kant simply adopts the scientific method for philosophy unmodified and without qualification; Kant is interested in a properly metaphysical *analogue* of science's method.

In the B-preface, Kant alludes to the criteria for 'the secure course of a science' (Bvii), of the 'royal path' (Bx) of science. These are: (1) a commonly agreed upon goal (unanimity); (2) steady progress; (3) consolidation of success; and (4) universal access (science must be exoteric, not esoteric) (see Bvii; cf. Aix, Bxiv–xv, and Bxxxii ff.). Traditional metaphysics does not appear to comply with any of these standards for science, according to Kant. For Kant, traditional metaphysics is still characterized by a 'battlefield', where various parochial factions and competing schools are engaged in 'mock combat' (Bxv). Kant thinks that logic and mathematics, and also the newer physical (natural) science, set the example, having reached a level of success very early on in their history, although in the case of physics this took a little longer—notwithstanding the various competing theories, also in the sciences; nevertheless, unlike philosophy all these schools of thought in the sciences share the same single, incontestable basic scientific method, with which they conduct their research.

As regards the sciences, Kant points out (Bxiii ff.) that 'a sudden revolution in the way of thinking' (Bxii) enabled these disciplines to establish themselves as rigorous sciences. The fundamental principle of the sciences rests on a general pattern of thought in virtue of which one acquires an understanding of the object in their respective fields of inquiry. Such an insight is possible to the extent that certain results hang together in conformity with previously stipulated rules. For a physicist it holds that the laws of nature cannot simply be read off nature. Nature must obey the way in which the scientist charts nature, that is, determines it in accord with predetermined procedures.[40] Paradigmatically, the physicist formulates a hypothesis concerning a connected whole of data, framed in theoretical terminology, which is subsequently put to the test, whereby one establishes whether the test data conform to the hypothesized theoretical framework. This results in the formulation of a theory or law that becomes standard unless the hypothesis is falsified by counter-evidence. Kant interprets this in such a way that also the physicist, albeit implicitly,[41] must be taken to understand that the rationally acquired insight is obtained only because the result is produced or brought forth 'according to its [i.e. the physicist's reasoning] own design' (Bxiii). The rationality of the experimental procedure lies precisely in the fact that the hypothesis exactly matches, or agrees with, the result of the subsequent tests, absent falsifying evidence. The experiment that a scientist carries out is characterized by a certain non-trivial tautology: what is determinately known as law-governed is known in accord with pre-determined, pre-given, rules or procedures.

Mutatis mutandis, the same holds for mathematics and any science modelled after the mathematical method. For mathematics, the experimental method as such does of course not apply. However, as Kant points out in the B-preface, for the mathematician holds too, just as much as for the physicist (cf. Bxiii ff.), that he does not

> trace what he [sees] in this figure [i.e. 'the isosceles triangle'], or even trace its mere concept, and read off, as it were, from the properties of the figure; but rather ... *produce[s] the latter from what he himself thought into the object and*

presented (through construction) according to a priori concepts, and that in order to know something securely a priori he had to ascribe to the thing nothing except what followed necessarily from what he himself had put into it in accordance with its concept.

Bxii, emphasis added; cf. A713/B741

This is significant for an appreciation of the exact sciences and mathematics as exemplars for Kant's own thought apropos of the status of metaphysics (or philosophy more generally). Kant's Copernicanism resides precisely in there being a philosophical analogue of this rational-experimental procedure that is characteristic of the sciences.[42]

Analogous to the exact sciences and to Copernicus's thought-experiment in particular, Kant introduces, in the passages in the B-preface just prior and directly following the famous Copernican analogy, a thought-experiment for metaphysics ('[t]his experiment of reason', Bxx note; cf. Bxvi), so that in a similar way metaphysics pursue the secure course of science. The passage in question reads:

Up to now it has been assumed that [C] all our cognition must conform to the objects; but [D] all attempts to find out something about them *a priori* through concepts that would extend our cognition have, on this presupposition, come to nothing. Hence let us once try whether we do not get farther with the problems of metaphysics by [E] assuming that the objects must conform to our cognition, which would agree better with [A] the requested possibility of an *a priori* cognition of them, which is [B] to establish something about objects before they are given to us . . . .[43] [D] If intuition has to conform to the constitution of the objects, then I do not see how we can know anything of them *a priori*; but if [E] the object (as an object of the senses) conforms to the constitution of our faculty of intuition, then [F] I can very well represent this possibility to myself.

Bxvi–xvii[44]

The thought-experiment expressed in this quotation can be put in the following way (the letters that have been inserted in the above text are presented in the order of the argument steps):

(A) Metaphysics is a priori cognition of objects.

(B) In order to have a priori cognition of objects we must know something about objects *before* we experience them.

(C) Knowledge corresponds to objects in the way we experience them as empirically given. (*standard correspondence theory of truth*)

Taking (A) as the standard view of metaphysics (which Kant accepts), we see that (B) is implied by definition and (C) is the paradigmatic background assumption of traditional theories of knowledge, which results in

> (D) If knowledge of an object x conforms to x as it is experienced as empirically given (viz. a posteriori), then *ex hypothesi* knowledge cannot be a priori.

We discern in (D) that on (C) a contradiction with (B) ensues. In fact, on (C) a priori cognition, and thus metaphysics, is impossible. Now suppose that instead of (C) we advance hypothesis

> (E) Objects correspond to our manner of cognizing them. (*hypothesis of transcendental cognition*)

If we accept (E), we can avoid the contradiction shown in (D), for

> (F) 'we can cognize of things *a priori* only what we ourselves have put into them' (Bxviii), that is to say, we have a priori cognition of things insofar as they agree with the a priori forms of cognition, or, have some kind of cognition of them *before* we experience them.

Since (F) means that the contradiction shown in (D) is avoided and (C) is thereby disconfirmed, the hypothesis (E) is to be accepted on the grounds of it yielding a more logically coherent theory showing greater explanatory force than on (C) (although of course it is still not an *apodictic* proof of its truth).

In this thought experiment Kant shows himself to be in basic agreement with the traditional view of truth: to wit, truth as *adæquatio rei et intellectus* (cf. B82ff./A58ff.). Yet according to the traditional interpretation of *adæquatio* thought must correspond to the thing (as in [C]), such that, given certain empirical conditions, the thing x, which affects the senses, must be seen as isomorphically identical to the forms of the understanding y, so that y maps onto x. In the case of empiricism this means that y's representation of x is in fact an exact copy of, and as such produced or caused by, represented x. However, the relation between x and y can on such a causal account of knowledge only be an a posteriori knowable one, for x must first affect the senses in order for the relation to y to obtain, so that y corresponds to x (only a divine mind could thus know a priori a thing's properties).[45]

With a view to the possibility of an a priori analysis of knowledge Kant inverts the above perspective, without however relinquishing the notion of truth as correspondence.[46] This now concerns the so-called 'transcendental turn': we must take the thing such that *it* conforms to thought. The reversal of thought implies that, *from within the perspective of thought*, a rigorous relation is established between, on the one hand, the necessary conditions or rules[47] under which a thing *x* must stand in order for it first to count as an object *for me*, viz. for the cognizing or thinking subject, and, on the other hand, the conditions or rules of thought or the understanding itself (*y*). Only in this case, Kant argues, is a priori cognition of *x* possible and in fact *ex hypothesi*, for those two sets of conditions or rules are specified by *y* and thus the relation of correspondence between them can be grasped a priori by the cognizing subject (F) (cf. A114). This idea is in agreement with the thought that 'nothing can be ascribed to the objects except what the thinking subject takes out of itself' (Bxxiii).[48]

By means of this thought experiment of pure reason Kant believes he has provided a 'touchstone' (Bxviii) for establishing the legitimacy of metaphysical claims, and for establishing it apodictically to boot. The hypothesis of inverting the relation between the intellect (understanding) and the object first makes metaphysics possible as a genuine a priori mode of cognition. In this way, from within the purview of reason itself, through the 'self-knowledge' of the understanding, a one-to-one a priori relation can be identified between the elements of cognition, that is, between on the one hand the necessary concepts employed by the cognizing subject and, on the other, the pure forms of the empirical object which she cognizes. This one-to-one relation obtains if and only if objects conform to a priori concepts and pure intuition, more precisely, if and only if an isomorphic a priori identifiable relation exists between the *form* of knowledge or experience, which by definition is conceptual, and the necessary *form* of objects of our experience (namely, pure intuition). Only in this way can the claim to truth (as correspondence, *adæquatio*), with which metaphysics is essentially concerned, be legitimated.

The most important outcome of this thought experiment is that thus a more harmonious, indeed rational coherence can be discerned between the various elements of cognition from the perspective of a priori analysis, hence from within the 'self-knowing' perspective of pure reason, precisely as metaphysics claims to be doing as regards a priori cognition.[49] *It is exactly herein that we must locate Kant's Copernicanism*. The result of the analysis of knowledge with a view to determining the conditions of truth is inextricably bound up with the way the analysis is manifested in and by thought itself (hence my characterization 'self-explanation' or Kant's 'self-knowledge'). Put differently, the a priori insight acquired into the intimate relation between thought and object, i.e. truth as correspondence, is connected to the way the object must be considered conformable to how thought conceives of it in accord with its own self-understanding, just as with Copernicus the hypothesis of earth rotation, more generally, the inversion from geocentrism to heliocentrism, yielded greater insight into planetary motion and moreover could clarify not a few irregularities in the existing astronomical models. The strong similarity between Copernicus's revolution and Kant's lies uniquely in a significant increase in rationality, understood in its root sense as proportion or relation, within the explanatory framework as a direct result of a change in perspective. For Copernicus, this meant that a more secure astronomy became possible, which was no longer vulnerable to ad hoc revisions. Kant's fundamental concern was the possibility of a priori insight into the grounds of knowledge, indeed the possibility of rational thought as such, and thus in the conditions of truth. In the closing section I briefly elaborate on the aspect of rational thought in respect of Kant.

The analogy between Kant's and Copernicus's way of reasoning therefore lies in the two-fold feature of hypothetico-deductive reasoning underpinning their thought, which concerns (1) a proposal to change the perspective or frame of reference, which, when accepted (2) leads to an increase in insight into a particular technical problem, that is, yields more rationality in terms of explaining pressing problems in a particular field of inquiry. The result (2) confirms the propriety of the hypothesis (1) and justifies its acceptance. It is clear that, on this reading of the analogy, Kant's Copernicanism is not about a theory of perspectivism per se (*perspectivism*), nor *merely* a proposal for a paradigm shift (AH), for both readings entirely neglect to account for what appears important for Kant and Copernicus in equal measure: an increase in rationality in respect of solving a technical problem, which is expressed by (2). It is this *methodical* likeness that warrants Kant's analogy with Copernicus.

2.6 'Forma dat esse rei'

The rational structure of knowledge that Kant envisions is paradigmatically expressed by his formula introduced in the B-preface of the *Critique*, which is often cited, but seldom understood. This is the earlier quoted dictum 'that we can cognize of things a priori only what we ourselves have put into them' (Bxxiii). This passage expresses the hypothetico-deductive way of thinking, the 'altered way of thinking', underlying Kant's Copernicanism. What this means is that the structure of the analysis of the relation between thought and object (the question of truth) takes on a conditional form, whereby the acquired insight *eo ipso* implies a certain limitation.[50] In other words, the modality of the argument regarding truth concerns a conditional necessity, even though the conclusion of the argument is anything but hypothetical, that is, vulnerable to revision (cf. Axv, where Kant likens hypotheses to 'forbidden commodity' [*verbotene Ware*]).⁵¹ This is affirmed by Kant's assertion that

> this attempt [*Versuch*] [i.e. the 'alteration in our way of thinking'] succeeds as well as we could wish, and it promises to metaphysics the secure course of a science.... For after this alteration in our way of thinking we can very well explain the possibility of a cognition a priori, and what is still more, we can provide satisfactory [*genugtuenden*] proofs of the laws that are the a priori ground of nature ... which were both impossible according to the earlier way of proceeding.
> Bxviii–xix, trans. modified

The hypothesis or 'attempt' of a reversal of procedure, of 'our way of thinking', enables us to give a satisfactory philosophical proof of the possibility of a priori cognition, which was hitherto not possible. However, that Kant's *reasoning* manifests an implicit hypothetical or conditional structure does not in the least prevent the resultant *proof itself*, to be given in the body of the *Critique* (cf. Bxxii), from being a '*deduction* of our faculty [*Vermögen*] of cognizing a priori' (Bxix, emphasis added) and not, as is the case in the empirical sciences, a demonstration merely based on induction (epagogic proof).

This hypothetico-deductive or conditional form of reasoning was already expressed by the way in which Kant's thought experiment, which we analysed above, proceeded. I shall attempt to clarify this point a bit more by having recourse to a standard dictum that Kant cites in a late essay, titled *On A Recently Prominent Tone of Superiority in Philosophy*, published in the *Berlinische Monatsschrift* of May 1796 (see VT, AA 8:387–406). This at first blush highly rhetorical essay is customarily ignored in the literature on Kant's theoretical philosophy. However, it contains some interesting allusions that throw light on the central planks of Kant's theoretical thought. In this respect, it is worthy of note that Kant there cites the scholastic dictum *forma dat esse rei*, which he accepts in principle. Kant reads this dictum such that

> in the form lies the essence of the thing [*Sache*]⁵² insofar as this [i.e. the essence of the thing] is to be known through reasons.
> VT, AA 8:404 [Kant 2002:443]⁵³

What does Kant mean here? What Kant has in mind can be rephrased as a conditional:

> The thinking self or the epistemic agent is able to know something essentially about the thing (to know the *esse* of the *res*, the *Sache*) *if and only if* the thinking

self or the epistemic agent provides (*dat*) a certain form (*forma*) to that which it cognizes, viz. the thing or state of affairs (*res*, the *Sache*), in accordance with the general principles of reason itself.

In this case the thinking self knows the thing *through reason*, which for Kant means as much as *necessarily* and *a priori* (B4), and hence *apodictically* (but not in a mathematical sense). The implication of this is that the form (*forma*) that the thinking self puts into, or gives to (*dat*), the thing (*res*), in conformity with the rules of reason, corresponds to the essence (*esse*) of the thing that is being cognized (by the thinking self). Thus, thought corresponds to the thing *insofar and only insofar as it is being cognized*. The form of thought is therefore the essence of the *known* thing.

That is why Kant believes that reason determines the form of what it knows with certainty and a priori, for *it itself* puts in the form to which the known object must conform; this is in line with what Kant says in the above-quoted passage at Bxviii. Consequently, we may claim that as thinkers, and *mutatis mutandis* as moral agents, we are our own authors of the conditions under which we know things or act according to maxims, respectively. In the context of his practical philosophy, Kant asserts that we are subject to no law or cognitive constraint which we have not legislated or prescribed to us ourselves.[54] It is in this sense that, taken generally, reason is self-legitimating and, accordingly, self-explicatory. That is to say, reason a priori puts a structure into that which is 'perceived' or that which it posits, the object of thought (and *mutatis mutandis* the object of the moral will), in order to subsequently legitimize that structure as the necessary form both of what is cognized, the thing as object, and the manner in which it is cognized. Kant often talks about the same conditions that are the conditions of the experience of objects and the conditions of the objects of experience (A158/B197).

Kant thus demonstrates that a self-legitimating analysis, a 'self-knowledge' of sorts, is the kind of explanatory model for adequate and coherent philosophical cognition, which may lay claim to being scientific in the same way as Copernicus's hypothetical construction by way of the postulate of earth rotation yielded a new, more coherent standard in astronomy in terms of computing planetary motions. Therefore, Kant's allusion to Copernicus's 'first thoughts' (Bxvi) is not, as many interpreters of Kant claim or intimate, just a *façon de parler* concerning the introduction of a new paradigm. It rather indicates a systematic, substantial connection with Copernicus's scientific hypothetico-deductive methodology, which Kant considered paradigmatic for any science, and thus, *mutatis mutandis*, also for metaphysics.

But as noted earlier, in a note towards the end of the preface Kant makes it clear that the hypothetical nature of his argument in the B-preface must make way for an apodictic proof of the *truth* of the hypothesis regarding the conformity of objects to the a priori forms of intuition and thought. What in the preface had been proposed 'as a hypothesis' must 'in the treatise itself ... be proved not hypothetically but rather apodictically from the constitution of our representations of space and time and from the elementary concepts of the understanding' (Bxxii note). In the body of the *Critique* itself, Kant must thus show, in accordance with the progressive, synthetic method that is adopted for the *Critique* (Prol, AA 4:263, 274ff., 278ff.), that for the proof, which for philosophy must always be ostensive (A789/B817), no data 'except reason itself' are accepted so as to 'develop cognition out of its original seeds' (Prol, AA 4:274 [Kant 2002:70]). This is because metaphysics 'must always be dogmatic, i.e., it must prove its conclusion strictly a priori from secure principles' (Bxxxv), '*from the nature of the understanding itself*' (Prol, AA 4:308 [Kant 2002:101]). However, against the sheer dogmatism of the School metaphysics, this means for Kant that reason must first critically inquire 'in what way and by what right it has obtained' the principles by means of which it acquires a priori knowledge of objects. This does not mean that the thought experiment in the B-Preface was just that; rather, the hypothesis of the conformity of objects *to* thought itself is apodictically confirmed in the body of the *Critique*, in particular through the analysis of the faculty of understanding, that is, in the Transcendental Deduction, which shows that indeed the a priori knowledge of objects flows analytically from the understanding knowing itself.[55]

3

'A representation of my representations': Apperception and the Leibnizian-Wolffian Background

3.1 Introduction

To provide some historical and contextual background to Kant's theory of apperception—which is to be discussed in the following Chapter 4—in this chapter, I explore to what extent, and in which context, transcendental apperception and the notion of 'consciousness' are featured in Kant's metaphysics lectures and what, in this regard, changes (or not) from the pre-Critical to the Critical phase of Kant's lecturing activity, also by looking at inchoate senses of self-consciousness in his published work prior to the First *Critique*. My interest is chiefly in the metaphysics lectures, both before and contemporaneous with Kant's Critical phase, but to a lesser extent I also refer to the anthropology and logic lectures.

It is in the metaphysics lectures that one gets a clearer picture, compared to the *Critique* itself, of the Leibnizian and Wolffian background of Kant's theory of apperception, as well as of the usage and context of the term 'consciousness', and why that term should be approached with some caution, also in the *Critique*, as it might lead one to believe that Kant, or indeed Leibniz and Wolff, are simply talking about a 'merely' psychological notion of consciousness, even considering that the term of course occurs within the context of what is traditionally called empirical psychology. Kant's chief motivation for coining the term 'transcendental apperception' is, I believe, because he precisely wanted to avoid confusion between the psychological and epistemological meanings of consciousness, a confusion one easily sees in the accounts of Leibniz, Wolff, and Baumgarten.[1] Although Kant already expounds on apperception and its epistemic function in his unpublished *Reflexionen* from the mid-1770s, in the so-called *Duisburg Nachlass*, in the lectures the notion 'apperception' only first crops up in the

Metaphysik Mrongovius, from just after the publication of the first edition of the *Critique*. One can safely say that *transcendental* apperception is a specifically Critical coinage, which one will not find any earlier outside Kant's corpus. By contrast, Kant's rationalist predecessors identified inner sense with self-consciousness or *apperceptio*. Kant is the first who explicitly differentiates between inner sense or empirical apperception and apperception as a logical, formal self-consciousness. But it is also clear that even in the *Critique* Kant confusingly continues using the term 'consciousness', when it is evident from the context that unitary consciousness or transcendental consciousness or apperception is at issue, not mere psychological consciousness (self-awareness or lower-level awareness).

Although the notion of transcendental apperception as such is original to Kant, the term 'apperception' is of course owed to Leibniz, and there are parallels especially to Wolff's idea of consciousness of self as derivative of object consciousness, as a kind of reflexive consciousness that accompanies the consciousness of objects. For Wolff, an aspect of consciousness is that it expresses a two-way relation to objects: consciousness is not just consciousness of things but also, and at the same time, a consciousness of self. There is always a reflexive element involved in the perception of an object, and this element is consciousness or apperception (*apperceptio*), which points to the subject of representation or perception. Apperception is the consciousness of the self's own activity present *in perceiving objects outside of herself*. This idea of apperception is based on Wolff's definition of consciousness as the capacity to distinguish. In being conscious of things, one differentiates things from one another, but also from *oneself* as the agent of differentiation. So the subject is differentiated from objects precisely in her being conscious of those various objects through differentiation. This fundamental and specifically non-psychological concept of self-consciousness as reflexivity, which has its roots in Wolff, is to become central to Kant's thought and that of the later German Idealists, not least Hegel's. Kant's view of self-consciousness is similar to Wolff's: the derivative model of consciousness of Wolff (Thiel 2011:308) is *mutatis mutandis* applicable to Kant's view of transcendental consciousness as constitutive of the objective unity of representations as defining an object. While Kant's view is much less explicitly characterized in terms of explicit subject-object oppositions, as are later Fichte's and Hegel's, transcendental apperception must not be seen as prior to the perception of objects, but, to put it in terms proposed by Robert Pippin (1997a), as adverbial to it. Transcendental consciousness and consciousness of objects are equiprimordial. As Kant puts it at A108, the original and necessary consciousness of the identity of oneself is <u>at the same time</u> a consciousness of an equally necessary unity of the synthesis of all appearances in accordance with concepts ... for the mind could not possibly think of the identity of itself in the manifoldness of its representations, and indeed think this *a priori*, if it did not have before its eyes the identity of its action, which subjects all synthesis of apprehension (which is empirical) to a transcendental unity, and first makes possible their connection in accordance with *a priori* rules.

A108, my underlining

The 'necessary unity of the synthesis of all appearances' is—as explained in this section of the A-Deduction—what first constitutes a possible object of experience. However, this necessary unity is nothing but the necessary unity of the act of synthesis of representations that also, simultaneously, first constitutes one's identity as self-consciousness. There is no discrepancy between the application of a priori rules that bring unity to one's representations of an *object* or objects and the a priori rules that unify one's very representations *as one's own*. They are the same set of rules. Both the representation of objects and self-consciousness rest on the very same act of synthesis, i.e. transcendental apperception. Transcendental apperception could then be said, similarly to Wolff's reflexive understanding of consciousness, to be that which lies at the origin of the differentiation between subject and object,[2] and is, in a sense, 'derivative' of, or adverbial to, the consciousness of objects, since it does not exist other than in the act of synthesis that enables the perception of objects.

3.2 Apperception and Consciousness

The notion of transcendental apperception is without doubt one of the cornerstones of the transcendental philosophy. In the A-Deduction in the *Critique of Pure Reason*, Kant calls it the *Radikalvermögen* of all our cognition (A114), a term not easily translatable into English. The German term refers to the Latin *radix*, meaning 'root', so 'root capacity' would be a potential translation for it.[3] It is associated closely with self-consciousness, more in particular with the well-known phrase with which the Transcendental Deduction of the Categories (hereafter 'the Deduction' for short) proper, in its B-version, is introduced in §16, namely 'The *I think* must *be able* to accompany all my representations' (B131). This 'I think' is, as Kant says at A354, 'the formal proposition of apperception', and concerns the transcendental unity of self-consciousness, and so the 'consciousness of oneself' (*Bewußtsein seiner Selbst*) (B68[4]).

Crucially, as Kant proceeds to argue in the Deduction, transcendental apperception, as an act of the understanding, provides 'the legislation for nature' (A126), and is the subjective ground on which nature's lawfulness depends (cf. A127).[5] Transcendental apperception is not only the necessary condition, or the subjective condition, under which we can *experience* nature and its objects, but, as Kant argues, also the sufficient, or objective, condition for nature and its objects, insofar as nature *qua* nature or the objectivity of objects is concerned.[6] In other words, transcendental apperception is also an objective condition of experience. Kant's position might seem extreme, and smacking of phenomenalistic idealism, when he argues, in the conclusion of the A-Deduction, that the objects of which we have knowledge 'are one and all in me, that is, are determinations of my identical self', which is 'only another way of saying that there must be a complete unity of them in one and the same apperception' (A129, trans. Kemp Smith). However, what I believe Kant is claiming here is that, very generally put, knowledge of objects is intimately and necessarily bound up with a form of self-consciousness, an idea that I contend he picks up, at least partly, from the Wolffian tradition but on which at the same time he puts his own Critical slant. I return to this perhaps surprisingly Wolffian aspect in Section 3.3.

In this chapter, I do not yet discuss the theoretical details of Kant's theory of apperception and its pivotal role in the foundation of empirical knowledge, which is what I do in the next chapter. To provide some historical context before going on to delineate the systematic features of apperception in the argument of the Deduction, I merely wish to focus here on the extent to which Kant addresses transcendental apperception in the lectures on metaphysics that he gave in the 1780s and early 1790s, which have been published in volumes 28 and 29 of the *Akademie Ausgabe*. (I shall also refer to relevant passages in the contemporary anthropology lecture notes.) This provides an opportunity to look at the background of Kant's theory of apperception in his predecessors, something into which the *Critique* itself does not give us insight.

Noticeable, first, is that, in the lecture notes, Kant hardly ever uses the term 'apperception' (it occurs roughly 36 times in all of the extant metaphysics notes) and that where he uses it he never calls it '*transcendental* apperception', but always merely 'apperception'. More often, though, he refers to it just by the label that his rationalist predecessors in the German school used: 'consciousness', which presents a potential problem of confusing transcendental apperception with consciousness as such. This is mostly a matter of terminology, but, at least at first sight, it might be that Kant's view on consciousness in the lecture notes is still very much informed by the Wolffian conflationist view of consciousness, and that this is even carried over into the *Critique*, at least in the A-version, to the extent that Kant does not always carefully distinguish between the terms 'apperception' and 'consciousness'. This is an important issue, as from the very first reception of the First *Critique*, many commentators from Reinhold up until recent times[7] have taken Kant's principle of apperception to be a principle of consciousness, which confuses a chiefly epistemological principle with a psychological condition. In the *Critique*, Kant makes it clear that transcendental conditions must be seen strictly separately from conditions that have to do with psychology (cf. e.g. B152). But I believe that there are clear indications, also in the lecture notes, that Kant's use of the term 'consciousness' must be read as meaning 'apperception', in the Critical sense of transcendental apperception, or as meaning 'unity of consciousness', not just consciousness in any (mere) psychological sense (in terms of 'awareness' or 'sentience' or 'feeling of self').

Secondly—and this is related to the first issue—contrary to what the great majority among commentators of Kant believe (e.g. Wolff 1973, Allison 1983, Collins 1999) I contend that Kant does not think, as might be concluded from some of his statements, that in sensibility or inner sense, independently of transcendental apperception, there is no consciousness at all, more precisely, that mere sensible representations are unconscious or not conscious representations. Notice that, as far as I know, in most of its occurrences Kant does not use the term 'unconscious' and cognates intransitively but more in the sense of 'not being conscious of'. In fact, he hardly uses it at all. At one point in the anthropology lecture notes, he associates absolute unconsciousness with death.[8] In the *Critique*, Kant quite explicitly—and implicitly in some passages in the lectures of the Critical period (but see below Section 3.4)—keeps inner sense and *transcendental* apperception apart, where the former must be seen as equivalent to *empirical* apperception, which is 'forever variable' and consists merely of a 'stream of inner appearances' (A107). The Critical Kant clearly distances himself from what was 'customary in the systems of psychology' (B153), referring to the broadly Wolffian tradition, which viewed inner sense as identical to apperception *simpliciter*. For the Critical Kant, inner sense is thus merely psychological, whereas transcendental apperception refers to a logical, formal consciousness.[9]

But the pre-Critical Kant just takes over whole the standard notion of 'inner sense' as referring to the consciousness of self generally or what later on is called 'self-consciousness' (or what in his Latin writings Wolff calls *apperceptio*), which as said the Critical Kant first specifically differentiates as *transcendental* consciousness or apperception, on the one hand, and inner sense and empirical apperception, on the other. And given that in the rationalist systems of psychology inner sense was identified with 'consciousness strictly speaking', i.e. 'the state of my soul' (Baumgarten, *Metaphysica*, §535), it does not seem unreasonable to expect Kant, in the Critical phase, to continue to associate his successor notion of transcendental apperception with 'consciousness strictly speaking', thus giving rise to an ambiguity over the use and meaning of 'apperception' in contrast to 'consciousness' in the more technical, psychological sense.[10] But we must note that, already early on, and in a way that comports with his later distinction between inner sense and apperception (more precisely, *transcendental* apperception), Kant also distinguishes between psychological and logical, formal consciousness.[11] And most often it is also only this latter sense of consciousness that he is referring to when he uses the term 'consciousness'.

In the next section, I explore the Leibnizian and Wolffian background of Kant's developing views, and examine also some of the very few passages in which Kant hints at self-consciousness in published work from the pre-Critical period. To get a clearer idea of Kant's views in this regard, I also briefly look at the Leibnizian-Wolffian theory of obscure representations, which Kant adopts.

3.3 Self-Consciousness in the Pre-Critical Kant and the Leibnizian-Wolffian Background

As Reinhard Brandt (1994:2) has pointed out, prior to and including the *Inaugural Dissertation* of 1770, apart from metaphysical questions regarding soul-body interaction, Kant appears uninterested in the topic of consciousness or self-consciousness as such or as a grounding faculty for knowledge in his published works in the pre-Critical period, which is evidenced by the infrequent occurrence of the very term 'consciousness'.[12] Heiner Klemme (1996:55ff., esp. p. 59) has shown that Kant's subjective turn takes place in the early 1770s, which first becomes manifest in particular in the anthropology lectures of 1772–73 (Collins and Parow).[13] However, Kant does speak of 'inner sense' and hints at the cognitive function it has already in earlier published works, such as in the conclusion to his essay *The False Subtlety* of 1762, where he reflects on the 'mysterious power ... which makes judging possible' as that which makes the difference between animals and human beings. He identifies this power as 'the faculty of inner sense', which is 'the faculty of making one's own representations the objects of one's thought' and is 'a fundamental faculty' (*Grundvermögen*) that 'can only belong to rational beings', and on which 'the entire higher faculty of cognition is based' (DfS, AA 2:60 [Kant 2003:104]). Likewise, in the 1763 essay *Negative Magnitudes*,

Kant refers appreciatively to Leibniz's view of the soul's faculty of representation, or activity of the mind, as the foundation for conceptuality:

> There is something imposing and, it seems to me, profoundly true in this thought of Leibniz: the soul embraces the whole universe with its faculty of representation, though only an infinitesimally tiny part of these representations is clear. It is, indeed, the case that *concepts of every kind must have as the foundation on which alone they are based the inner activity of our minds. … The power of thought possessed by the soul must contain the real grounds of all concepts*, in so far as they are supposed to arise in a natural fashion within the soul.
>
> NG, AA 2:199 [Kant 2003:237], emphasis added

And in the *Inquiry* of 1764, when comparing the method for metaphysics with Newton's method for natural science, he sees an important foundational, or at least facilitating, role for 'inner experience' or 'self-evident inner consciousness'. Kant writes:

> The true method of metaphysics is basically the same as that introduced by Newton into natural science and which has been of such benefit to it. Newton's method maintains that one ought, on the basis of certain experience and, if need be, with the help of geometry, to seek out the rules in accordance with which certain phenomena of nature occur. Even if one does not discover the fundamental principle of these occurrences in the bodies themselves, it is nonetheless certain that they operate in accordance with this law. Complex natural events are explained once it has been clearly shown how they are governed by these well-established rules. Likewise in metaphysics: *by means of certain inner experience, that is to say, by means of an immediate and self-evident inner consciousness*, seek out those characteristic marks which are certainly to be found in the concept of any general property.
>
> UD, AA 2:286 [Kant 2003:259], emphasis added[14]

The above-quoted reference to Leibniz's view of the soul as the faculty of conscious representation or activity of the mind warrants a look at the backdrop against which Kant eventually, in the 1770s up to the *Critique*, develops his own theory of transcendental (self-)consciousness, or transcendental apperception. It is unlikely that on this point Kant was directly influenced by either Leibniz or Wolff apart from inheriting the existing terminology. Most probably, the theory of transcendental apperception is original to Kant himself. Udo Thiel (2011:372–6) suggests that Mérian's account of 'original apperception' might have had some influence on Kant's conception of transcendental apperception. Kant must have known about Mérian's conception of apperception through Tetens' account of

Mérian in his *Philosophische Versuche über die menschliche Natur und ihre Entwicklung* (1777), which Kant read. But notice that Kant's first use of the term 'apperception', whilst pointing out its epistemic grounding function that is later associated with its transcendental role, in the *Duisburg Nachlass* (Refl 4674, AA 17:646–7 [1773–75]), predates his reading of Tetens. One of the very first occurrences of the term 'apperception' in the Kantian corpus is in *Reflexion* 4562 (AA 17:594), dated by Adickes between 1772 and 1775/6.

What is clear though is that Kant appropriates Leibniz's notion of 'apperception', which is first mentioned in the *New Essays* (G 5:121, II.ix.4), by its cognate *s'appercevoir*, and later in the *Principles of Nature and Grace* (G 6:600, §4) and *Monadology* (G 6:608–9, §14). Apart from one occasion (§93) where he employs the term *apperceptibilitas*,[15] Baumgarten does not use the term 'apperception' or its cognate 'apperceive' in the *Metaphysica*, although he does mention the Latin equivalent in his *Acroasis logica*,[16] a copy of which Kant had in his possession (Warda 1922:45). Baumgarten barely even discusses consciousness. Wolff employs the Latinized *apperceptio* in his *Psychologia empirica*.[17]

Leibniz distinguishes between perception, which is 'the inner state of the monad', and apperception, the latter defined as consciousness (*conscience*), or 'the reflexive knowledge of that inner state' (*Principles*, G 6:600, §4; cf. *Monadology*, G 6:608–9, §14).[18] Leibniz criticizes Locke's view of the ineliminably reflexive nature of perception, which is the view that it is 'impossible for any one to perceive without perceiving, that he does perceive' (Locke, *Essay*, Book II, Ch. XXVII, §9). As Leibniz points out, the view that any perception is a conscious perception is vulnerable to an infinite regress. In his response to the Lockean position, he writes:

> [I]t is not possible that we should always reflect explicitly on all our thoughts; otherwise the mind would reflect on each reflection *ad infinitum*, without ever being able to move on to a new thought. For example, in apperceiving some present feeling, I should have always to think that I think about that feeling, and further to think that I think of thinking about it, and so on *ad infinitum*.
>
> *New Essays*, G 5:108, II.i.§19, trans. emended

Leibniz's objection that an infinite regress threatens if all of our thoughts were always reflected upon is a valid one. However, concurring with this does not necessarily mean that the possibility that the first-order perception has some degree of (non-reflexive) consciousness, i.e. a consciousness that is not an apperception (understood as reflexive consciousness), is thereby excluded. In fact, one could argue that the first-order perception must be conscious, in the non-reflexive sense, in order for a second-order, reflexive consciousness of that state at all to be possible.

For Leibniz, by contrast, apparently the perceptions that are not apperceived are themselves *ex hypothesi* unconscious. He calls these perceptions minute perceptions (*petites perceptions*) in the *New Essays*. In one notable passage, Leibniz writes about these perceptions in relation to apperception: '[A]t every moment there is an infinity of perceptions in us, but without apperception and without reflection, that is, changes in the soul itself, which we do not apperceive [*dont nous ne nous appercevons pas*]' (*New Essays*, G 5:46, preface, trans. mine). The standard reading takes Leibniz here to deny these minute perceptions the feature of 'being conscious'. Notice though that Leibniz here appears to equate 'apperception' with 'reflection', which suggests that a higher-order consciousness is at issue, not thereby excluding the possibility that the infinite amount of perceptions in us which we do not apperceive, are nonetheless conscious perceptions at least *to some degree*. Jorgensen (2009:242) argues indeed that 'consciousness arises with sensation', not first with a higher-order reflection, pointing to a passage in the *Monadology* (G 6:610; §23), where Leibniz writes that 'on being awakened from a stupor, we *apperceive* our perceptions'. Here, apperception clearly indicates first-order consciousness, not consciousness of the reflexive kind.[19]

However, as Thiel (2011:300) justly observes, the official reading of Leibniz's position on the unconsciousness of minute perceptions raises the question of 'how the conscious can arise from the unconscious'. This is all the more problematic since, in conformity with the Law of Continuity (cf. Jorgensen 2009),[20] Leibniz believes that 'noticeable [conscious] perceptions arise *by degrees* from ones that are too minute to be noticed' (*New Essays*, Preface, G 5:49, emphasis added). Hence, Thiel rightly asks: 'How can consciousness develop "by degrees" from something that is totally unconscious ...?' (2011:300). I shall come back to this central problem further below. I believe that the Critical Kant is able to avoid this problem precisely by disentangling the notion of inner sense, or consciousness strictly speaking (which Kant interprets as consciousness in a more determinate psychological sense), from apperception as a formal consciousness or *conscientia logica*, namely, as *transcendental* apperception.

For Wolff, as we have seen, consciousness implies the capacity to distinguish. In the German Metaphysics, first published in 1720, his view is that we are conscious of things in so far as we distinguish them.[21] A representation is clear (*klar*) if we are able to distinguish various things from each other, and if in addition the parts of a thing are clear, then the representation is distinct (*deutlich*). Where a representation is not clear, it is obscure (*dunkel*), meaning that it is not conscious, which is similar to Leibniz's position on minute perceptions, which are not apperceived. Thus, since clarity consists in the distinction in the manifold of things and distinctness results from the clarity of their parts, clarity and distinctness of representation 'ground' consciousness (VG, §732, p. 457).[22] This definition of consciousness entails the view that isolated representations cannot be conscious ones. Given that consciousness is the capacity to distinguish, representations can be conscious only in their relation or coherence. That is, isolated and simple representations could not be differentiated from each other, since given their isolation a network of connectivity that is required for differentiation is missing; hence I could not be conscious *of* representations as isolated representations, and so isolated representations cannot be conscious. This is an important element of Wolff's view of consciousness.

But given that Wolff thinks that '*complete* obscurity...cancels out consciousness [*hebet die völlige Dunckelheit das Bewustseyn auf*]' (VG, §731, p. 457, emphasis added) and given the Leibnizian view that there are degrees to which a thought is more or less obscure,[23] it would appear to follow that while, as Wolff believes, consciousness seems to consist in the *relation between* representations, that is, in the way that they are differentiated, each representation itself must have a degree of some intensity that is *relative to* some degree that another, differentiated representation has. That is to say, the consciousness as relation consists in one degree being relative to another degree, so that the relation as consciousness would seem to lie in the degree to which one representation is conscious relative to another conscious representation on a scale of decreasing or increasing magnitudes. If the relation constitutes consciousness, then the *relata* constituting the relation must to some degree also amount to consciousness, on a scale of intensive magnitudes ranging from a total lack of consciousness (=0) being equivalent to complete obscurity, as Wolff himself suggests, to clear consciousness (=1). I shall return to this problem when I discuss Kant's view of consciousness in Section 3.4.

Another important element of Wolff's view of consciousness—a topic that we already broached earlier—is that it concerns a two-way relation: consciousness is not just consciousness of things but equally, and simultaneously, a *self-consciousness*. Any representation that is a perception of an object also always has a reflexive part, which is the element of apperception, and points to the *subject* of representation. Apperception is the consciousness of the self's own activity *in the consciousness of things*. This is again based on the definition of consciousness as the capacity to distinguish, for 'in distinguishing objects from one another we become conscious of ourselves as distinct from the objects of which we are conscious' (Thiel 2011:307–8).[24] The subject is differentiated from objects precisely in her being conscious of those objects.[25] Thiel talks about self-consciousness as being 'doubly derivative', that is, 'it depends on the consciousness of objects, and on the consciousness of our mental act of distinguishing that is involved in the consciousness of objects' (Thiel 2011:308). But it also means that, reciprocally, we could not be conscious of objects if we were not self-conscious. Notice that consciousness is broader in scope than apperception: consciousness can be of external objects or of one's own thoughts, whereas apperception is always an inner-directed consciousness that feeds off the consciousness of things (Wolff, VG, §730, pp. 455–6).

The Wolffian view of self-consciousness as derivative of the consciousness of representations of objects seems to be reflected in what Kant is reported as having said in the early *Metaphysik* L1, namely that the consciousness of self is 'a knowing of that which belongs to me [*ein Wissen dessen, was mir zukommt*]', namely that it is 'a *representation of* my representations' (V-Met-L1/Pölitz, AA 28:227, trans. mine and emphasis added). The reflexivity inherent to representation, that is, the second-order representation of one's first-order representations of objects, is even more clearly expressed in a later lecture note (the *Metaphysik Vigilantius*; 1794–95), where the reflexivity ('the representation of my representation to myself') is also directly linked to apperception, a notion still absent from the early lectures:

> [W]hat representation is in itself, is inexplicable. A definition of that cannot be given because a representation can be explained only and in no other way than when one again represents a representation to oneself .... This action of the mind can be described as something in me that refers to something other. Now this relation of this something other in me is representation taken subjectively. The representation is aimed in part *at the object*, to which I am referring, in part *at that action of the mind* through which I compare something in me with the object. {Then one is occupied with the object in itself and its constitution, which must be wholly distinguished from the manner of representation of the subject, which involves the second, the action of the mind.} This latter is called consciousness or the representation of myself insofar as I exhibit the representation of my representation to myself.[26] ... Consciousness is also called apperception, which accompanies the represented object.
>   V-Met/Vigil, AA 29:970 [Kant 2001:441], my underlining

Corey Dyck (2011:48) contends that Wolff's derivative conception of self-consciousness is 'certainly a long way from Kant's well-known claim of an *original* apperception'. But unlike Dyck, and despite the terminological contrast, I believe that, notwithstanding some crucial differences, Kant and Wolff are much closer in this particular respect, and not just the pre-Critical Kant of the Pölitz lectures quoted earlier (V-Met-L1/Pölitz, AA 28:227), but the Critical Kant too. In the Critical view, transcendental consciousness or apperception is after all an *objective* unity of consciousness defining an object in general (B137). *Mutatis mutandis*, this is similar to Wolff's view of self-consciousness being derivative of objective consciousness, in that for Kant there is an original or transcendental consciousness only insofar as there is an a priori synthesis of representations that defines an object (in general) simply because the transcendental unity of self-consciousness *constitutes* the objective unity of representations *in virtue of* a priori synthesis of one's own representations (B139) (see Chapter 4).[27] So, one could say that the self of transcendental self-consciousness is derivative of the synthesis that constitutes the objective unity among one's representations. The 'originality' of transcendental apperception must thus not be interpreted as if it were somehow *prior to* the objective unity of representations, nor is there, as Dyck claims, a 'priority of the identity of the subject disclosed in transcendental self-consciousness to the mind's synthesis of its representations' (Dyck 2011:49). In my view, this, Dyck's view is too redolent of a Henrichian reading of the status of the analytic identity of transcendental self-consciousness, which is putatively independent of, and prior to, an a priori synthesis of one's representations and a fortiori the *objective* unity of consciousness (see Henrich 1976, 1988). Rather, it is the analytic unity of the identical self that is first grounded on the 'antecedently conceived' (B133n.) synthetic unity that results from a priori synthesis. No identity of self obtains independently of, or prior to, the a priori synthesis that first constitutes an original-synthetic unity of self-consciousness, and hence grounds an objective unity of consciousness. In fact, the analytic and synthetic unities are mutually implicative aspects of the function of unity that underlies the identity of the self as the agent of any judgement, which is defined by the objective unity of apperception.[28] So Kant's original apperception is not prior to or more fundamental than the objective unity of apperception, but it is contemporaneous with it, just as for Wolff apperception of oneself is derivative of the objective unity of representation of objects and is first constituted in the differentiation of objects.

To some extent, Kant is also indebted to Wolff's theory of clear and distinct representation, though with some significant changes—i.e. unlike Wolff, for Kant the opposite of distinct is not confused, but indistinct; he equally opposes the view that the contrast between confusion/indistinctness and distinctness maps onto the distinction between sensibility and the understanding.[29] Relatedly, the pre-Critical Kant adheres to the Leibnizian-Wolffian theory of obscure representations and the traditional view that consciousness is a characteristic of the understanding and reason and not of sensibility.[30] Hence, '[o]bscure representations are those of which one is not conscious', 'although I can infer that such representations, of which I am not conscious, are in me' (V-Anth/Fried [1775–76], AA 25:479 [Kant 2012a:55]). In various passages in the logic[31] as well as the anthropology lecture notes[32] Kant recounts the well-known example of the Milky Way, which I see clearly 'as a white strip', but of whose individual stars I have no immediate awareness but only obscure representations; or also the example of the improvising musician who 'must direct his reflection upon every finger he places, on playing, on what he wants to play, and on the new [music] he wants to produce', but is thereby not *directly* conscious of every single note he plays (V-Anth/Fried, AA 25:479 [Kant 2012a:55]).[33] On this account, of representations that are obscure, such as individual stars or notes, I can become conscious only by inference, but as such they are unconscious. Consciousness and obscurity are mutually exclusive since clarity, the opposite of obscurity, is the definition of consciousness. In the early Pölitz metaphysics notes we see this confirmed:

> As concerns objective consciousness, those representations which we have of objects of which one is conscious are called *clear* [*klare*] representations; those of whose features [*Merkmale*] one is also conscious, *distinct* [*deutliche*]; those of which one is not at all conscious, *obscure* [*dunkle*].
> V-Met-L1/Pölitz, AA 28:227 [Kant 2001:46–7][34]

However, later, in the *Critique*, at least in its B-edition, Kant is critical of the traditional view that consciousness equates with clarity and that therefore we cannot at all be conscious of obscure representations, although in the Mrongovius anthropology (V-Anth/Mron, AA 25:1221), from 1784–85, and in e.g. the later Pölitz lectures (V-Met-L2/Pölitz, AA 28:584) Kant still states the view, in conformity with the traditional viewpoint, that I am *not* conscious of my obscure representations. It should be observed though that these statements were recorded before the publication of the B-edition of the *Critique* of 1787, where in the revised Paralogisms chapter Kant first presents his critique of the view that clarity equates with consciousness, and that by implication obscure representations must be unconscious ones (B414–15n; see further below). Here in the Anthropology notes, however, Kant also says that I am not *immediately* conscious of these obscure representations, that is, conscious of each individual star, not thereby excluding the possibility that some degree of consciousness must be involved even in the obscure representation of individual stars.

That obscure representations are not *eo ipso* unconscious representations may also be illustrated by Kant's view on sleep in early works such as *Inquiry* and *Dreams of a Spirit Seer*, as well as contemporaneous metaphysics lectures notes. Since *Inquiry* is a pre-Critical work, it is unsurprising that Kant here confirms the standard Leibnizian-Wolffian view that '[o]*bscure* representations are representations of which we are not conscious'. However, he talks about 'obscure concepts' such as those we have in deep sleep and, interestingly, observes that the term 'consciousness' is ambiguous, for either 'one is not conscious that one has a representation, or one is not conscious that one has had a representation' (UD, AA 2:289–90 [Kant 2003:263]). As Kant points out, the former means merely that one's representation is obscure, whereas the latter that one does not remember it. Now from the fact that one does not remember that one had a representation it does not follow that one was not conscious, to some degree, of the representation *while* asleep, e.g. while sleepwalking. In *Dreams of a Spirit-Seer* (1766) Kant recounts the same example and surmises that 'these representations may be clearer and more extensive than even the clearest of the representations we have when we are awake' (TG, AA 2:338n [Kant 2003:325]). Similarly, in the contemporaneous account in the *Metaphysik Herder* of 1762–64, Kant is reported to have said:

> The states of the soul while sleeping are not exhausted by dreams [*Die Zustände der Seele im Schlafe erschöpfen nicht die Träume*]. *We can have clear representations, which we do not know and therefore we think were not there*[.]—There is a kind of sleep, where sleeping persons perform certain arbitrary acts in accordance with their fantasies. The fact that they are sleeping shows their lack of sensation (e.g. one who had mere feeling but no consciousness at all) and *from the fact that we do not remember* [*anything*] *when we awake from a deep sleep, it does not follow that we were then not conscious of this.*
>
> V-Met/Herder, AA 28:86, trans. mine and emphasis added

In the *Critique* itself, Kant more clearly states his view that consciousness has a greater extension than the scope of clarity strictly speaking (cf. Wunderlich 2005:141), or put more precisely, that clarity, and thus consciousness, comes in degrees, *relative to* obscurity. That is to say, also obscure representations that are accompanied by a weak consciousness which suffices to make certain distinctions between representations but falls short of second-order reflexive consciousness, or, apperception, must be possible. This is the position that Kant takes in the

B-edition of the *Critique*, in a well-known note in the Paralogisms in which he criticizes the Wolffians. In contrast to the Wolffian conception—and this also relates to my point earlier about the essentially relational nature of consciousness—in the *Critique* Kant argues, in line with Leibniz's Law of Continuity, that between clear consciousness and total unconsciousness—an 'absolute absence' of consciousness, or a 'psychological darkness' (*psychologische Dunkelheit*) (Prol, AA 4:307 [Kant 1977:50])—infinitely many degrees of consciousness exist:

> Clarity is not, as the logicians say, the consciousness of a representation; for a certain degree of consciousness, which, however, is not sufficient for memory, must be met with [*anzutreffen sein*] even in some obscure representations, because without any consciousness we would make no distinction [*Unterschied*] in the combination of obscure representations; yet we are capable of doing this with the marks of some concepts (such as those of right and equity, or those of a musician who, when improvising, hits many notes at the same time). Rather a representation is clear if the consciousness in it is sufficient for *a consciousness of the difference* [*des Unterschiedes*] between it and others. To be sure, if this consciousness suffices for a distinction [*Unterscheidung*], but not for a consciousness of the difference [*des Unterschiedes*], then the representation must still be called obscure. So there are infinitely many degrees of consciousness down to its vanishing.
>
> B414-15n.

Because 'a certain degree of consciousness ... must be met with even in some obscure representations', Kant here no longer identifies clarity with consciousness *simpliciter*, but rather with a second-order consciousness, namely a consciousness *of* the differentiation of representations.[35] The differentiation itself of representations is still accompanied by a degree of consciousness, which may range in intensity anywhere on a scale between 0 to 1, but one which falls short of the clear consciousness (=1) that accompanies a *recognition* of the differentiation (of which transcendental consciousness is the necessary condition). This gradual view of consciousness is confirmed in the contemporary and later metaphysics lecture notes, i.e. the *Von Schön* (1789/91), the *Mrongovius* (1782/83), and the *Vigilantius* (1794/95):

> Each sensation is considered as if it originated from zero just as much as it can also decrease again to zero; the sensation will never become completely nothing, even though for us it is dwindlingly small [*verschwindend*]: our sensations become gradually weaker until the lack of consciousness. Consciousness always requires a degree of differentiation [*Grad des Unterscheidens*]; now even if *this*

consciousness [of the differentiation] vanishes, the sensation therefore still has a degree.

V-Met/Schön, AA 28:509, trans. mine and emphasis added

All reality has degree. There are degrees from sensation to thought, i.e., up to apperception, where I think myself with respect to the understanding. Something can have so little degree that I can scarcely notice it, but nonetheless I am still always conscious of it. There is, properly speaking, no largest and smallest in experience.

V-Met/Mron, AA 29:834 [Kant 2001:192]

It follows now from this, that the real, since it has its ground in sensation, therefore in the object of the senses, could not have its abode in the merely intellectual, therefore the degree of the real can thus be thought neither as greatest <*maximum*> nor as smallest <*minimum*>. On the other hand, it is certain that the modification of the degree of the intensive magnitude of the real quality must be infinite, *even if it can also be unnoticeable*. Therefore between the determinate degree A until 0=zero there must be found an infinite multitude of qualities of the real, *even if in an unnoticeable degree, e.g., knowledge, representations, yes even the consciousness of human beings have many degrees, without one being able to determine the smallest*.

V-Met/Vigil, AA 29:1000 [Kant 2001:468], emphasis added

The crucial note to B414 in the B-edition Paralogisms is important for an assessment of Kant's relation to the traditional view of consciousness and the theory of obscure representations, and the development of his Critical notion of transcendental apperception, which we see reflected in the changes between his conception of inner sense and consciousness from the lectures on metaphysics in the 1770s (the Herder and early Pölitz notes) and the later lectures. I discuss this in the next section, while I return to the issue of obscurity in Section 3.5.

3.4 From the Metaphysik Herder to the Lectures from the Critical Period: A Developing Conception of Consciousness

In the early, pre-Critical lectures, the *Metaphysik Herder* and *Metaphysik L1*, Kant still holds a view of consciousness that is largely Wolffian. Consciousness of inner sense is a consciousness of self or self-consciousness, and comes down to a concept of the 'I' as intelligence, which is the soul of which in addition we have provable knowledge as a substance separate from the body (V-Met-L1/Pölitz, AA 28:224–5). Kant simply distinguishes between, on the one hand, *conscientia psychologica*, 'where one is conscious merely of one's subject [*sich nur seines Subjects bewußt ist*]' (V-Met-L1/Pölitz, AA 28:227, trans. mine), and which is intuitive, and, on the other hand, a discursive *conscientia logica*, which is directed at objects and which as objective consciousness is therefore constitutive of knowledge strictly speaking.[36] In line with Baumgarten's definition of inner sense as 'consciousness strictly speaking' (*Metaphysica*, §535), Kant takes over the standard idea that existed among his rationalist predecessors that consciousness is to be identified with inner sense (V-Met/Herder, AA 28:901), which animals lack despite possessing a soul (V-Met-L1/Pölitz, AA 28:274);[37] animals only have '*prævisio* without consciousness' (V-Met/Herder, AA 28:862), and given that Kant associates consciousness with judging (V-Met/Herder, AA 28:853), animals are a fortiori not capable of judging either (cf. DfS, AA 2:60).[38]

After the publication of the *Critique*, the picture in the metaphysics lectures that we know from the Critical period changes accordingly. As already indicated in my introduction, Kant's view of inner sense changes, as well as his idea of the role of consciousness, which is more explicitly connected to the capacity to judge. Notice, however, that whereas Kant's view regarding inner sense changes, even in the *Critique* and especially in the A-version he continues to employ the general term *Bewustseyn* for the judgemental capacity of the understanding, which is unique to human beings.[39] Yet in almost all cases where Kant uses the term *Bewustseyn*, he means a higher form of consciousness, that is, transcendental apperception. Consciousness is now connected to the logical topic of the rules for unifying various representations in a judgement. For instance, in the *Metaphysik Volckmann* from 1784–85 we read that judgement is 'the consciousness of the manifold representations of a unity in one consciousness [*das Bewustseyn der mannigfaltigen Vorstellungen einer Einheit in einem Bewußtseyn*]' (V-Met/Volck, AA 28:395, trans. mine).[40] In other words, consciousness is more clearly connected to epistemology: cognition or knowledge is, according to the *Metaphysik von Schön* (mid-to-late 1780s), 'the representation with consciousness, in relation to some object [*in Beziehung auf irgend ein Objekt*]', which must be contrasted with 'subjective representations or sensations', by means of which we do not cognize anything (V-Met/Schön, AA 28:471, trans. mine). The connection between knowledge, the unity of consciousness, and objectivity is emphasized thus:

> Everything which we call knowledge [*Erkenntnis*] agrees with the fact that it is a unity and a connection [*Verbindung*] of the manifold of representations. That is,

many representations must be connected [*verbunden*] in one consciousness. The universality must concern the unity of consciousness in the synthesis, and this now is the thought of an object [*Objekte*], for I am able to think only by means of the fact that I bring unity of consciousness into the manifold of my representations....

> V-Met/Schön, AA 28:471, trans. mine

Consciousness, more specifically the unity of consciousness, now defines the form of thought itself (V-Met/Schön, AA 28:472.3–5). In the later *Metaphysik Dohna* Kant says that 'pure consciousness is found already in logic', and that accordingly 'all judgments are representations of whose unity we are conscious' (V-Met/Dohna, AA 28:671 [Kant 2001:372]). Indeed, unity of consciousness, more precisely the consciousness of *objective* unity, now defines judgement, in conformity with the crucial passage at B137 in the B-Deduction (which confirms that the *Metaphysik von Schön* must be dated after 1786)[41]:

> Now judgement is the consciousness of the objective unity of various representations. Consequently, they [i.e. all acts of the understanding] contain the ways in which representations can be universally connected in one consciousness.
>
> V-Met/Schön, AA 28:472, trans. mine

And, accordingly, the unity of consciousness corresponds to the set of categories:

> [A]ll pure concepts of the understanding [are] nothing ... but concepts of the unification of the manifold in one consciousness.
>
> V-Met/Schön, AA 28:482, trans. mine

Consciousness, more in particular the consciousness of myself, as 'a mere act <*actus*> of thinking' (V-Met/Vigil, AA 29:978 [Kant 2001:448]), is now seen to be constitutive of the synthesis among the manifold representations in intuition and hence of the a priori concepts of knowledge, the view that Kant expounds in the *Critique*[42] and is broadly reflected in the metaphysics lectures of the 1780s and 90s, such as in this passage in the late *Metaphysik Vigilantius* (1794–95):

> Concepts can also be thought *a priori* if they contain nothing but the concept of synthesis, i.e., of the composition of the manifold in representation in order to constitute a cognition, and this synthesis has unity, i.e., <u>the consciousness of myself</u> of the connection of the manifold in my representation.... The understanding alone has connected the manifold in the representation, and the concept arose through the consciousness of the connection. On this rests the pure concept of the understanding: or *a priori* concept. The subject or the understanding maintains the consciousness itself of the connection of the manifold through

the pure intuition of space and time. One thus calls the pure concepts of the understanding those which contain *synthetic unity* or the consciousness of the connection of the manifold in representation, or concepts of the unity of the manifold in synthetic representation. One predicates the pure concept of understanding as category—therefore this is the consciousness of the synthetic unity of the given manifold in representation.

V-Met/Vigil, AA 29:978–9 [Kant 2001:448], my underlining

In the same Vigilantius notes, consciousness is identified as a 'logical function', namely as a consciousness 'of the unity of the manifold according to concepts' (V-Met/Vigil, AA 29:984 [Kant 2001:453]).

Although the term 'apperception' itself only first appears in the lecture notes from the Critical period, Kant already used, and reflected on the epistemic role of, the term in the 1770s, most explicitly in the *Duisburg Nachlass*:

> The condition of all *apperception* is the unity of the thinking subject. From this flows the connection of the manifold in accordance with a rule and in a whole, since the unity of the function must suffice for subordination as well as coordination.
> Refl 4675 [May 1775], AA 17:651.13–16 [Kant 2005:163]

> Everything that is *thought* as an object of perception stands under a rule of *apperception*, self-perception.
> Refl 4677, AA 17:658 [Kant 2005:167]

But these reflections did not carry over to the contemporary lectures (at least, the ones we have notes of): in *Metaphysik* L1 (the 1770s Pölitz) no mention is made of apperception. But in the *Mrongovius* lecture notes, the first extant metaphysics lecture notes from right after the publication of the first edition of the *Critique*, explicit mention is made of the *Critique*,[43] which makes it likely that Kant used or at least referred to the *Critique* in his metaphysics lectures. By far the most occurrences of the term 'apperception' or the Latin *apperceptio* are, accordingly, in the *Mrongovius* lectures (by my count, 18 times out of roughly 36 times in all of the metaphysics lectures).[44] In contrast to the traditional (rationalist) view of inner sense as self-consciousness *tout court*, pure apperception is now clearly differentiated from inner sense: in a *Reflexion* on anthropology (from around 1783–84) Kant notes that apperception is in fact not a 'sense' (*Sinn*), 'but [that] by means of [which] we are conscious of representations of both outer and inner sense'. He writes further:

> It [i.e. apperception] is merely the relation of all representations to their common subject, not to the object. The form of inner sense is time. The form of

apperception is the formal unity in consciousness in general, which is [a] logical [unity].

Refl 224, AA 15:85, trans. mine

In conformity with Kant's position in the *Critique of Pure Reason*, inner sense is now identified as *empirical* apperception, as consciousness in the materially psychological sense, which sharply contrasts with a *formal* consciousness, i.e. transcendental apperception. In the *Metaphysik Dohna*, from the early 1790s and roughly contemporaneous with the published *Anthropology*,[45] Kant points out that the distinction between empirical and intellectual or pure apperception reflects the idea that it is the latter (pure apperception) which is 'self-determining' and the former (empirical apperception) which concerns myself as a 'being whose existence is determined in time', i.e. in inner sense (V-Met/Dohna, AA 28:670-1 [Kant 2001:372]; cf. B151-2); or, in the words of *Metaphysik* K2 (also early 1790s), empirical apperception is 'when I am conscious of myself by means of inner sense ... (whereby I am *given* to myself [*hier muss ich mir selbst gegeben sein*])' (V-Met-K2/Heinze, AA 28:712-3, trans. mine and emphasis added), which suggests the contrast between the spontaneity of transcendental apperception, which does the 'self-determining', and the receptivity of empirical apperception that is highlighted in the *Critique* (B151-2).

An important passage in the Mrongovius notes in the section on empirical psychology (rendered *Erfahrungspsychologie* in Meier's 1766 German translation of Baumgarten's *Metaphysica*), where Kant speaks explicitly of apperception, gives an excellent précis of the central line of reasoning of the Transcendental Deduction, that is, that the unity of consciousness, or transcendental apperception, constitutes the general rule for concept formation and hence for the possibility of the representation of objects:

> A concept is the consciousness that the [same] is contained in one representation as in another, or that in multiple representations one and the same features are contained. This thus presupposes consciousness or apperception. ... Understanding is the faculty for bringing various representations under a rule. It rests on apperception. (It is the faculty for determining the particular by the general. With the higher cognitive power the cognitive faculty is considered not in relation to intuition, but rather to the unity of consciousness. This is the representation of one's representations and therefore is also called apperception. Without the consciousness of the sameness of a representation in many representations, no general rule would be possible. For a rule is a necessary unity of consciousness of a manifold of representations, relation of the manifold of

representations to one consciousness.) But how are concepts possible through apperception? In that I represent to myself the identity of my apperception in many representations. The concept is a common perception <*perceptio communis*>, e.g. the concept of body. This applies to metal, gold, stone, etc. In this I represent to myself a one in a manifold. The logical function of this consists in generality. This is the analytic unity of apperception, and many in one is its synthetic unity. The analytic unity of apperception represents nothing new to us, but rather is merely conscious of the manifold in one representation. The synthetic unity deals with many, insofar as it is contained in one. As long as the understanding judges according to this it is a pure understanding. The understanding makes rules. From the multiple representations it draws out the general, that which is met in all. It is consequently also called the faculty of rules. Experience presupposes understanding because it is a connection of perceptions according to rules. It has *a posteriori* and *a priori* rules.

        V-Met/Mron, AA 29:888–9 [Kant 2001:256–7], trans. emended

Here, all the fundamental aspects of Kant's mature theory of knowledge, specifically the pivotal role played by transcendental apperception, come to the fore. Consciousness or apperception is explicitly linked to the theory of concepts, namely to the idea that by means of a general rule many particular representations are united under a general or common one, and a fortiori to the capacity to judge about objects, thus to the possibility of experience. The grounding role of consciousness is acknowledged in the sense that the activity of judging consists precisely in the consciousness of the unity among the manifold of one's own representations.[46] Herein, I believe, the connection with the quintessentially Wolffian reflexive conception of apperception as the 'representation of one's representations' becomes apparent, which *mutatis mutandis* shows the reciprocal or mutually implicative relation between the subject of consciousness and the objects that it represents.

3.5 Transcendental Apperception, Consciousness and Obscure Representations

A lingering ambiguity remains about the relation between inner sense and transcendental apperception in the Mrongovius notes, which might however have to do with an ambiguity affecting Kant's overall position on apperception, also in the *Critique* (see e.g. B140). For example, when in the Mrongovius lecture Kant says that '[a]pperception is the ground of inner sense' (V-Met/Mron, AA

29:882 [Kant 2001:251]), he apparently means transcendental apperception, given that he equates inner sense with empirical apperception. But what does it mean that transcendental apperception is the ground of inner sense? Does it mean that it would not be possible to have an inner sense (according to the Critical meaning) that is not grounded on transcendental apperception—in the case of animals, say? That seems odd given that inner sense is *always* variable (A107), and transcendental apperception is supposed to provide a measure of permanence to inner sense. If transcendental apperception provides a measure of permanence to inner sense, and inner sense were unconditionally grounded on transcendental apperception, then inner sense cannot be variable. But inner sense *is* variable, as Kant explicitly says, therefore inner sense is not unconditionally grounded upon transcendental apperception. However, Kant's Critical argument is to be taken in a modally moderate sense: inner sense is grounded on transcendental apperception *if and only if* inner sense is determined in time. This implies that there is thus a real possibility that inner sense is not coextensive with transcendental apperception for some occurrent mental state.

In addition to the aforementioned ambiguity regarding inner sense and pure apperception, it is also still claimed in the Mongovius that '[c]onsciousness is the principle of the possibility of the understanding, *but not of sensibility*' and that the 'self underlies consciousness and is what is peculiar to spirit' (V-Met/Mron, AA 29:878 [Kant 2001:247], emphasis added). This is reminiscent of the pre-Critical view of consciousness, which says that consciousness is exclusive to the understanding, and the idea that inner sense is identified as self-consciousness *tout court*, were it not for the occurrence of the term 'apperception' a bit later in the text (Kant 2001:248), a term that, in the lecture notes that we know, was not used by Kant in his lectures prior to the publication of the *Critique*, and, as is clear from a later passage in the Mongovius (V-Met/Mron, AA 29:888), refers strictly to unity of consciousness, not consciousness *simpliciter*.[47]

Whatever the case may be regarding these ambiguities, and to return to the topic of obscure representations that are supposedly unconscious, a notable passage from the Vigilantius notes reveals Kant's Critical view regarding the continuous and gradual nature of consciousness:

> Just as the clarity of a representation can gradually become obscure so that finally the soul slumbers in it and thus its consciousness is lost little by little, so can all degrees of the powers of the human soul give way little by little, and when they have been diminished through all degrees, finally pass over into a nothing. Here is no leap <*saltus*>, but rather it observes the laws of continuity by

descending through ever smaller degrees, between which there is always again a time.

V-Met/Vigil, AA 29:1037–8 [Kant 2001:503]

Like the passages from the *Mrongovius*, *Von Schön* and elsewhere in the *Vigilantius*, quoted earlier in Section 3.3, this excerpt demonstrates that Kant has abandoned the official Leibnizian-Wolffian line[48] that obscure representations of which one is not (or not immediately) conscious are therefore unconscious. For in conformity with the Law of Continuity clarity and obscurity are not absolute values,[49] but signal a lesser or greater comparative degree of intensive magnitude on a scale of 0 to 1, given that each individual representation, being a sensation ('each sensation is only a singular representation' [V-Met/Schön, AA 28:507, trans. mine]), is *eo ipso* conscious qua it necessarily having a certain intensive magnitude. This position is echoed in the Jäsche logic, where Kant maintains that the intensive magnitude (concerning the 'matter') of the different representations in the manifold of which I am aware can decrease, implying a *weaker* consciousness, not an instantaneous total lack of consciousness:

> And even with compound representations, too, in which a manifold of marks can be distinguished, indistinctness often derives not from confusion but from *weakness of consciousness*. Thus something can be distinct as to *form*, i.e., I can be conscious of the manifold in the representation, but the distinctness can diminish as to *matter* if the degree of consciousness becomes smaller, although all the order is there.
>
> Log, AA 9:35 [Kant 2004a:546]

The *Wiener Logik* (c. 1780) confirms such a gradual view of obscure representations: representations 'are called obscure *in comparison with* ones that have the degree of clarity' (V-Lo/Wiener, AA 24:840 [Kant 2004a:295], emphasis added). However, in the same passage in the *Wiener Logik* it is stated that 'logical obscurity ... is distinct from psychological obscurity, *of which one is not at all conscious*', and that while '[l]ogical obscurity is *comparative, the latter* [i.e. psychological obscurity] *is absolute*' (trans. emended and emphasis added). This would appear to conflict with the view, expressed in the earlier quoted passage in the *Metaphysik Vigilantius* and the note to B414 in the *Critique*—which we discussed in Section 3.3—of the relative degree to which a representation can be psychologically obscure (or clear), as is also suggested in the above-quoted Jäsche passage with regard to the *matter* of consciousness. Given this ambiguity arising from the logic lectures, it is not crystal clear what Kant's definitive stance on psychological obscurity is.

But what is clear is that, in the Critical philosophy, it is the formal consciousness of transcendental apperception which is responsible for the objective *determination*, by means of the categories of quality (specifically, the category of negation), of the qualitative nature of representations, that is, their being conscious states in a psychologically material sense. Transcendental apperception is thus a necessary condition for *determinate*, clear empirical consciousness of objects (including oneself), but that does not imply that, absent transcendental apperception, it is impossible to have obscure representations that are conscious to *some* extent, but fail to be registered in normal, categorially governed experience.[50] There are occurrences of mental states such that when one is in the state one does not have an *experience* in the strict Kantian sense but nonetheless is, in some subcognitive, indeterminate manner, immediately aware of one's environment or oneself, if perhaps in a way that is barely noticeable. For instance, consider the activity of driving a car, where each function required for doing so skilfully is necessarily performed with some degree of consciousness, but obviously not to the extent that one is constantly reflexively aware of (all of) one's actions, on pain of causing an accident. The degree of intensity of one's empirical consciousness (the 'distinctness ... as to matter') varies depending on psycho-physiological circumstances, triggered by actual events in the spatial world around us. As Kant says, 'consciousness has various degrees of clarity, which become ever weaker, e.g., in falling asleep' (V-Met-K2/Heinze, AA 28:764 [Kant 2001:404]), which, of course, one surely hopes not to do while driving! In the act of falling asleep, most evidently, the weakening of one's consciousness amounts to a gradual diminution of one's consciousness to a degree that is no longer noticeable by oneself as a putative self-conscious self, and is not an absolute change from a state of consciousness to unconsciousness, an 'absolute absence' of consciousness (Prol, AA 4:307 [Kant 1977:50]). In conclusion, then, like the *Critique* itself the metaphysics lectures contemporaneous with it reveal that Kant has moved away from the conflationist view of consciousness and self-consciousness that, at least on the traditional reading, some of his predecessors espoused.

4

Apperception, Self-Consciousness, and Self-Knowledge in Kant

4.1 Introduction

Kant's theory of transcendental apperception, which concerns the rules for unitary self-consciousness, is a central part of the Critical project for establishing the necessary (and formally sufficient) conditions of cognition or knowledge.[1] The principle of transcendental apperception, in Kant's words, is 'the supreme principle of all use of the understanding', and, since the understanding is the 'faculty of knowledge', transcendental apperception is the principle of all knowledge (B136–7, trans. emended). This is a relatively uncontroversial aspect of Kant's theory of apperception, although it should be said that there is hardly even general agreement about the details of its central tenets.[2] But there does seem to be a general agreement about the view that Kant's theory of transcendental apperception is first and foremost constitutive of *objective* knowledge, and not so much a theory about the possibility of *self*-knowledge or a *sui generis* theory of self-consciousness. It is generally held that the Kantian principle of unitary self-consciousness may be about the rules for uniting one's representations, which enables the knowledge of objects, but is not about *self-consciousness* per se.[3] That is to say, transcendental apperception is more about what enables us to think *about something other than thought* than it is about how we are aware of *ourselves*, whether as thinkers or just as having *some* kind of self-awareness (self-feeling, proprioception). In the past, Dieter Henrich (1967:10) has spoken of the 'grounding function' (*Begründungsfunktion*), for Kant, of self-consciousness for something else, namely objective knowledge. That means that self-consciousness is the ground of something else, namely that it is a function of *objective* cognition, or more precisely, cognition of the objective, and not cognition of the subjective.

The view that Kant's theory of apperception is less concerned with self-consciousness per se than it is with self-consciousness as the ground of objective knowledge is often motivated by Kant's remark, in the introductory section of the Paralogisms chapter of the *Critique of Pure Reason*, that we can think of the self only in terms of the predicates that we think, never *an sich*, in abstraction from these predicates of thinking. We can never really think the self itself, *qua* self, as it is apart from any necessary constitutive conditions under which alone, like any other entity or object, it can be thought. We only think our thoughts, and do not have thereby access to, let alone know, some putative underlying identical self, to whom these thoughts belong. That is to say, if I were to try to determine the identical underlying self *whose* thoughts are thought, I would move in a circle, 'since we must always already avail ourselves of the representation of it [i.e. the 'I'] at all times in order to judge anything about it'. Kant says that 'we cannot separate ourselves from this inconvenience' (A346/B404). Determining or judging about any object, so also about myself *as* my self, always already presupposes the thinking 'I' that I need to employ to so determine or judge.

Especially, this latter remark about 'this inconvenience' would appear to mean that the transcendental perspective of the 'I think', by means of which we think our thoughts, *prevents* us from having an immediate access to ourselves *qua* thinking selves, and so by implication prohibits a *sui generis* theory of self-consciousness. We cannot, so to speak, *objectify* our intrinsically *subjective* perspective. The only way of gaining cognition of one's self is by treating it in the same way as objects are cognized, which might create the impression that on Kant's account self-consciousness strictly speaking is only a derivative kind of self-consciousness. So it would seem that Kant's treatment of the 'I think'—which is what is being discussed in this particular section in the Paralogisms, but is in fact the principle of apperception (B132; see further below the account in Section 4.3)—does not provide us a theory of self-consciousness *an sich*. And indeed, as Kant says, the 'I' of the 'I think' is but a 'transcendental subject of thoughts = x'. The 'consciousness in itself' does not distinguish 'a particular object', but, 'insofar as it is to be called a cognition', is rather 'a form of representation in general' through which 'anything' can be thought (A346/B404). The 'I think', as the 'vehicle' of my thoughts, 'of all concepts whatever' (A341/B399), thus seems a neutral placeholder for thoughts that are being thought, by whoever thinks them. That is, 'the proposition *I think* (taken problematically) contains the form of every judgment of understanding whatever and accompanies all categories as their vehicle'. Moreover, the 'proposition *I think* is', as Kant says, 'taken here only problematically; not insofar as it may contain a perception of an existence (the Cartesian *cogito, ergo sum*)' (A347–8/B405–6). In the Paralogisms, Kant considers the 'I think' proposition only 'in order to see which properties might flow from so simple a proposition as this [i.e. the 'I think'] for its subject' (A347/B405).

It is clear, from these passages at least, that on Kant's account the function of the 'I' is squarely aimed at thought or thinking as such, in particular the understanding as the form of any possible knowledge, and not at self-consciousness (or at least self-consciousness in a narrower sense). The view expressed in the Paralogisms is not arbitrary, but is grounded in the discursive logic that underpins Kant's theory of knowledge, which is shown in the logic of transcendental apperception, which we shall discuss further below. Relatedly, as we saw in the last chapter, Kant also makes a crucial distinction between inner sense and apperception, unlike the rationalists, for whom inner sense *is* self-consciousness, and implies immediate cognition of the self *an sich*, as substance, through empirical experience (i.e. inner sense, empirical self-consciousness).

In this chapter, I wish to concentrate on two connected elements of Kant's theory of self-consciousness: the transcendental conditions for establishing the identity of self-consciousness, which first enable the awareness thereof, namely self-consciousness strictly speaking, and the relation between self-consciousness and self-knowledge. I contend that two mistaken assumptions underlie the critique of Kant's 'derivative' or so-called 'reflection-theoretical' view of self-consciousness, namely the belief that it does not accommodate a *sui generis* theory of self-consciousness: (1) that the identity of self is somehow a priori *given*, and presumably any act of transcendental apperception, which is interpreted as an act of reflection, always already presupposes this putative a priori self-identity, and (2) that the awareness of the identity of self-consciousness *ipso facto* amounts to self-*knowledge*, namely knowledge of an identical a priori given self. Concerning assumption (1), often it is thought that Kant's so-called reflective 'I think', which accompanies my representations, is secondary to, or derivative of, the transcendental unity of self-consciousness, or indeed, secondary to the putative *identity* of self-consciousness, whereby the latter is seen as identical to the transcendental unity of self-consciousness but should not be conflated with the 'I think'. In Section 4.3, I address this false assumption from an interpretative point of view, by looking more closely at Kant's argument in §16 of the B-Deduction (B131-6). This will show that Kant's view of self-consciousness is in fact not derivative, and that instead any account of self-consciousness and the identity of self is only *first* made possible by transcendental consciousness or transcendental apperception, *which is nothing but the act itself of accompanying, through the 'I think', one's representations as one's own*. Transcendental consciousness is an *original* consciousness, which *a priori* grounds any form of self-consciousness or self-knowledge, and is 'the consciousness of myself, as original apperception' (A117n). In brief, transcendental unity of consciousness=original apperception= the 'I think'. In Section 4.4, I consider (*ad* assumption 2) why, for Kant, awareness of the identity of self-consciousness does not *ipso facto* amount to self-*knowledge*, and explain that, in addition to transcendental self-consciousness, what Kant calls the 'affection' of inner sense is needed for self-knowledge to be possible. But first, in the next section, I address some more general, systematic issues, which directly bear on the aforementioned topics.

4.2 Self-Consciousness and Identity

Apart from interpretative grounds (which are addressed in Sections 4.3 and 4.4), there are also philosophical reasons for why Kant's account of self-consciousness does not account for self-consciousness in the sense of strict self-knowledge, which explains the misguidedness of the criticism that Kant's theory of apperception lacks the means to account for a *sui generis* self-consciousness. The general criticism is that if the identity of self is first established in the *reflection on* oneself—a turning back into oneself—then the self-identity and the knowledge thereof is not immediate, but secondary to the reflection. But at the same time, it is argued, the reflection *presupposes* the identity of the self in order to be able to carry out the reflection, for the reflection is of course done by the same person or self whose identity is reflected upon. This model of self-consciousness *ipso facto* cannot attain determination of self-identity per se because it fundamentally misconstrues the nature of self-consciousness or the 'I' as a function of thought or cognition. The difference between the 'I' as a function of thought and the 'I' as referring to self-consciousness strictly speaking can be indicated by seeing the former in terms of a proposition of the form (a) 'I know that I φ' or '(I know:) I φ'—what Ernst Tugendhat (1997:50) calls 'epistemic self-consciousness'—where φ stands for a predicate describing a generic conscious state, and the latter in terms of a self-relation that is expressed by the Fichtean identity proposition (b) '$I_y = I_x$',[4] where *y* stands for the agent or subject of the act of self-consciousness and *x* for the object of the act of self-consciousness. In proposition (b) there is an identity between the positions on both sides of the copula, between *the knowing* 'I' (I_y) and *the known* 'I' (I_x); (b) expresses self-consciousness, namely, an intimate and immediate, non-propositional knowledge of one's self-relation or one's being related to oneself.[5] In proposition (a) there is prima facie no expression of a self-relation, nor of an identity between 'I' and the proposition 'I φ', that is, an identity between *knowing* (the 'I') and *known* (putatively the proposition 'I φ'); the 'I φ' expresses a cognitive *act* performed by an 'I', rather than an *object* of knowledge for an 'I'. Kant's notion of self-consciousness, according to his theory of apperception (which I shall delineate in Section 4.3), would be describable as (a) but not as (b). It is significant that Tugendhat calls (a) a form of 'epistemic self-consciousness', as this is precisely the reason why Kant's view of self-consciousness is criticized for lacking the means to describe a *sui generis* self-consciousness.

Though the opposite is often claimed,[6] it should be clear that Kant's aforementioned circle is *not* the circularity of presupposing what one is supposed to be reflectively aware of, namely the identity of the self that is both known entity and knower of this entity (shown by the identity proposition '$I_y = I_x$').[7] This interpretation of the circularity to which Kant alludes in the Paralogism's introductory section sees self-consciousness in terms of the representationalist subject-object model '*s* represents *o*', where, in the case of *self*-representation, *s* is supposed to be identical to *o* in conformity with the Fichtean proposition '$I_y = I_x$'. But in Kant's case the problem does not concern the putative identity between the *subject* as the thinker ('I_y' or henceforth 'I_s') and *the thinker* as *her own* object ('I_x' or henceforth 'I_o'), but rather the identity between my thoughts as accidents and their substratum, putatively the *substance in which they inhere* (A349–50). The circularity, for Kant, concerns the unavoidability of having to employ the 'I_s' as the 'vehicle' of my thoughts, in whatever attempt to determine the substance underlying it (putatively, 'I_o'). That is to say, in order to determine the substratum to which my thoughts collectively belong, I need to employ the 'vehicle' with which I *think* these thoughts in the first place, which points to a circularity that is non-vicious and unavoidable.

This may *seem* to be the same circularity as the one that appeared so problematic to Fichte (and his contemporary followers), namely, that the subject doing the thinking *is also* the object of my thought whose identity I am trying to establish, which creates the vicious circularity of trying to determine the identity of that which one has already made an appeal to in the very attempt to determine it.[8] But for Kant the identity of the logical self of discursive thinking (the 'I_s') is unproblematic, and does not presuppose knowledge of the identity of 'I_o': I *know* that my thoughts are mine to the extent and to the extent only that I accompany them, as Kant says in the well-known proposition at the start of his argument for the conditions for self-consciousness in §16 of the B-Deduction; in fact, it is an 'analytical proposition', namely defining the rule that

> it is only because I can combine a manifold of given representations *in one consciousness* that it is possible for me to represent the *identity of the consciousness*

in these representations itself, i.e., the *analytical* unity of apperception is only possible under the presupposition of some *synthetic* one, [which thus first] ground[s] ... the identity of apperception itself.

B133–5

So, in one sense at least, I know about the identity between myself as the thinker of my thoughts and the thoughts I thereby accompany or think, just because the identity of my self is established in the very act of accompanying my representations, which, according to Kant, requires an a priori act of synthesis (more on this further below). I am aware of the identity of the synthesis that first establishes the identity of the representations I accompany, just because I am the one doing the accompanying, that is, performing the synthesis. Kant speaks of an identity in terms of an *analytical unity of consciousness or apperception* that obtains between all of the set of representations that are accompanied by an 'I think', for any such occurrent accompanying of representations (B133–4).

The circularity of which Kant speaks in the Paralogisms does not concern the alleged problem with establishing, along the s=o model, the identity between thinker and *what is thought*, whose identity is, as I argued, unproblematic for Kant, for any set of representations r accompanied by any instantiated 'I think' ('I_s') is identical to 'I_s' to the extent and to the extent only that r is accompanied by 'I_s'; there is thus an identity between the 'I' as subject ('I_s') and *its predicates* as its 'object' (cf. A197/B242: any representation can be called the 'object' of another representation). Rather, the circularity problem, for Kant, concerns the mistaken attempt to establish the identity between the thinker 'I_s' and any simple *substance* ('I_o') that may underlie the subject of thought ('I_s'). So what is at issue here is establishing the identity between the subject and its putative substratum in terms of an unconditional noumenal *substance*, and the possibility of this Kant categorically rejects. But *knowing the identity of an underlying substance*, hence knowledge about the identity between 'I_s' and 'I_o', is *not* presupposed in whatever self-conscious act of accompanying my representations which determines the identity of those representations as mine. To suppose it were would in Kant's view precisely reverse the order of what grounds and what is grounded; hence his circularity objection: putatively being able to determine the subject as grounding substance presupposes the transcendental act of apperception, and not the other way around, as Henrich, following Fichte, believes it does. To know the identity of 'I_o' would mean to know the identity of *all* possible thoughts that the 'I_s' has, not just those that 'I_s' occurrently accompanies, but also those that 'I_s' accompanied in the past and those that 'I_s' were to accompany in the future—and it is at any rate impossible for 'I$_s$' to know all of the possible thoughts that she could have or have had. Moreover, 'I$_s$' does not know if the substance that corresponds to 'I$_s$' is exhausted by the set of all of 'I$_s$'s possible thoughts, and not identical to a non-mental body. (Presupposing the Fichtean identity between 'I$_s$' and 'I$_o$' appears to imply the presupposition of a metaphysical dualism between mind and body.)

I should point out again, though, that the identity between the thinking 'I$_s$' and its predicates—the identity at issue in Kant's argument about apperception—is not one strictly between two propositions 'I know' and 'I φ' which relate to each other as main and subordinate clauses in the proposition 'I know that I φ'. Rather, the identity is one between *the 'I'* in the main clause and *the 'I'* in the subordinate clause, based on the idea that, when I φ, I know that I *am* the one φ-ing. The *knowledge*—if that is the proper term—that I have of the identity concerned here is non-propositional because it is prior to, and presupposed by, knowing the propositional content of 'I φ'. This kind of non-propositional knowledge of one's identity comes with φ-ing, for any act of φ-ing which I am aware of as doing—this is perhaps expressed better in the formulation '(I know:) I φ'. It is the consciousness of oneself in terms of the identity of an action or function that unites a manifold of representations. This is illustrated by Kant's claim in A108, also quoted by Henrich in this context,[9] where Kant writes:

> Thus the original and necessary consciousness of the identity of oneself is *at the same time* a consciousness of an equally necessary unity of the synthesis of all appearances in accordance with concepts, i.e., in accordance with the rules that not only make them necessarily reproducible, but also thereby determine an object for their intuition, i.e., the concept of something in which they are necessarily connected; *for the mind could not possibly think of the identity of itself in the manifoldness of its representations, and indeed think this a priori, if it did not have before its eyes the identity of its action*, which subjects all synthesis of apprehension (which is empirical) to a transcendental unity, and first makes possible their connection in accordance with *a priori* rules.
>
> A108, emphasis added

Kant may seem to say here that the apperceptive mind has an a priori awareness of the identity of the self, suggesting that the awareness of its identity is somehow prior to the action of synthesis, which is central to the argument in the context of this passage. But what Kant in fact says is that the identity of the mind is *simultaneous with* 'its action' of subjecting the synthesis of apprehension to a transcendental unity. The awareness of the self's identity is dependent on an 'action' of synthesis or unification of representations (I return to this argument in Section 4.4), and is not a priori given and as such immediately intuitable.

By contrast, the Fichtean position ('$I_y = I_x$') assumes an intuitive evidence of the identity of the 'I' in any act of self-awareness—hence, Fichte employs the term *Selbstanschauung* to indicate this, whereas Kant specifically and consistently says that our mode of cognizing is not one based on self-intuition in terms of an intellectual intuition, thus *presupposing* a priori knowledge of an identical 'I' across various instances of consciousness, that is, an identical substance underlying self-consciousness, to which I have an intuitive and thus immediate access (see, for example, B153, B157–9; cf. B135, B138–9, B148–9). Kant acknowledges a kind of immediate intuition underlying the intellectual 'I', in apperception, but this is only an undefined or indeterminate *empirical* intuition, a 'feeling' (Prol, AA 4:334n), of the existence of myself as the one thinking for *any one particular instantiation* of the 'I think', not across a manifold of such instantiations let alone for *all* possible instantiations of the 'I think' (see B422–3n). Importantly, the Fichtean self-intuition assumes an awareness of the identity of the self qua self, whereas, for Kant, any intuition that were involved as implied by or underlying the act of apperception would as such be merely a fleeting, instantaneous sensation. Kant's own term *Selbstanschauung*, which he uses in a footnote in §25 of the B-Deduction, is precisely the opposite of Fichte's, since it is not an intellectual intuition. For Kant, self-intuition is a *sensible* intuition under the a priori form of time, which, if I were to attain knowledge of my self's phenomenal identity (as an observable person), is required *in addition* to the *intellectual* awareness that I have of myself in the apperceptive act that accompanies my φ-ing, which is an awareness of myself purely as an intelligence, as a logical subject. (This subject is, as such, empirically or psychologically speaking, empty, for the representation of oneself in the act of apperception, namely the consciousness '*that* I am' in the very act, is 'a *thinking*, not an *intuiting*' [B157].) As Kant says, 'the determination of my existence can only occur in correspondence with the form of inner sense', which is time. As a result, in Kant's view, I do not have '*cognition* of myself *as I am*, but only as I *appear* to myself' (B158). Apart from this sensible self-intuition,

> I do not have yet another self-intuition, which would give the *determining* in me, of the spontaneity of which alone I am conscious, even before the act of *determination*, in the same way as time gives that which is to be determined, thus I cannot determine my existence as that of a self-active being, rather I merely

represent the spontaneity of my thought, i.e., of the determining, and my existence always remains only sensibly determinable, i.e., determinable as the existence of an appearance.

B157–8n.

This departs significantly from the Fichtean notion of immediate evidence of self-identity in an intellectual intuition. In the *Wissenschaftslehre nova methodo*, however, Fichte appears to deny that his notion of intellectual intuition is different from what Kant in fact means when speaking of the way we think of ourselves. According to Fichte, the immediate intuition of myself as a thinker, whereby the *thinking* 'I' and the *thought* 'I' are one, is the inner intuition of the active 'I', and is intellectual; it forms the immediate ground or basis on which I am able to think of myself. Fichte says that 'this does not contradict the Kantian system, [and that] Kant only rejects a *sensible intellectual intuition*, and rightly so' (GA IV, 2:31). Importantly, Fichte says here—and this might be seen as contrasting with my suggestion earlier—that the 'I' at issue here is only the 'I' 'for me', 'insofar as I conceive of its concept through an immediate consciousness'; 'another *being* of the "I", as substance, soul etc. *is not at all at issue here*' (GA IV, 2:29, emphasis added). Therefore, the intellectual intuition provides one awareness only of the *activity* of thinking of oneself, not of one's putative substantial self or soul (what Fichte refers to as a 'fixed' or 'resting' 'I', in contrast to an 'acting' 'I' [GA IV, 2:31]). It would thus appear that neither Kant *nor Fichte* have in mind a conception of the substantial 'I', when they refer to the thinking 'I'. But despite Fichte's criticism of Kant as beholden to a reflexive $s=o$ model of self-consciousness, I should like to stress that Kant, too, believes that the 'I' is *first produced* in the activity of thinking (see B132). It remains to be seen, however, to what extent Fichte's and Kant's views in fact concur, since Kant explicitly sees the 'I' of thinking as a mere logical 'I', which is empty, whereas Fichte portrays the 'I' as self-positing, not as 'beforehand already a substance', but *as such* still positing its own 'essence' (GA IV, 2:31; all translations from Fichte are mine). This latter element goes beyond what Kant would endorse. For in the proposition 'I know that I φ' or '(I know:) I φ', as an expression of what Tugendhat calls epistemic self-consciousness, one does not just *assume* the identity between the 'I' in the main clause and the 'I' in the that-clause, based on putative intuitional evidence. There are a priori rules that govern knowledge of the identity between them, by means of which this knowledge is established, and not somehow assumed on the basis of putative immediate intuitional evidence. These are the transcendental rules, namely the categories, of which Kant speaks.[10]

For Kant, in the mere employment of the deictic expression or indexical 'I' no person is *identified*. Hence, there is no risk of misidentification. To identify myself *as a person*, I need to have an empirical intuition of myself beyond the mere representation 'I', in the same way as this would be required for any other object in space and time. In employing the indexical 'I'—which is not a universal representation in terms of a concept under which other representations can be subsumed (in the way that the concept 'red' is)—I am not specifically referring to '*Dennis Schulting*', but merely reflexively referring to *myself* as the one who has any particular occurrent representation by self-ascribing that representation to myself. The representation 'I' does not in and of itself single out *me* in particular, namely myself as *this* person with the name '*Dennis Schulting*', precisely because it is or can be employed by *anyone* who self-reflexively ascribes his or her representations to him or herself, for any actual occurrence of such self-ascription. 'I' is merely a formal representation by means of which one self-ascribes *one's own* representations to *oneself*, for *any* representer who so self-ascribes representations (cf. A122). The rules that govern this use of the formal representation 'I', or 'I think', is what Kant calls the conditions that make up transcendental apperception. Kant argues for this in §16 (B131–6). This will be delineated in the next section.

The identity at issue in 'epistemic' self-consciousness (and which I shall argue is the right *model* for self-consciousness *simpliciter*) is the identity of which I have knowledge in the following way: I know that I φ but this does not mean that there is a *separate* act of knowing in addition to the act of φ-ing, or that I have a second-order reflection upon myself as having certain knowledge, let alone that I need to have knowledge of my substantial self-identity in order to be able to φ. Tugendhat is right that there is strictly speaking no identity between the 'I' in the main clause and the proposition 'I φ', in the sense that 'I' as knowing is identical to the content of whichever act of φ-ing I do (unlike in the Fichtean proposition '$I_y = I_x$'). But there is an identity of sorts between the 'I' that *knows* she is φ-ing and the *very act* of her φ-ing. In other words, the identity lies between the *act* of knowing and the *act* of doing: in φ-ing I am simultaneously aware of *myself* as φ-ing, or, I know *of myself as* φ-ing, while φ-ing. I am not aware of myself as my own *object* (as in the quasi-tautological proposition '$I_s = I_o$'), but I am aware of myself as *doing* something, namely thinking this or that. The relation between knowing that I φ and the fact that I φ, between the knowledge of φ-ing and the act of φ-ing, is not dyadic, as the reflection-theoretical model suggests. Rather, the expression of an identity lies in the adverbial nature of the relation between knowledge and act.[11] To put it in Kantian terminology, I *apperceptively* know that I φ while φ-ing. The relation between the apperceptive knowledge and the act of φ-ing is one of identity nonetheless.[12]

4.3 Transcendental Apperception and Self-Consciousness

In §16 of the B-Deduction, as a first step in the argument toward the formulation of the conditions of possible knowledge, Kant elucidates his theory of self-consciousness. I am here not interested in the grounding function of self-consciousness for knowledge, as Kant sees it, though it is directly implied by the theory of self-consciousness.[13] Kant argues that the identity of self-consciousness is grounded in an act of original apperception, which he calls pure or also transcendental apperception, to contrast it with empirical apperception, which I shall not consider further here (though I do discuss some aspects of inner sense, an alternate term for empirical apperception, in Section 4.4).[14] Kant starts famously with the proposition which says that the

> *I think* must *be able* to accompany all my representations.
>
> B131

In this proposition, Kant states that there is a necessary unitary relation between the representation 'I think' and the manifold of all those representations that are accompanied by it. The unitary aspect of the relation is made clear by Kant in stating that representations can be '*my* representations' only if they 'all together belong to one self-consciousness [*zu einem Selbstbewußtsein*]' (B132, trans. emended[15]). The state of together belonging to me signifies a certain kind of necessary unity among the representations that are accompanied by the 'I think', which, as we shall see, *first* constitutes the identity of self-consciousness. This unity of their belonging together is what Kant calls 'the *transcendental* unity of self-consciousness' (B132). All too commonly, one is committed to reading this transcendental-unitary relation between the 'I think' and its representations in too strong a modal sense. The strong modal reading of the principle of transcendental apperception says, roughly (whereby PTA stands for Principle of Transcendental Apperception):

> PTA = *Necessarily*, all representations of which I am conscious are subject to the unifying act of apperception.

This definition of transcendental apperception is problematic. The principle of apperception, that is, the 'I think' proposition, specifically does not state that, *necessarily*, for any and all representations *r* there is an actual or potential instance of self-consciousness or a self-aware agent S, so that *r* is *eo ipso* unified with all other representations represented, either potentially or actually, by S. That would be a rather intemperate claim, and it would also conflict with several of Kant's statements about the possibility of representations or even instances of consciousness which an arbitrary representer R is not apperceptively aware of having—for example, the representations had by infants, who are not yet able to employ the very concept of 'I' (see Anth, AA 7:127–8).[16] It does not follow that if some occurrent representation *r* were not accompanied by the 'I think', that is, represented by S, R does not represent *r* or is not in some non-apperceptive sense minimally aware of *r*.

Stressing the necessary *potentiality* of apperception does not help here, for infants represent without *ever* apperceiving their representing, so that for them there is not even a potentiality of apperception.[17] However, many interpreters do take this route. Some read the principle of apperception as saying that all my representations must *be able* to be accompanied by the 'I think', expressing the necessity of a possibility, whilst at the same time it is not the case that all of one's representations need *effectively* or *actually* be so accompanied. On this reading, one could thus have representations that are not actually accompanied by the 'I think', but representations must still have a real potential for such accompaniment. In other words, representations have an inbuilt disposition towards apperception; they cannot fail to possibly being accompanied. This potentiality is not a mere hypothesis but implies a necessary entailment of apperception for *all* possible representations (though it is not clear, on this reading, what the conditions of satisfaction are for what is in the first instance deemed merely a potentiality or possibility). These interpreters believe that it is supposedly in this way that one attends to the peculiar modal aspect that appears to be implied by Kant's words 'must be able'. That is, for every instance of a representation A there is a parallel instance of an 'I think'-accompaniment B, and B is always already formally, though not existentially, instantiated in A. This means that it is not the case that for any instance A there necessarily obtains an *actual* reflection of the kind B, but it does mean that there can be no instance A that does not already imply, formally, and so entail a possible instance of B. This position holds that some representations that one has could and sometimes do in fact go un-accompanied by the 'I think'. Some representations do exist without an 'I think' strictly speaking having been instantiated. Representations are then not non-existent per se, but they are non-existent before the 'I' (cf. B132). However, a complication arises for this reading: how does it account for the difference between unaccompanied and actually accompanied representations if *all* representations must at least entail possible accompaniment? That is to say, when is the 'I think' actually instantiated and when only formally? Put differently, which condition or conditions in addition to transcendental apperception, as a putatively merely possible condition, is or are supposedly required for the instantiation of the reflective 'I think'? What we thus see is that this reading has in fact not explained the modal phrase 'must be able' in the 'I think' proposition at all, but has merely added a further layer of confusion.[18]

I suggest that we read the 'I think' proposition differently. On a more moderate reading, the principle of apperception states that for any and all representations r to be part of the set of *all my* representations, r must be part of the set of representations that are conjointly accompanied by my identical self as the agent of representing, by means of an analytic unity of consciousness, which is common to all those representations accompanied by the same self, that is, *my* same self. This reading is in line with the criterial principle expressed at B138:

> All *my* representations in any given intuition must stand under the condition under which alone I can ascribe them to the identical self as my representations, and thus can grasp them together, as synthetically combined in an apperception, through the general expression *I think*.
>
> original emphasis

Notice that Kant puts emphasis on the indexical 'my'. The criterion for the unity among the representations that makes them 'belong to me',[19] and relates them to my identical subject, is the '*analytical* unity of apperception' (B132–3, my underlining). There lies a strict reciprocity, or analytic unity, between the indexical 'I' of the act of apperception or self-ascription and the possessive determiner 'my' as the indexical contained in the accompanied manifold of representations, of all the representations that I ascribe to myself. This makes sense, as the only representations that 'I' ever accompany, *or am able* to accompany, will be 'my' representations, not yours, hers, or *x*'s, not even those that happen to be occurrent in my head, but to which I do not currently direct my attention.[20] Therefore, the relation between the 'I think' and *its* (my own) representations is a bi-conditional one. The moderate reading of apperception can be defined thus:

> PTA* = A representation r is accompanied by subject S *if and only if* r is analytically united with all representations that have the same relation to S and S accompanies these representations conjointly, for which a certain condition of combining must be fulfilled.

The condition of combining mentioned in the above definition, as well as in the earlier quoted passage at B138, is the condition of *a priori synthesis*, which is the explanatory ground of the analytic principle PTA* (B135). The 'thoroughgoing identity of the apperception of a manifold given in intuition' (B133), which is expressed by PTA*, is first made possible by a priori synthesis, or the original-synthetic unity of apperception; 'thoroughgoing identity of self-consciousness could not be thought' without the presupposition of a necessary synthesis of the representations given in intuition (B135). This means that for Kant the identity of my representations as belonging to me in virtue of their analytic unity, that is, *my* self-identity as thinker, is not a priori *given*, of which I would have a priori knowledge (through immediate intuitional evidence, say), but must be established by a spontaneous act of unification of my representations—Kant calls the 'I think' 'an act of *spontaneity*', which 'cannot be regarded as belonging to sensibility', and so is not given in or with it, and is in fact the self-consciousness that accompanies all other representations, and 'cannot be accompanied by any further representations' (B132), which constitutes it as spontaneity proper.[21] The 'I think' or self-consciousness is spontaneous, original, properly basic, yet it *rests on* an a priori synthesis, which is the aforementioned *transcendental* unity of self-consciousness, which, as an 'original combination' (B133), holds the representations accompanied by the 'I think' together as self-same representations. Does the originality and spontaneity of self-consciousness or the 'I think' and the fact that it rests on an a priori synthesis not amount to a contradiction? No. For the 'I think' and the a priori synthesis or the transcendental unity of self-consciousness, or also called the 'original-synthetic unity of apperception' (B131, heading §16; B135), are equiprimordial. Kant explains:

> The thought that these representations given in intuition all together belong *to me means* ... *the same as that I unite* them in one self-consciousness, or at least can unite them therein, and although it is itself not yet the consciousness of the *synthesis* of the representations, it still presupposes the possibility of the latter, i.e., only because I can comprehend their manifold in one consciousness do I call them all together *my* representations. ... Synthetic unity of the manifold of intuitions, as given *a priori*, is thus the ground of the identity of apperception itself, which precedes *a priori* all *my* determinate thinking.
>
> B134, trans. emended and my underlining

The a priori synthetic unity as the 'ground of the identity of apperception itself' is a *logical* ground. It is not as if it *preceded* the act of apperception; rather, it enables it in the very act of apperception. Identity of self-consciousness consists in the act of unifying or accompanying (in the above-described sense), *by means of a priori synthesis*, one's self-same representations, which is the unification of one's own representations in a transcendental unity of self-consciousness (B132). This act of unifying *is* in fact the act of a priori synthesis, for it is an act that puts representations together in a synthetic unity as *originally* belonging together—originally, to the extent that they are all equally mine in accordance with the rule of unification that is the transcendental unity of apperception. Hence, Kant calls it, in the heading to §16 (B131), the 'original-synthetic unity of apperception', which combines the unity and act aspects of a priori synthesis. The sharing of the analytic unity (the indexical 'I') among the representations accompanied by the 'I' is rigorously coextensive with the a priori putting them together in a synthetic unity, a representational whole of representations as *together* belonging to the 'I', whose same (analytic) feature they share, namely by being *my* representations—of course, these representations belong together synthetically, in an a priori way, *only* to the extent that they share this same analytic feature (for they can be quite different in every other respect). The element of togetherness is emphasized by the synthesis, while the sharing of the same indexical 'my' is made manifest by the element of analytic unity. This identity among *my* representations is first made possible through the fact that *I* put them together by accompanying them *all* as *my* representations, 'by my *adding* one representation to the other and being conscious of their synthesis' (B133).²² The reciprocity between the analytic and synthetic unities of apperception is specifically asserted by Kant in the following passage:

> It is only because I can combine a manifold of given representations *in one consciousness* that it is possible for me to represent the *identity of the consciousness in these representations* itself, i.e., the *analytical* unity of apperception is only possible under the presupposition of some *synthetic* one.
>
> B133, my underlining²³

All of this comports with my earlier statements in Section 4.2 that there is a relation of identity between the 'I' of 'I know' and the 'I' of 'I φ' in the proposition '(I know:) I φ'. The possibility of the so-called 'epistemic' self-consciousness expressed here (as Tugendhat terms it) is the *transcendental* unity of self-consciousness, which first constitutes the thoroughgoing identity of self-consciousness, that is, self-consciousness *simpliciter*, which is not based on, or grounded in, an intuitional evidence of an a priori self-sameness, but in an original, spontaneous *act* that first establishes '*identity of the consciousness in these representations*' (B133), namely, the representations in any manifold in intuition which I accompany and take as together belonging to me. For Kant, through the 'I' neither a manifold nor its combination is given that I could intuitively represent, as in an intellectual intuition (B135), so I am not intuitively aware of my own a priori identity—which is what Fichte does suggest is the case in the background of his proposition '$I_y=I_x$'. I have to combine the representations in any given empirical intuition in order to first attain awareness of my identity, namely of myself as the self accompanying *these*—namely my— representations.[24] Hence, Kant says that

> I am therefore conscious of the identical self in regard to the manifold of the representations that are given to me in an intuition because I call them all together *my* representations, which constitute *one*. But that is as much as to say that I am conscious *a priori* of their necessary synthesis, which is called the original synthetic unity of apperception, under which all representations given to me stand, but under which they must also be brought by means of a synthesis.
> B135–6

The necessary synthesis which a priori grounds the identity of my self-consciousness is obviously not manifestly present in the *proposition* '(I know:) I φ', and neither am I of course literally (psychologically) conscious of the a priori synthesis as such. Yet in any apperceptively accompanying my φ-ing I am implicitly aware of the necessary combining of the various representations as *mine* in whatever cognition I have, that is, regardless of the specific content of my φ-ing. It is this apperceptive implicit awareness of a priori synthesis that paradigmatically constitutes *self-consciousness*, that is, an awareness of my identity of the action of combining my representations as my own for any case of cognition or φ-ing—it is the mind's consciousness of '*the identity of the function* by means of which [a] manifold is synthetically combined into one cognition' (A108, emphasis added). But, importantly, the consciousness of the identity of this combinatory function of the cognitive mind does not constitute *knowledge*, strictly speaking, of my self's identity, that is, knowledge of the self in a more traditional sense of self-consciousness. For knowledge of the self something more is required, on Kant's account, in a way that is parallel to what establishes possible knowledge of spatiotemporal *objects*. This I address in the next section.

4.4 Self-Knowledge

One of the central aspects of Kant's transcendental theory of self-consciousness, which crucially separates his from previous theories, is the distinction between transcendental apperception and inner sense, the latter also called empirical apperception (A107). Philosophers in the rationalist tradition of rational psychology (Leibniz, Wolff, Baumgarten) did not distinguish between inner sense and transcendental apperception. For them, inner sense *was* self-consciousness *simpliciter*. They did not differentiate pure from empirical forms of self-consciousness (for more discussion, see Chapter 3). For the rational psychologists, this meant that the experience in inner sense amounted to a self-consciousness that is identical to the experience of self as a substance, and as a person. This identity is conveyed by the idea of immediate evidence of one's self through inner sense, which provides knowledge of one's immaterial soul. For the rational psychologist, the empirical experience of oneself in inner sense or self-consciousness amounted to an intimate, empirically manifest self-acquaintance that, on this very basis, grounds any further rational knowledge claims about the soul (i.e. its immateriality, substantiality, personality).[25]

At the end of the previous section, I pointed out that by contrast, for Kant, self-consciousness does not *ipso facto* entail self-*knowledge*. As Kant says, 'the consciousness of oneself is … far from being a cognition of oneself [*ein Erkenntnis seiner selbst*]' (B158). This is precisely because, for Kant, transcendental apperception is *not* to be identified with inner sense, which, if it were, would yield an intuitional knowledge of the self's innermost nature, by means of an intellectual intuition (B159), namely, knowledge of how I would be in myself (B157), just as his rationalist predecessors believed. However, Kant acknowledges, his differentiation of self-consciousness as transcendental apperception from inner sense does create a paradox, for it seems to divide the self into an active and a passive part, which raises the question, as Kant says (B153), of how it is at all possible that we 'relate to ourselves passively' (as is the case in inner sense, which Kant calls the '*passive* subject' at B153). It also invites the question as to why it is that we are not able to attain cognition of ourselves as we, *qua thinking beings*, are in ourselves if it is the case that we do have a direct awareness of what makes us thinkers, namely of the original synthetic unity of apperception in any act of cognition. This paradox regarding the active and passive subjects is addressed in an excursus in the B-Deduction (§24), but it is described by Kant in more detail in a long crossed-out passage from his manuscript for the 1798 *Anthropology from a Pragmatic Point of View*.[26] It is worth quoting that passage in full here (the crossed-out passage is appended to §7 in the *Anthropology*):

> How then is the great difficulty to be removed, in which consciousness of oneself still presents only the appearance of oneself, and not the human being in himself?

And why does it not present a double I, but nevertheless a doubled consciousness of this I, first that of mere *thinking* but then also that of inner *perception* (rational and empirical); that is, discursive and intuitive apperception, of which the first belongs to logic and [the] other to anthropology (as physiology)? The former is without content (matter of cognition), while the latter is provided with a content by inner sense....

And no one doubts that we could not equally make inner observations of ourselves and make experiences in this way, but if we dare now to speak of objects of inner sense (which as sense always provides appearances only) it is because we are able to reach only cognition of ourselves, not as we are, but as we appear (internally) to ourselves. There is something shocking in this proposition, which we must consider more carefully.—We allow a judgment of this kind regarding objects outside us, but it looks quite absurd to apply it to what we perceive within ourselves.—That some word-twisters take appearance and *semblance* (*Erscheinung und Schein*) for one and the same thing and say that their statements mean as much as: 'it seems (*scheint*) to me that I exist and have this or that representation' is a falsification unworthy of any refutation.

This difficulty rests entirely on a confusing of *inner sense* (and of empirical self-consciousness) with *apperception* (intellectual self-consciousness), which are usually taken to be one and the same. The I in every judgment is neither an intuition nor a concept, and not at all a determination of an object, but an act of understanding by the determining subject as such, and the consciousness of oneself; pure apperception itself therefore belongs merely to logic (without any matter and content). On the other hand, the I of inner sense, that is, of the perception and observation of oneself, is not the subject of judgment, but an object. <u>Consciousness of the one who *observes* himself is an entirely simple representation of the subject in judgment as such, of which one knows everything if one merely thinks it. But the I which has been observed by itself is a sum total of so many objects of inner perception that psychology has plenty to do in tracing everything that lies hidden in it</u>. And psychology may not ever hope to complete this task and answer satisfactorily the question: 'What is the human being?'

One must therefore distinguish pure apperception (of the understanding) from empirical apperception (of sensibility). The latter, when the subject attends to himself, is also at the same time affected and so calls out sensations in him, that is, brings representations to consciousness. These representations are in conformity with each other according to the form of their relation, the subjective and formal condition of sensibility; namely, intuition in time (simultaneously or in succession), and not merely according to rules of the understanding.

Kant 2007:253, my underlining

As is made clear in this passage, Kant makes a distinction between the logical conditions for pure self-consciousness, and the conditions for a *concrete* self-consciousness, for 'observation of oneself' or self-perception. The former conditions are dealt with in §16 of the B-Deduction, which I addressed in the previous section: it concerns the consciousness or a priori cognition of the pure apperceptive 'I', who is always implicitly aware of herself as φ-ing. In pure self-consciousness, we do not perceive ourselves as we are in ourselves, but merely as intelligences (B158n.), as subjects aware of their φ-ing. The latter conditions, by contrast, concern the perception of the self as an object, which is to be treated in the same way that objects outside of oneself are perceived—this concerns Kant's view of the strict parallelism between the knowledge of the self as an object and the knowledge of outer objects, a topic that resurfaces in the Refutation of Idealism (B274–9). In fact, there is no difference in principle between the way I can know, strictly speaking,[27] about myself and how I cognize objects *outside* me: in both cases, I know only an appearance, not the intrinsic nature of how I am in myself or things in themselves, based on the notion that this knowledge, in both cases, is constrained by empirical intuition (B156). This solves the paradox that Kant noted at the beginning of the excursus at B152–6. Kant writes:

> But how the I that I think is to differ from the I that intuits itself (for I can represent other kinds of intuition as at least possible) and yet be identical with the latter as the same subject, how therefore I can say that *I* as intelligence and *thinking* subject cognize my self as an object that is *thought*, insofar as I am also given to myself in intuition, only, like other phenomena, not as I am for the understanding but rather as I appear to myself, this is no more and no less difficult than how I can be an object for myself in general and indeed one of intuition and inner perceptions.
>
> B155

In order to perceive oneself in terms of self-observation or self-knowledge, that is, when I am 'an object for myself', 'a determinate sort of intuition', more in particular, a 'self-intuition' (B155, B157, B157n.) is required 'in addition to that which I think myself' (B158), that is, in addition to the purely logical original-synthetic unity of apperception or the faculty of combination, of which I am aware as the 'I' of pure self-consciousness. This self-intuition 'is grounded in an *a priori* given form, i.e. time, which is sensible and belongs to the receptivity of the determinable' (B157n.). Through the synthesis of the understanding in sensibility, which is a '*transcendental synthesis of the imagination*', it is then possible to determine 'sensibility internally', by ordering the time determinations in inner sense. This determinative synthesis is exercised 'on the *passive* subject', that is, on inner sense (B153). Kant calls this the affection of the inner sense or internal affection (in the literature sometimes referred to as 'self-affection', though Kant himself does not use this term as such; he speaks of being 'internally affected *by our selves*' at B156).[28] Inner sense is 'mere *form* of intuition', which 'does not yet contain any *determinate* intuition at all' (B154),[29] while pure apperception is 'the source of all combination' (B154; cf. B129–30) and is what provides the determination to the mere manifold in inner sense (the passive subject). What Kant means by the fact that the understanding, through the determining act of pure apperception, *affects* the inner sense by 'bringing it under an apperception' (B153), is that the combination that first yields *knowledge* of an object is *produced* by the understanding—hence, the name '*productive* imagination', while the imagination is the 'effect of the understanding on sensibility and its first application' (B152). This affection of inner sense, as the way manifolds of representation in an empirical intuition are determined, holds true, *mutatis mutandis*, for internal as well as outer objects, so for knowledge or determinate perception of *oneself* as well as of objects outside me—again confirming Kant's strict parallelism between subject and object as far as the epistemology of knowledge is concerned. Insofar as the conditions of its possibility are concerned, self-observation or self-perception is thus no different, and no more problematic, than the perception of outer objects.

In and of itself, the a priori synthesis, which determines, and thus affects, the mere manifold in inner sense, 'is nothing other than the unity of the action of which [the self of understanding] is conscious as such even without sensibility' (B153). The self-intuition is merely empirical, but the internal affection mentioned earlier is nothing but the *determination* by the understanding of this intuition in inner sense—the affection itself is thus nothing psychological, as the term might suggest. I do not have 'yet another self-intuition, which would *give* the *determining* in me, of the spontaneity of which alone I am conscious, <u>even before the act of *determination*</u>' (B158n., my underlining). Therefore, 'I cannot determine my existence as that of a self-active being, rather I merely represent the spontaneity of my thought' (B158n.).[30] This is crucially different from any kind of self-knowledge that assumes that we have an immediately, intuitionally evidential cognition of ourselves as intelligences, along the lines of Fichte's *Selbstanschauung*, whereby I a priori intuit my 'determining' self, even before I exercise it in whatever act of determinative cognition. Kant categorically rejects the idea of an intellectual intuition (B159; see also B68, B135, B138–9, B148–9, B153, B157–9). For Kant, self-knowledge does not consist in, nor does it presuppose, intuitive knowledge of a strict identity of subject and object in the sense of Fichte's quasi-tautology '$I_y=I_x$'. Rather, it concerns merely an identity relation between the apperception as the determining act and a sensible intuition insofar as the latter is determined by it, which consequently yields a cognition of myself as an appearance only, not as a thing in itself, that is, not *essentially*, nor a cognition of the supposed essence of my determining self. This identity rests upon, *and is first constituted by*, a function of synthesis of a given empirical manifold in inner sense, and consists strictly speaking in the *analytic unity* of apperception (B133). I have no prior intuitive acquaintance with my determining self; I am acquainted only with my self as the subject of apperception, through affecting manifolds of representations in inner sense. Only the representations that I combine as together belonging to the unity of my apperception, which defines an objective unity of consciousness (and hence an object for thought) (B137), constitute an object of my thought, regardless of the question whether this concerns an outer or inner object (myself as an object of self-perception). I do not have privileged knowledge of my own *determining* self as an inner object.

Of course, the 'I think' does imply the existence of the 'I', for every instantiation of the 'I', in every act of apperception, but it does not yet determine or give thereby the 'I' as an *object* of immediate perception (cf. B157n., B422n.). As Kant says, 'in the synthetic original unity of apperception, I am conscious of myself not as I appear to myself [as an object of empirical perception], nor *as* I am in myself [as in a Fichtean *Selbstanschauung*], but only *that* I am' (B157).[31] This comports with the distinction between the self-consciousness of pure apperception and the self-intuition in inner sense, which enables self-perception or self-knowledge. The de facto *existence* of the thinking self as 'the *determining* in me' (B158n.), that is, the act of transcendental apperception, is logically implied in the act: the apperceptive 'I' that is φ-ing is instantiated *in an existing person* doing the φ-ing, namely my occurrent thinking self. But to *determine* the existence of this person, that is, if I were to determine myself as *this particular person doing my occurrent φ-ing, namely, 'Dennis Schulting'*, requires more than self-consciousness. In transcendental self-consciousness, I am not aware of myself as *this particular person, 'Dennis Schulting'*; I am just aware of *myself* as φ-ing, where 'myself' rigidly refers to *me*, that is, to the person that φ-s, but at the same time does not thereby rigidly designate me as *this particular person, 'Dennis Schulting'*.[32] For the latter, an additional act of self-affection is required, which determines a certain manifold in my sensibility that identifies me, objectively, as *this particular person, 'Dennis Schulting'*. This identifying information is objective, in that it concerns information that is objectively valid, and thus, at least potentially, intersubjectively available (in the same way that any empirical evidence for outer objects would be intersubjectively available). This information is not private. I myself was told or came to know when I was much younger, that that was my identifying name. But the identifying information does not play the central role in identifying myself *as myself* (though it may play *a* role). I could identify myself as myself even if I did not know *who* I was strictly speaking, or what name I had (bar severe cognitive malfunction, whereby I had lost, not just my memory, but also my apperceptive capacities); or indeed if I were thoroughly mistaken about who I was. Indexicals such as 'myself', 'mine', 'my', and 'I' are instantiated by *any and all* subjects of acts of φ-ing who are apperceptively aware of themselves as φ-ing, regardless of their particular names, histories, personalities, and so on.

The internal affection by the understanding of one's inner sense is the 'concretization', as it were, of the combinatory capacity of pure apperception, of my pure intelligence or the a priori act of synthesis in any act of φ-ing. This holds for inner as well as outer objects of perception. It is clear, both from the accounts of pure, transcendental self-consciousness, or pure apperception, and the inner affection of one's inner sense *by oneself*, which enables self-observation, that Kant is not concerned with the psychological or anthropological aspects of subjectivity, the aspects that most people associate with subjectivity, with our innermost, purely subjective or private experiences or mental states. Indeed, as Kant says in the above-quoted crossed-out passage from the *Anthropology*, 'the I which has been observed by itself is a sum total of so many objects of inner perception that psychology has plenty to do in tracing everything that lies hidden in it'. Transcendental philosophy's view of self-consciousness, and even of self-knowledge, is more limited in its scope and need not concern itself with all these 'many objects of inner perception'. It is merely concerned with the a priori constraints under which both self-consciousness and self-knowledge can take place, the conditions namely that first define what it means to be able, in the strictest sense, to have consciousness or indeed knowledge of oneself at all.

5

Reflexivity, Intentionality, and Animal Perception

5.1 Introduction

The central argument of the Transcendental Deduction of the Categories concerns the core Copernican belief that there exists a deep intimacy between the self and the object at the conceptual level. It is Kant's claim that the very principle of thought, that is, transcendental apperception, is not just the necessary condition of the cognition of objects, but in fact also the sufficient condition of the very notion of an object, of what it means to refer to an object. This means that we can trace the fundamental characteristics of an object as such back to thought itself. This might seem a crafty way of reintroducing unadulterated rationalism by the backdoor. There is something prima facie odd about the claim that objectivity can be derived from thought itself. But the hint is in the adjective 'conceptual'. The argument pivots on the distinction that Kant upholds between, on the one hand, the object 'as far as its existence is concerned' (B125), and the object *for* thought, on the other. The existence of the object can never be established by means of a priori contemplation; we rely on an empirical intuition of the object in order to be immediately related to the object and thus first know about its existence or its real possibility, and this is what marks out Kant's empirical realism in contrast to the rationalism of his predecessors. The relation between the object as it is the object of thought and thinking is one we can establish a priori precisely because we *take* the object, in whatever further determinable way it may manifest itself, as existing at least before our thought—how could we otherwise talk about it? This simple reflection on the intimate relation between thought and object as a reflexivity of thought itself—thought takes the other than itself, that is, the object, as existing before or for itself—constitutes the core of the Copernican revolution. The reflexivity lies in the way thought implicitly relates to itself in relating to what is not itself, in positing something as an object.

Empiricists never seem to realize that in their very insistence on the independency of the given object, outside of and apart from thought, a relation to, and at the same time also a separation from, the outside object *qua* outside is first posited and then not reflectively acknowledged. As Hegel later noticed in his critique of reflection philosophy including empiricism—and this is a quintessentially Copernican thought—positing a dualism of thought and object, whereby both are as such considered entirely independent of each other and self-standing, neglects the fact that it is *thought* that posits this dualism in the first place: thought a priori places or projects the object outside the frame of thought and as separate, and it does this precisely *by means of thought* so that a conceptual relation of some sort to the object is ipso facto established. Insisting on the dualism without acknowledging the a priori relation that thought itself puts between itself and its own outside, the object, comes down to a philosophical oversight, if not philosophical bad faith. A proper philosophical analysis should recognize that insofar as the object is an object of thought—and *it is that* insofar as we are able to talk about it philosophically—an a priori determinable relation obtains between thought and object. The object is therefore in principle knowable to the extent that it is in principle conceivable. There is of course no sense in which the object is reduced to a rational conception of it, for its independent existence, its in-itselfness, apart from the conceptual relation is beyond question. For empiricists, there is always the assumption of an apparently unbridgeable gap between thought and object, no matter how profound the theory of perception, reference or what have you, because unconsciously they take thought itself, in terms of the performative act that lies at the root of any theory, out of the equation. An empiricist thus fundamentally lacks *self*-reflexivity, a reflection of his own assumptions and performativity.

There is thus nothing odd in making the claim that objectivity can be derived from thought itself if we take the idea seriously that thought itself posits a relation to the object even in the very possibility of the object as conceptually something *outside and independent of* thought. If we parse—as Kant does in the Deduction from §16 onwards, leading to the definition of an object at B137, with the pages B138 and B139 as corollary conclusions from that derivation—the characteristics of the capacity to think, expressed in the ability to attach an 'I think' to all of one's representations that one may ascribe to oneself, then we see, in a dense step-by-step argument, that the concept of an object is analytically derived from the unity that lies at the root of our self-consciousness.[1] A deep intimacy thus exists between the self and the object at the conceptual level. This intimacy, which I have referred to in terms of reciprocity in other work (Schulting

2018b), finds expression in the following illuminating and crucial passage in the paragraph following the one in which Kant provides the definition of an object:

> The synthetic unity of consciousness is...an objective condition of all cognition, not merely something I myself need in order to cognize an object but rather something under which every intuition must stand *in order to become an object for me*.
>
> B138

It is claimed here that the unity of consciousness is not a necessary *psychological* condition of experience (in the colloquial sense of experience), but a necessary condition of the possible experience of objects (whereby experience should be read in the technical Kantian sense of *Erfahrung*), that is to say, a condition of how something can be an *object* of experience. I have provided detailed assessments of the claims that Kant makes here elsewhere, and I am not going to rehearse them here. What is important is to retain the idea that experience of objects and objects of experience are relata within the same domain that is governed by the unity of consciousness or the principle of apperception; objects are nothing *outside* this domain.[2] Transcendental apperception establishes, in virtue of the unity of the consciousness of one's representations, not just the experience, by subjects, of objects, but also the very objects that subjects experience.

However, Kant also wants to make a point of the fact, in the concluding paragraphs of §17—and this is the element that I want to expand on further in this chapter—that the scope of this principle of apperception is restricted. He writes:

> This principle [of apperception] is not a principle for every possible understanding, but only for one through whose pure apperception in the representation in the representation *I am* nothing manifold is given at all. ... [F]or the human understanding it is unavoidably the first principle, so that the human understanding cannot even form for itself the least concept of another possible understanding, either one that would intuit itself or one that, while possessing a sensible intuition, would possess one of a different kind than one grounded in space and time.
>
> B138–9

What Kant wants to draw attention to here is the contrast between human discursive understanding and any non-discursive forms of understanding (either one who has an intellectual intuition of given objects, or an alternative discursive understanding that, unlike us, relies on a non-spatiotemporal sensible intuition). But Kant also observes that the principle of apperception is uniquely characteristic for beings that have a representation of themselves as subjects: as an 'I' that thinks and is thereby aware of herself as existing as thinker ('I am'). This implies that non-human animals do not apperceive the representations that they have. In early work and in the lectures, Kant clearly sided with his rationalist predecessors in denying animals inner sense, that is, a consciousness of self, which he identified with inner sense (V-Met/Herder, AA 28:901) (see Chapter 3). But commentators have read this as saying that animals have no consciousness *simpliciter*. That belief appears to be informed by the standard interpretation of the principle of apperception as a principle of mere consciousness. If animals do not have apperception, then by implication they do not have consciousness. But this reading of apperception is mistaken on purely interpretative grounds, as I have argued in detail elsewhere.[3] Transcendental apperception is not a necessary nor a sufficient condition of consciousness. Scientific evidence moreover supports the view that most vertebrates do arguably have at least creature consciousness and some mammals such as dolphins and elephants have shown evidence even of some form of bodily *self*-awareness. Another implication of the claim that animals do not have the capacity for apperception is that, because apperception grounds objective cognition, animals also do not have awareness of, or represent, objects. But this seems a rather unwelcome consequence of Kant's claim about the intimacy between self-consciousness (apperception) and the experience of objects. Animals are as much part of, and interact with objects in, phenomenal nature as we are, one should think. Let me explore this implication further.

5.2 Objectivity and Consciousness

In a recent article, in the context of a discussion of Kantian nonconceptualism, Sacha Golob differentiates the notion of 'objectivity*' from the notion of objectivity as it is defined in the Deduction (§17). He defines objectivity* in the following way:

> A visual experience E is objective* iff E represents a distinction between spatiotemporal particulars and the mental states of the subject of that experience.
> 2018[4]

This notion of objectivity is supposed to enable a conception of objectivity that is not a function of the unity of apperception (and thus of judgement)—which it is on Kant's understanding in §17 in the Deduction—but nonetheless guarantees a particular perspective by a subject or an ego-centric perspective vis-à-vis an object that can be differentiated from that perspective. On the one hand, I suspect that what Golob means by objectivity* is partly covered by what, in Schulting (2017a), I referred to as Kant's *Gegenstand*, which lies at the root of any intuition of a given object (A19/B33), is not a mental state but is rather that which is outside us spatially, and provides us with impressions, which are causally related to it. On the other hand, I do not think that objectivity* as a kind of primitive object-directed intentionality—animal perception or the intentionality of infants, say—is something that is compatible with the Kantian transcendental framework. Object-directed intentionality is the prerogative of the subject that, in Copernican terms, sees objects in terms of their conformity to the forms of her intuition and understanding. Anything outside that purview cannot count as objective or as having object-directed intentionality. But this does of course not mean that animals and infants, say, have no immediate awareness of their surroundings as a result of sensory input. Succinctly put, in my view it is *either* objectivity, as Kant defines it in the Deduction, *or* it is pure immediacy—that is, any set of representations that are sub-objective or merely subjectively valid do not qualify as objective or object-directed in the strict sense, but can and do involve being affected by objects and the behavioural responses that result from it. (I shall elaborate on the meaning of 'immediacy' in Section 5.3 below.)

Golob suggests, with good reason, that 'objectivity' is a technical term that has different meanings for different philosophers, and even Kant himself, as Golob notes, points to a loose sense of the term 'object' at A189–90. Though it would be perfectly legitimate in general to do so, I believe to differentiate between various senses of *objectivity* and to use the same term in all of these cases—even if annotated by an * or whatever other signifier is preferred—is to undermine one of the central arguments of the Deduction (in §17 of the B-Deduction, and A103–10 in the A-Deduction), namely, that objectivity is constituted first and *only* by the unity of apperception, and that there is no objectivity, strictly speaking, apart from the unity of apperception. To argue otherwise, or to weaken that link, is in my opinion to undermine the thrust of the Deduction, and the core claim of the Copernican turn: that objectivity is first constituted by the conformity to the forms of our intuition and understanding, which are constituted by the unity of apperception (or at any rate, insofar as the forms of intuition are determined by the understanding). There is also a philosophical reason not to go down the route of redefinition and modification in order to fit any sub-transcendental notion of objectivity into the Kantian transcendental framework (see below). But, as Golob observes, the issues are of course not merely definitional—on second thought, I should have refrained from giving the impression, on one occasion, that Kant rigorously distinguishes between the terms *Objekt* and *Gegenstand* (Schulting 2017a:21); as Golob correctly notes, Kant does not stick to such a strict differentiation and uses both terms interchangeably.[5]

If we look at the issues from a more systematic point of view, to posit an objective* intentionality for animals, in the sense that Golob proposes, strikes me as anthropomorphic and as revealing a conflation of the transcendental and empirical levels of reasoning. These levels are to be distinguished strictly on account of the Copernican turn, which proposed to look at the justification of the use of concepts from the perspective of the *self*-knowledge of reason, that is, from the perspective of rational self-legitimation without having to have recourse to empirical verificationism. It might be that Kant is not sufficiently phenomenologically sensitive to possible kinds of intentionality other than the one that is governed by transcendental laws (see Golob 2020). But it is important to point out, I think, that to try and imagine a non-human 'perspective' or 'intentionality' is still always an attempt *from our* human rational perspective, namely the perspective in which the very *idea* of a perspective is fundamental, that is, the perspective of the self-knowledge of human reason. I do not think an animal has a viewpoint—in the sense of what it is for something to be *for it*[6]—in the way that we have a viewpoint or perspective on some object. Obviously, animals engage with their environment, often in very intricate ways (an eagle, say, as Golob explains; I return to this example below), but they do not *represent to themselves* what they engage with in the way we are able to represent to ourselves what we see and interact with—and this representing to oneself one's own representing, being aware of one's representing is,[7] I suggest, essential to 'having a viewpoint'.

In other words, animals lack reflexivity, namely the capacity of representing one's representing to oneself, which *first* differentiates the subject of representation from the object of representation and vice versa, as Christian Wolff already made clear—this is an important element that Kant picks up from Wolff (see Chapter 3). Udo Thiel has rightly pointed out that for Wolff self-consciousness is 'doubly derivative', that is, 'it depends on the consciousness of objects, and on the consciousness of our mental act of distinguishing that is involved in the consciousness of objects' (Thiel 2011:308). But it also means that, reciprocally, we could not be conscious of objects if we were not self-conscious. This element of reflexivity is fundamentally lacking in animals.[8] See for example this early passage from the *Metaphysik Herder*:

> Animals (by hypothesis) have a faculty for acting according to choice, but they cannot *represent to themselves* the motivational grounds: they are not self-consciously acting on these at will.
>
> V-Met/Herder, AA 28:99, trans. mine, emphasis added

Of course, one could say that animals also have a particular outlook from which they have awareness of their surroundings, and that is certainly true, but this would not yet be an object-directed *intentionality* nor would it imply that animals have mental states which contain an intended object within themselves. An animal represents, but it is a *substantia bruta repræsentativa*, not an *intelligentia*. That animals do not have intentionality, according to Kant, is clearly shown by a passage in a lesser work of the mid-80s—hence, in the Critical period:

> For there is in cattle, as well as in the human being, that remarkable faculty we call imagination, the principle of perception and motion by which things that are absent can really exist in the mind as though they were present, as can things that never have been and perhaps never can be. But in cattle, *this force is not directed by any choice or deliberate intention of the animal* [*haec vis non arbitrio quodam ipsius animalis et deliberato proposito*[9] *regitur*], *but is put into play by stimuli and impulsions implanted by nature itself*, apart from any influence of the will.
>
> De medicina corporis, AA 15:944 [Kant 2007:186], emphasis added

As to animal consciousness, Kant often seems to deny that animals have consciousness. In a passage in the *Philosophical Encyclopædia* of 1775, he writes:

> The main, and nearly the only, difference between animals and humans is consciousness, but that is also so great that it can never be replaced with something else. Many animals behave and build so craftily that they come quite close to humans, but all are without consciousness.
>
> PhilEnz, AA 29:44–5, trans. mine

But it should be noted that the consciousness Kant likely means here is transitive consciousness (see Chapter 3). See also the following passages in the Pölitz lectures and in a later lecture note:

> Accordingly we attribute to [animals] a faculty of sensation, imagination, etc., but all only sensible as a lower faculty, and not connected with consciousness. We can explain all phenomena of the animals from this outer sensibility and from mechanical grounds of their bodies, without presupposing consciousness or inner sense. The philosopher must not increase the principles of cognitions without cause.
>
> V-Met-L1/Pölitz, AA 28:277, trans. mine

> [C]onsciousness is wholly lacking in animals, their behaviour occurs according to laws of the power of imagination, which nature has laid in them.
>
> V-Met/Dohna, AA 28:689–90, trans. mine

In a late letter, Kant writes:

> First, the division of the faculty of representation in the mere apprehension of the representation, *apprehensio bruta* without consciousness, which is solely for animals [*das Vieh*], and the sphere of apperception, i.e. of concepts; the latter comprises the sphere of the understanding in general.
>
> Br, AA 11:345, trans. mine

When Kant denies animals consciousness, it is self-consciousness (or inner sense) or transitive consciousness what he denies them, not creature consciousness and a certain awareness of their surroundings. Objectivity in Kant's sense is, however, a function of apperceptive subjectivity (this is basically the thesis of subjectivism that I defend in Schulting 2017a). Animals are not self-conscious in Kant's sense, i.e. apperceptively subjective. Because they are not subjects, animals by implication do not have a sense or 'idea' of objects in the strong Kantian sense—that is, objects *qua* objects; they perceive objects, but do not perceive them *as* objects. But it should also be borne in mind that there are in fact no objects strictly speaking outside of the objectivity that is born of apperceptive subjectivity, that is, objects external to the transcendental self. It concerns here the essential, philosophical meaning of the term 'object' (for Kant at least): that which is positioned 'over against' (A104–5); an object is as it were projected over against the subject *by* that subject,[10] and does not exist outside that subject—*qua* object, that is, since as a thing in itself it does of course exist outside the subject.[11]

This is the whole point of Kant's transcendental (Copernican) turn: there is no object just given over there, to which we, perceivers, cognizers, knowers, subsequently simply latch on, let alone could have *a priori* knowledge of if it were given beforehand. Of course, in a way *something* is given that we can label 'an object' in the ordinary (manifest) sense of the word (what I referred to as *Gegenstand*), but specifically not in the philosophical sense of the word. To put it differently, we cannot just assume that there is an *object sensu stricto* given, with respect to which animals, infants, human beings or what have you *then* go on to adopt, each in their own way, a subjective perspective.

The transcendental perspective does not apply to the animal case. To say that animal experience or perception refers to an object in a way that differentiates the object from their perspective on it, as Golob suggests, is, as I pointed out earlier, to mix up the transcendental and the empirical levels. On the empirical level animals are naturally as much part of the objective world as human beings are, and they interact with objects in similar or not so similar ways as human beings, but they are not *subjects* in the transcendental way, that is, they do not interact with objects *qua* objects of experience, as differentiatable from subjects.[12] Though I am not committed to a particular standpoint about which kinds of consciousness can be attributed to animals—and I think we need to differentiate here between types of animals (ants are sentient as much as dolphins are, but their levels of consciousness are uncontroversially very different)—I think that from a Kantian point of view animals cannot be said to have a type of consciousness other than intransitive. Animals have creature consciousness and some form of awareness of objects simply by being sensibly affected by them, but no transitive consciousness. They are not conscious *of* an object as differentiated, *by* themselves, from themselves. This does not of course imply that as creature-conscious animals they do not interact with objects in multiple complex ways. They are surely aware of the particulars, animate and inanimate, that they encounter and with which they interact in their surroundings by tracking these particulars in their different spatial locations (Golob calls these particulars 'objects[3]' in Golob, forthcoming). So I concur with Golob that as conscious beings animals have a spatial phenomenology, but I diverge from his view in that I do not think that this entails that animals have an awareness *of* the distinction between a perceived object and *themselves* (see further Section 5.3).

I should point out that denying animals a higher-order form of consciousness might be seen as at least controversial because it has been demonstrated in research that certain higher species of mammals, such as elephants, dolphins and hominids, apparently show signs of some form of self-reflexivity—that is, they seem to have some 'bodily self-awareness' when, for example, they see and react to a mirror image of a blob of paint that is painted on a particular side of their bodies in a way that suggests that they recognize it to be a blob of paint on their *own* bodies. But I think this 'bodily self-awareness' still falls way short of the kind of self-consciousness that is conditional on the possibility of transcendental self-consciousness as mutually constitutive of explicit consciousness of self *qua* self and experience of objects *qua* objects.[13] The awareness of their own bodies might be likened to Sartre's 'non-thetic consciousness (of) the body', which is of course in the first instance applicable to our own bodily self-awareness, but can be extrapolated to animals.[14]

Obviously, animals can make a distinction between, say, a stall and its door, as Kant himself points out (DfS, AA 2:59–60),[15] but that capacity for differentiation is not allied to an awareness of themselves; or, as Kant says, the ox can differentiate the stall from its door, but it does not recognize the differentiating as *its* own act: Kant makes a distinction between physically and logically differentiating. Now Golob would of course immediately rejoin that while an animal obviously does not make judgements about the objects it sees (by making *logical* distinctions), it does make physical distinctions, not just between objects, *but also between the objects and it itself*. But while we agree on the fact that animals are capable of making physical differentiations, on the point of what it means to make logical differentiations I think we disagree fundamentally, for in my interpretation apperception and the capacity for self-awareness in that strict reflexive sense cannot be decoupled from the capacity to judge, i.e. the capacity for making logical distinctions. So even if it is true that explicit judgements need not—and in the animal case, *cannot*—be made, the *capacity* to judge must still be there for beings to have the capacity for transcendental apperception as the *necessary* condition for strict awareness of self as well as of objects as different from self. And, as we agree, animals do not have that capacity. Physically differentiating, by contrast, is just the empirical act of differentiating, by locating and tracking spatially arrayed objects in virtue of certain causally determined dispositions, without having the capacity for being aware of, or recognizing, that one is doing so—which, as Golob nicely points out, involves the ability to 'recognize generic properties or marks' (Golob 2020:73–4). This last act Kant calls, in this early work, the act of *logically* differentiating. Later, in the Critical period, this is more accurately associated with the recognitive synthesis of the imagination, which is the necessary ground of the capacity for conceptualizing (and so for judging). While Golob appears to agree that this synthesis is not a capacity that animals share with humans, he does appear to believe, as said, that animals have some way of differentiating, not just between different objects such as a stall and its door, but also between objects and *themselves*. But I think that the capacity for physical differentiating is insufficient for this latter type of recognition of differences, and by implication the recognition of an object *as* an object—i.e. intentionality, or object*-directedness. And it is here that Golob and I disagree. Let me elaborate in the next section on the point of determinate space that Golob brings up, which is relevant to having the capacity to differentiate between objects.

5.3 Animal Perception and Spatial Determination

When I wrote about the elephant calf taking a shortcut through the wooden fence of an elephant sanctuary (Schulting 2017a:308), this was meant to underline that it is not as if animals cannot perceive, in their own characteristic ways, complex arrangements in nature just because they do not share our transcendental, i.e. objectively valid, perspective in terms of being *subjects* of experience—animals *are* of course part of the category-governed mechanical nexus of nature. My point was intended to counteract arguments by strong conceptualists, who tend to argue that outside the transcendental perspective, so absent transcendental apperception, there is just 'chaos'. But both strong conceptualists and nonconceptualists appear to mix up the empirical and transcendental perspectives. Obviously, purely seen from the empirical perspective, it is undeniable that animals as well as human beings interact in multiply complex and variant ways with objects. But, as I argued above, it is also undeniable that animals do not have knowledge of objects *qua* objects and *qua* their interactions with them: they just interact with them in accordance with the laws that govern the phenomenal, natural world.

The transcendental perspective that is introduced by Kant concerns the question of how it is possible that we have knowledge of objects and why the judgements we make about them are objectively valid. He shows, in the Transcendental Deduction and then in the Analogies, that objects are functions of our very thought, and not things that are just out there for us to subsequently latch onto so that as a result of this we acquire knowledge of them as objects. This is what the transcendental perspective means. For animals, by contrast, objects are not functions of their experience, let alone of their thought. Animals merely *encounter* objects with which they are programmed, as it were, to interact in specific ways. The entire Copernican perspective is not relevant to the case of animals. *For us*, of course, the way that animals do so interact is part of the natural realm that is constituted by the transcendental perspective because *everything* that happens in the phenomenal realm, in nature, is part of the nature that is determined by transcendental laws. But it would be a category mistake of the highest order to believe that since this is so, animals too have a subjective (let alone a transcendental) way of looking at things, or a close analogue of it. It would be anthropomorphic to project the conditions of our necessary way of experiencing—which, importantly, are also the conditions of the objects of our experience—and of cognizing phenomenal nature onto animals. The creature consciousness that animals have is nothing like our subjective, transitive kind of consciousness that we have when we experience or cognize our surrounding environment, which entails the possibility of making judgements about it and accounting for our beliefs. (It should be noted that there is also a level of creature consciousness in ourselves, which is for example the kind of immediate awareness that we have in what Kant calls the 'feeling' of our bodily existence, i.e. proprioception—see the excellent analyses in this regard by Longuenesse 2017.)

Golob misconstrues the context in which I wrote that it is 'difficult to *understand* [*note the emphasis!*] though what it could mean for one to have intuitions that are *not* synthesised, that is, to have "merely [a] manifold" ... of representations' (Schulting 2017a:326). The context here is the conclusion of the proof in the B-Deduction, namely the argument that categories are necessary conditions of the perception of spatiotemporal objects, and that thus the objective validity of the categories has been proven. But this is clearly the conclusion of an argument that aims to explain the possibility of *human* cognition of objects, not the *impossibility* of animal perception. The combination or synthesis that is the necessary enabling condition of such cognition is *necessary* combination, not just any contingent binding of perceptions. I have analysed the difference between necessary combination and categorially arbitrary binding, and also why the argument in B130, which Golob cites, should *not* be read as if the two were conflated by Kant, in detail elsewhere (see Schulting 2018b:186–93). When Golob quotes me as denying, supposedly, that 'animals "can have relation to an individual *object*, even if only indeterminately"' (Schulting 2017a:21)', and that 'animals are unable to perceive "objects as determinate spaces" (2017a:22)', in both cases he interpolates the word 'animals', where in the context of those quotations—which is the introduction to the book—I do not at all talk about animals (animals first briefly appear in Chapter 3 of the book), but about possible human perception independently of the workings of synthesis. In fact, Golob's charge is directly contradicted by another passage, where I do discuss animal perception. It is useful to quote this in full:

> *This does not imply that, in the absence of the categories, there cannot be a nonconceptual intuition of particulars, e.g. when an animal or an infant sees a spatially located thing, which it is able to discriminate from among other things, and which it can track* (see e.g. Allais 2011:103). The animal or infant does not need to think the thing 'as a persisting and causally unitary substance' in order to perceive a relatively distinct particular. This is just because animals or infants have no conception of objects in the strict Kantian sense of persisting and causally related substances. And mere perception is not dependent on the employment of the categories, or indeed the application of empirical concepts or ascription of properties. I concur with Allais on this (see Chap. 5). But it would be wrong to conclude from this—it being contrary to the specific goal of TD—that for adults with properly functioning cognitive abilities, who do employ concepts in judgements, categories would merely be conditions for thinking

about objects, by virtue of 'apply[ing] empirical concepts to objects in judgments' (Allais 2011:103). Rather, the goal of TD is precisely to explain how categories, not only enable the application of empirical concepts to given objects, but also first determine manifolds of representations in an intuition as objects, namely, as determinate appearances. The categories must thus be seen as also establishing the necessary conditions under which there can be said first to be objects, to which then empirical concepts can be applied.

Schulting 2017a:170–1, emphasis added

Another passage he quotes, in which I talk about 'a recognition of the manifold ... *as* qualitatively or quantitatively complex' (Schulting 2017a:266), is linked by Golob to animal perception, but I do not discuss animal perception at all there. Again, the discussion there is to be seen in the context of the possibility of human perception of objects in the analysis of the Deduction (specifically, the A-Deduction), and what the counterfactual possibility of the categories not being instantiated in intuition would imply for *human* perception. Golob's linking of that counterfactual possibility and the animal case might seem justified, but that assumes that *our* mere sensibility is equivalent to animal sensibility—this is an assumption underlying what James Conant (2016) has recently dismissed as 'the layer-cake-conception' of the relation between sensibility and the understanding, whereby the understanding is a human rational add-on to a sensibility that is in large part shared by humans and animals alike; Golob indeed appears to endorse the layer-cake-conception, at least in some form, whereas I concur with Conant's critique of this view. The difference is crucial. Even if our sensibility were comparable to that of animals, *for us* it is difficult to imagine what it would *mean* to have mere sensibility because doing so lands us in an inevitable circle: to be able to imagine to have mere sensibility we would need the very tools, namely, the synthesis of the imagination, that deny us that immediacy. By contrast, sensible immediacy is precisely the default disposition for animals. To try and imagine the animal's situation is just that, an attempt to put oneself imaginatively in the position of a being that we cannot be. (We can of course act in ways similar to animal behaviour in some of our subcognitive activities or sensible 'coping'.)

Again, Golob himself appears to conflate two levels here: the transcendental or constitutive level and the empirical level. And I think this partly explains the problem he has with my reading, and also partly allays the worries he has. Though Golob makes it seem we do, in fact we do not disagree on the fundamental, empirically provable fact that animals and human beings alike—as holds for any *object* in nature—interact with objects in space in variant and multiple complex ways. There is nothing arbitrary, in an empirical sense, about the manner of these interactions: these are bound by the empirical laws of nature and diverse species-related biological embodied dispositions and behavioural patterns. Thus, if we take the excellent example that Golob takes, namely the 'eagle who picks out the rapidly moving body of a mouse, who tracks that body as it passes bushes and grasses and strikes precisely it and not the similar coloured rock next to it': the eagle is aiming at 'a determinate space' in the sense that the determinate space in question concerns another animal that is distinct from the object adjacent to it so that, wholly in virtue of contingent empirical laws of nature, the predator can 'aim' accurately (or indeed less accurately) at its prey. This is entirely independent of the transcendental question about the possibility of determining a space from the vantage point of human reason for the purposes of analysing knowledge, the issue that Kant is interested in in the Deduction and the Analogies.

There is often the misconception that on Kant's view the world would *de re* not be the phenomenal, natural world that we know if it weren't for the transcendental laws of human understanding. This misconception, again, conflates the transcendental and empirical levels of the analysis in the *Critique*. What is being analysed in Kant's transcendental analysis is the *possibility* of empirical objects and events insofar as they are possible objects and events of our experience, not with respect to their factual existences and occurrences or their empirical status as such (this holds for empirical natural laws too). The question is always and across the different sections of the Aesthetic and the Analytic in the *Critique* the question of *how* something is really possible or exists, never *that* or *if* it is the case or exists—or *why*, for that matter—and then only from the specifically human standpoint of reason. (To be sure, this is not a *relativist* premise on Kant's part, but the premise of an analysis that purports to be rational and a priori, and not merely descriptive or empirical.)

This means that criticisms—for example such as are currently en vogue in 'speculative realist' circles—that the Kantian transcendental perspective is a limited (and biased, reductionist) humanist perspective wholly miss the mark. If human beings were no longer around, or in ancestral times when there were in fact no humans around, the eagle would still be able to precisely aim at the mouse, and not accidentally hit at the rock, because it is able, in virtue of empirical laws of association and location in space, to accurately track the body of the mouse that is in a distinct place in space; the associated connections directly map onto the way in which the prey is a spatially arrayed body in phenomenal nature relative to the predator's own body. And to be sure, in those situations void of human beings there to observe events of interacting objects the transcendental perspective would still be universally valid, for that perspective is about the *possibility* of our cognition of objects and their conformity to our forms of cognition; spatiotemporal objects and events happen independently of our *actual* observations, but they do not and cannot happen independently of *possible* experience.[16]

This is why we argued in Onof & Schulting (2015) for the nonconceptualist position that spatial relations per se must not be seen as necessarily grounded on the a priori synthesis of the understanding. When Kant talks about 'determinate' space in the context of the Deduction, he means space as determined (*bestimmt*) by the human understanding in virtue of the synthetic act of apperception, i.e. via imagination. Determinate space (*bestimmter Raum* or a 'formal intuition' [B160n]) strictly speaking, i.e. as such, exists only on condition of there being a determination by the understanding. There is no determinate space absent determination by the understanding: these are two sides of the same coin that cannot be decoupled on pain of misapprehending the implications of Kant's idealism that is born of the Copernican turn. (And likewise, nature *formaliter spectata* exists only on condition of there being a determination by the understanding, but the empirical laws of nature, nature *materialiter spectata*, are of course as such independent of such an a priori determination, though they must conform to it, lest there be a gap between apperception and space.)[17] But determinate space as defined by the determinative act of the understanding is not metaphysical space, nor does the understanding define the sui generis properties of space. Of course, the two are not two different kinds of space, as ontologically speaking there is just one space and there is no gap between the understanding's determinative *capacity* and space itself; but metaphysical space is *as such* independent of the way it is necessarily *determined* by the understanding if space is to be determined as one particular place adjacent to another. Determinate space is always finite with respect to the larger space of which it forms a part, i.e. metaphysical space. Metaphysical space is in that sense independent, and can exist independently, of *actual* instantiations of the understanding's capacity of determining space as consisting of particular determinate spaces.

The ability of an animal to track its prey *in* space is itself therefore independent of the determination by an act of a priori synthesis, but the space in which it tracks its prey can be determined by proxy, i.e. vicariously *by us*, to be a determinate space (on the animal's behalf, as it were); in fact, it *must* be determinate space, for animals interact with phenomenal objects in the same (metaphysical) space in which we human beings do so.

But, by analogy with the thought experiment of which Kant speaks in his 26 May 1789 letter to Marcus Herz, if I 'imagine myself to be an animal', my (animal) representations of something in space would still 'carry on their play in an orderly fashion, as representations connected according to empirical laws of association, and thus even have an influence on my feeling and desire [which Kant allowed for animals],[18] without my being aware of them', i.e. not being aware of the representations' 'relation to the unity of representation of their object, by means of the synthetic unity of their apperception' (Br., AA 11:52 [Kant 1999:314]). Thus, animals have awareness of spatial objects, but not *in virtue of* an intentional awareness of the object of a unified representation that constitutes an object as 'a determinate space' (B138), but rather in virtue of their ability to associate merely according to empirical laws.

Where Golob and I diverge is with respect to the fact that I firmly believe that, on Kantian grounds at least, one cannot state that animals themselves, on account of their putative sui generis intentionality (object*-directedness), are responsible for the *determination* of an object in space or have such an intentional object in their mental states; that is, they are not *reflexively* directed at a determinate space such that they (can) become aware of themselves as the agents of their perceiving a determinate space; they rather just *interact* with what are in effect, on account of a transcendental analysis, determinate objects in space (or, put differently, they interact with determinate spaces). Animals do not apperceive, synthesize, nor cognize, let alone apply categories, which means they do not have an intentional object. They simply perceive, with more or less accuracy, in virtue of binding certain representations that map one to one onto the objects they come to represent. (These binding relations can be perfectly studied in zoology, or ornithology for that matter, to remain with the example of eagles.)

The animal example I gave (Schulting 2017a:308) was meant to illustrate the fact that, contrary to what Thomas Land (2014) (whose conceptualist views on spatial determination I discuss critically in that section) believes, there can be an intuition of something spatial without a priori synthesis being involved. I used the example of an elephant calf to illustrate this. Not all perception requires synthesis. But there the analogy stops with human perception; I certainly did not want to suggest that our sensibility is in all or even most respects like that of animals. And Golob's critique of my position suggests that I accept the structural similarity between animal sensibility and our own; but I deny this. So when I gave the example of hearing a sudden noise coming from a particular direction (Schulting 2017a:309), this was, again, of course an example of our human perception that is not (yet) a determinate perception of a distinct object—though I admit it might be a ground for confusion that it directly followed the paragraph in which I provided the animal example. But there is a similarity between that example and how an animal reacts to a noise coming from a certain direction in the same way as humans do but then does not, unlike human beings, apply categories (synthesize representations, apperceive) to become aware of a distinct object *as* distinct *from itself*. But that does not mean that the animal only sees chaos, and cannot make distinctions on an empirical level, just as a human being would be able to do upon hearing a sound from the left without thereby directly invoking the categories.

That Golob thinks my example of hearing a sudden noise as indicative of the real possibility of an intuition of a spatially located but *perceptually indistinct* object independently of the activity of synthesis entails a 'surely empirically false' claim about animal perception indicates that he conflates the necessary combination that is required for human cognitive perception of objects, *qua* distinguishable objects, and the contingent *empirical* nature of the connections that hold between objects—including the specific ways in which an animal tracks an object—regardless of our determination of the necessary character of these connections which makes it possible for us to cognize objects in nature—this includes the determination of them *qua* objects as functions solely of our determination. The empirical world does not need the categories *to exist* or for some causal event *to happen*, nor are empirical laws dependent on the categories *to obtain*; they obtain regardless of whether we apply the categories or not. The determination of the necessity in them does of course require the categories: nature is nature *qua* nature only in virtue of the categories. Only as objects of possible experience are things in nature categorially determinable, and necessarily at that. This, to be sure, does not imply that things *must* be determined or experienced, rather it means—and this is what the Transcendental Deduction aims to show—that there is no discrepancy between things in nature and transcendental apperception, i.e. *possible* experience, insofar as these things can be apprehended as objects for thought (objects of experience) for any possible instance of experience.[19] But no animal or inanimate object for that matter needs the categories to interact in the specific contingent empirical ways that they do. The fine-grainedness argument that Golob brings to the discussion is irrelevant. That animals are capable of 'tracking far finer-grained spatio-temporal relations than we are' is besides the point of the discussion in the Deduction (and the Analogies) concerning the determination of spatiotemporal relations. The sharper eyesight of an eagle, compared to that of our eyesight, is not a ground for claiming that surely the eagle can aim at a determinate space as much as a human being, if not more so. For the determinacy in question in the Deduction is not empirical determinacy but necessary combination. But, again, the eagle does in fact aim at a determinate space, however not in virtue of its own intentionality, but because it is part of phenomenal nature that is constituted by transcendental as well as empirical natural laws.

Golob ignored my discussion, in Schulting (2017a) chs 6 and 7, of the distinction that needs to be made between determining a complex manifold *as* complex and the complexity of the manifold as such. Golob's critique of my position makes it appear as if the complexity were solely born of the determination in virtue of the synthesis of the imagination, and not already there in the manifold, as if indeed the spatially arrayed manifold that an animal perceives did not allow of very specific complex, fine-grained relations that the scientific evidence shows an animal such as an eagle can track. As I noted in my analysis of the synthesis of apprehension, a 'mere manifold of isolated representations is not ipso facto qualitatively or quantitatively simple', but 'unsynthesised representations of outer sense are already quantitatively complex', that these are 'not recognised *as* complex' (2017a:287n.13), and that the complexity of a mere manifold does not depend on the synthesis of apprehension (2017a:265). This is in line with for example Stefanie Grüne's view that sensibility 'delivers complex representations, whose content is however not represented as something complex' (Grüne 2009:161).

5.4 Concluding Remark: Either Objectivity or Immediacy

I want to close with a remark on the 'immediacy' of intuition, which bears on animal perception. Absent transcendental apperception and the application of categories the object of intuition is still categorially indeterminate, or indistinct, but, importantly, given the absence of transcendental apperception there is no 'me' strictly speaking, and hence there is no clear transcendental distinction between *me* and the object—in other words, there is no 'for me', so there cannot be an *object* for me. This follows from the analysis of Kant's concept of self-consciousness and the related definition of an object in general in the first half of the B-Deduction (cf. the 'transcendental object' in the A-Deduction). The relation to the object of intuition I have *in intuition* is immediate, and therefore as such indistinct because it is by definition not mediated by a conceptual differentiation—that does not imply that the object is not something spatially arrayed outside me, with specific determinable boundaries, at a specific distance, with which other objects in the adjacent spaces interact in ways that are governed by universally valid natural laws. Animals are likewise orientated towards objects that are outside them in space, and in this sense I concur with Golob's claim that 'a three dimensional egocentrically orientated awareness of space within which something is seen as more or less distant is sufficient to sustain a distinction between spatio-temporal particulars and the subject's own states, such as sensations', so long as this is seen purely on the empirical level (though I would not use the term 'egocentrically'). And this is an important proviso: we should not mix up the transcendental and empirical levels; only the former constitutes objective intentionality or objectivity in the strict sense.

What is important here is to realize that Kant, as well as his successors in German idealism who built on this aspect of the Critical philosophy, were keenly aware of the mutually conditioning relation between an *object* and the *subject* of experience in the philosophically precise sense of those terms. If there is no explicit subject, i.e. no category application and a priori synthesis, such as in the case of animals, there is no object strictly speaking either. This follows from the transcendental logic of what it means to have an intentional object: 'object' is a function of subjectivity, the intentional object is a transcendental object that is nothing but a synthetic unity of representations, an object in the mind (the transcendental subject) (see e.g. A104–9).

Does that mean that there is no object *simpliciter*, a thing or things *de re*? No, of course not—this is what I tried to convey by making the distinction *Gegenstand/Objekt* (Schulting 2017a:21), pointing to Kant's own use of the generic, non-technical sense of *Gegenstand* that he employs at B1, where he states the empiricist principle that all cognition starts with experience. However, without category application/a priori synthesis/transcendental apperception there is no object *for* a subject just because there is no subject *for* which there would be an object. There is of course a certain orientation in space, necessarily for any rational or non-rational animal that is part of nature. However, while the orientation in space for humans is necessarily guided by the understanding—by way of the figurative synthesis—in order to determine the *objects* towards which one is orientated for the purpose of cognitive experience or judgement, for animals the orientation is sufficiently guaranteed by the way they are wired to interact with spatially arrayed objects; their orientation does not depend on a subjective act of synthesis or the binding of representations in such a way that the objects are determinate *for them*, as it were. The objective space within which they track other animals and objects is just the space of which they are part as much as objects are. To say that there is something for an object to be *for* an animal other than that an object sensibly affects that animal, and prompts sensations in the animal and consequently certain behavioural patterns, is an anthropomorphic projection. Rather, the animal's 'experience', if it can be called that, is one of pure immediacy.

Pure immediacy must be understood in the way that Hegel understood it: the identity that is constitutive of both subject and object, and thus at the same time enables their differentiation, is 'in intuition ... totally immersed in the manifold [*im Anschauen ganz und gar in die Mannigfaltigkeit versenkt*]' (GW 4:327 [Hegel 1977:70]). Hegel, just like Kant, has of course human sensible intuition in mind here, but this can be extrapolated to the animal case. Pure immediacy means that having a mere intuition of an object does not differentiate the object from its being represented; the representer's identity and the relative difference of the represented object are 'immersed' in the manifold of representations; but that does not mean that the difference between the representation or sensation (mental states) and an object that is being represented is not there, it is rather 'immersed' in the manifold representations. The metaphor that Hegel uses here is to make it clear that only the understanding is able to lift the relative difference (antithesis), and thus the relative identity, of subject and object out of that 'immersion'. Hegel refers to the blindness of intuition of which Kant speaks at A51/B75. That an intuition without concept is blind does not mean (as might be suggested by the term 'blind') that an intuition lacks awareness, but it means that without the involvement of the capacity for conceptual differentiation (and synthesis), i.e. apperception, an intuition cannot make out the distinction between representation and represented, and is thus blind with respect to the 'antithesis', as Hegel calls it. Hegel writes:

> Kant is therefore quite right in calling intuition without form [i.e. concept] [*Form (des Denkens)*] blind. For in [mere] intuition [without form] there is no relative antithesis [*Gegensatz*], and hence there is no relative identity of unity and difference. This relative identity and antithesis is what seeing or being conscious [*das Sehen oder das Bewußtsein*] consists in; but the identity is completely identical with the difference just as it is in the magnet.
> GW 4:327 [Hegel 1977:70]

I am not interested here in the validity of Hegel's interpretation of Kant, but at least one thing is right about this reading, namely that in intuition the 'relative identity' that exists *between* the unity of the understanding, with its characteristic forms (categories), and the difference (plurality) of the manifold of representations—an identity that is semantically expressed in a judgement (the very structure of a judgement S is P expresses the relative identity and antithesis of intuition and concept, 'something S is P')—has not yet come to the fore: this identity is the unity between, on the one hand, an experiencing subject that applies concepts and, on the other, the object to which, by way of the synthesis of an intuition of that object, those concepts are applied. Rather, the antithesis in empirical intuition 'besteht . . . in dieser Form des Versenktseins'.

This, then, is what nonconceptual content in a Kantian sense would mean: a content that has not yet been given the conceptual form which makes it a *determinate* content, whereby the opposition (and relative identity) between the subject and object of experience is first made manifest, *distinct*. Now of course we can redefine the terms of what we mean by objectivity or, more interestingly, differentiate various meanings of objectivity—which is what Golob aims for— but then we are no longer in the territory of interpreting Kant. The Copernican object is always an object *for us*, a transcendental object, and not something that exists or is already given apart from us. On Kant's view, animals do not have the Copernican perspective, so their perceptions involve neither a transcendental object nor some kind of intentional object-directedness. Animals are just part of the phenomenal realm as objects among other objects, with which they interact 'immediately', not as if they were intentionally aiming at them.

Kantian nonconceptualists thus cannot have their cake and eat it: it is *either* objectivity in the full Kantian sense *or* immediacy of intuition. On a Kantian account, in nonconceptual intuitions, or intuitions that are not or not yet categorially determined, there can be no sense of objectivity or objective intentionality, just because there is no subject which would take the object as existing *for* itself.

6

Disciple or Renegade? On Reinhold's Representationalism, the Principle of Consciousness, and the Thing in Itself

6.1 'Nothing But Representations'

It has been a long-standing problem in Kant scholarship how to conceive of Kant's notorious concept of the thing in itself, its inextricable relation to his idealism about appearances—which are what things are to us as representers—and the fact that, according to Kant, we cannot have knowledge of things in themselves, but only of objects as appearances (the so-called ignorance or unknowability thesis). It is important to note that the ignorance thesis does not imply that we know only our own private sense data, nor does it mean that things in themselves do not exist, or that there exist only thinking beings, that is, as Kant writes, that

> all other things which we believe are perceived in intuition are nothing but representations in the thinking beings, to which no object external to them in fact corresponds.

Kant insists that things that exist outside us 'are given'. What makes his view idealist is, not that he denies the existence of things that are independent of our minds (which he does not),[1] but that he denies that we have knowledge 'of what they may be in themselves'. We know only 'their appearances', which are 'the representations which they [i.e. the things] cause in us by affecting our senses' (all the above quotations from Prol, AA 4:288–9 [Kant 1977:32–3]).

There are certain elements of Kant's idealism that are foregrounded in this passage, and which are usually considered the most interesting (and also controversial) ones. These concern, first, the seeming fact that the objects that we know, i.e. appearances, are *mere* representations, a claim that Kant makes more often (see e.g. A30/B45, A120, A369, A371, A374–5n, A490–1/B518–19) and which has puzzled many commentators, for it seems to reduce empirically real objects to sense data after all.[2] That is, if appearances were really just representations, rather than the *objects* of representations, Kant's idealism about appearances would amount to a kind of phenomenalism. And it seems commentators believe phenomenalism is a Berkeleian spectre that just cannot be the right interpretative frame for reading Kant's emphatic empirical realism about objects of experience (cf. Langton 1998:141ff., Allais 2015).[3] Most commentators try to explain away this aspect of Kant's talk about appearances, i.e. that they are 'mere' representations. For example, since she wants to avoid a phenomenalist reading at all costs ('We have many good reasons for not taking at face value Kant's phenomenalist-sounding talk'), Rae Langton (1998:158ff.) misreads a controversial passage from the *Prolegomena* (AA 4:289), where whilst protesting against idealism (of the Berkeleian sort) Kant plainly identifies appearances with representations, which we call bodies. She suggests that we read the passage as saying that appearances are not to be identified with representations, but as saying that we 'know appearances *through* representations', relying on a phrase in the same passage. However, in this later phrase, Kant does not say that we know *appearances* 'through representations', but it is rather *things* which, 'though quite unknown to us as to what they are in themselves', we know 'through representations' (Prol, AA 4:289 [Kant 1977:33], trans. emended).[4]

Contrary to what Tobias Rosefeldt (2012:240–1) argues, I believe that in the *Prolegomena* passage at issue Kant does not take back the view expressed in the A-edition Fourth Paralogism that appearances as bodies are mere representations (A370). It is the *things* that we know *through* representations, which latter we call bodies; in other words, bodies *are* representations, and are not, strictly speaking, the things which we know *through* the representations, namely, *represent as* bodies. At any rate, the passage does not say that bodies are not representations, as Rosefeldt believes. We do indeed perceive objects (Kant's 'things' [*Dinge*]) as outside us *by means of* representations, and we perceive those objects *as* bodies (we do not just perceive our perceptions). But in the clause not quoted by Rosefeldt, which directly follows 'und denen wir die Benennung eines Körpers geben', Kant clearly identifies a body as 'bloß die Erscheinung', whilst a few lines before he identified appearances as 'the representations, which they [i.e. the things outside us] cause in us by affecting our senses'; hence, a body is a representation. So, strictly speaking, it is not a body which we know *through* representation, but the thing (in itself), which we *represent as* outside us, and *whose representation* we call body.[5] The *represented* thing, i.e. its appearance, is a body. The representations that are bodies are obviously not mere mental states, but represent*eds*,[6] that is, intentional objects—which are nonetheless nothing outside our thoughts. But, contrary to what Rosefeldt says, I would argue that even in the A-edition Fourth Paralogism, Kant should be taken to argue that bodies are represent*eds*, not mere mental states (significantly, he talks about 'Vorstellungs*arten*' at A372, emphasis added).

Like James Van Cleve (1999), who is one of the few exceptions in the literature to take phenomenalism seriously as an interpretation of Kant's idealism,[7] I believe not only that it is the only non-deflationary way to interpret Kant's explicit identification of appearances as representations, but also, unlike Van Cleve, that only a phenomenalist interpretation of Kant's idealism can explain his claim—the central argument of the Transcendental Deduction of the categories—that the necessary conditions of self-consciousness are sufficient for the objectivity of the objects of our experience, given sensory input. I cannot expand on this here.[8]

Secondly, there seems to be a problem with regard to the putative causal relation between things in themselves and appearances, which is often a ground for commentators to dismiss the causal reading of idealism as an appropriate interpretative approach (see e.g. Wood 2005). For the idea of a causal relation between things in themselves and appearances would appear (a) to conflict with the ignorance thesis, namely, that we do not have knowledge of things in themselves, so that we cannot know about any relations, causal or other, that obtain between things in themselves and appearances either, and (b) to suggest that things in themselves and appearances are not identical, for if things in themselves causally effect appearances, they cannot be identical to them (as Wood argues), raising the legitimate question that if they are not identical, in which other way appearances can be seen as the appearances *of* things in themselves.[9]

Thus, as regards (a), if we do not have knowledge of things in themselves, then neither can we have knowledge of their putative causal or affective relation to our representations. At most, it must be granted that it is analytic that if there is an appearance, there must be something appearing, which presumably is the thing in itself in terms of the thing that exists independently of what it appears as to us (cf. A251–2). From Jacobi onwards, Kant has been criticized for crossing the transcendental bounds of experience by applying a category of experience (causality) to something which *ex hypothesi* cannot be experienced, namely, things in themselves. There is, however, an undeniable generic dependence relation of appearances as grounded upon a thing in itself or things in themselves as an (in some respect) unconditioned or more fundamental ground, while causal relations are in some sense conceptually based on such ground-consequence relations. Nevertheless, the causal relation that Kant talks about is not just a logical ground-consequence relation, but genuinely a metaphysical relation of causal affection, as Kant says in the above-quoted passage from the *Prolegomena*.[10] It is not prima facie clear if Kant does not contradict his own restrictions here, as Jacobi and others alleged. But we can grant the appropriateness of assigning a role of sorts for causality even in the domain of things in themselves or in terms of the relation between things in themselves and appearances if this role is not seen as *constituting* causally determined objects or events governed by physical laws, that is, objects existing within the bounds of sense experience. It is thus doubtful—if not impossible on Kant's account—that any causal relation between things in themselves and appearances, if it is causal, would be one of *efficient* causation. The application of causality beyond the bounds of experience would thus at any rate be an unschematized use of the category.

With regard to (b), it would appear odd to claim that we know things in terms of '*their* appearances' (Prol, AA 4:289 [Kant 2002:84], emphasis added) if the appearances are not identical to that *of* which they are the appearances, namely, the things in themselves. At best, we would know the things' *appearances*, but nothing *of* the things in themselves that appear, or even *of how* they relate to us in the way that they appear to us—so that the possessive pronoun 'their' that Kant uses would then seem to be inapposite if it were indeed read strictly as signalling numerical identity. That is, we are not licensed to conclude from our acquaintance with or knowledge of the appearances, that we have knowledge of the appearances as *of* things in themselves that are putatively numerically identical to them. We are only licensed to infer, by logical implication, from our knowledge, or the existence, of appearances that there must be *something* that appears, without thereby identifying that something.[11] This is quite general, and does not give us any substantial clue as to the specific relation between any one appearance or appearances and thing in itself or things in themselves. The possessive pronoun 'their' that Kant employs thus should not be read as if it did any metaphysical lifting here: it does not signify numerical identity or one-to-one correspondence between appearance and the underlying thing in itself.

There are other passages which might seem to support readings that regard the distinction in terms of double aspects of the very same thing and so to confirm identity readings of the relation between things in themselves and appearances, e.g. at B69, where Kant writes:

> For in the appearance the objects, indeed even the properties [*Beschaffenheiten*] that we attribute to them, are always regarded as something really given; but

insofar as this property depends only on the mode of intuition of the subject in the relation of the given object to it is this object as appearance to be distinguished from itself as object in itself [*von ihm selber als Objekt an sich*].

trans. emended and my underlining[12]

More specifically, the double-aspect reading of things in themselves is often taken in terms of considering two disjunctive types of *property* of one and the same thing, where the properties are irreducible to each other, but still properties of one and the same thing, and where the thing to which these properties are attributed is considered the thing in itself. Such a reading is logically possible (think of Spinoza's view of different attributes as expressing the one substance). However, this reading, standard in the current so-called metaphysical two-aspect interpretation of transcendental idealism, is prima facie odd, if not flat-out contradictory, in the Kantian context. For Kant says that appearances do not exist *outside* our thoughts, whilst he asserts that things that exist outside us, and have an 'in itself' nature, are given independently of our thoughts; hence, because appearances are nothing but properties of our mind, i.e. *thoughts* or modes of *representation*, and do not exist *outside* our thoughts, they cannot be properties *of things in themselves* (as indeed Kant makes clear at Prol, AA 4:293)—which gainsays the view that appearances are somehow to be seen as the phenomenal or appearing properties *of* the very things in themselves underlying the appearances, even if these properties were to be seen as mind-dependent properties, that is, properties relativized to epistemic subjects, whose representations represent those things (Rosefeldt, ms.).

At B164, Kant writes that appearances do not 'exist in themselves, but only relative to the same being [the subject], insofar as it has senses'. This might, at first blush, be taken to mean either that, since appearances are mere representations, they exist only *in the particular subject* that has these representations, suggesting straightforward phenomenalism (empirical idealism), or that appearances are the properties of things in themselves that are relativized to an epistemic subject, as Rosefeldt suggests. I think that the 'relative to the subject' must be read neither reductively so as to suggest empirical idealism, nor as implying that, though not existing in themselves qua appearances, appearances are nonetheless the mind-dependent properties *of* things in themselves. The property of the object that we perceive outside us is the property of the given object 'only insofar as this property depends on the mode of intuition of the subject in the relation of the given object to it' (B69, trans. emended); in other words, the relation of the object to the subject, which enables its perception, is one that is first established by the subject's mode of intuition, in line with Kant's Copernican turn. This means that the appearances as properties attributed to the object are not just *partly* dependent on, or relativized to, the cognizing subject, but in fact wholly dependent on it, and so effectively wholly subject-internal.

Appearances thus cannot be properties, in any sense, *of* things in themselves, for this would mean that appearances existed *outside* the mind transcendentally. They of course do exist outside the mind empirically, but then they are empirical objects, bodies, not things in themselves, nor properties of things in themselves. An appearance as empirical object is a function of space, which is the transcendental condition under which objects can exist as being outside of me, that is, outside my mind (A23–4/B38–9). Space is not a property of things in themselves (A26/B42)—space (like time) is just 'in us' (A373)—so appearances cannot be properties of things in themselves. Therefore, appearances cannot exist outside the mind in the transcendental sense. Kant himself speaks of a contradiction, if *per impossibile* one were to regard objects in space and time, that is, appearances, as objects that are 'independent of this thought of mine [*ohne diesen meinen Gedanken*]':

> [F]or then I would contradict myself, since space and time, together with the appearances in them, are nothing existing in themselves and outside my representations, but are themselves *only modes of representation*, and *it is patently contradictory to say of a mere mode of representation that it also exists outside our representation*. The objects of the senses therefore exist only in experience; by contrast, to grant them a self-subsistent existence of their own, without experience or prior to it, is as much as to imagine that experience is also real without experience or prior to it.
>
> Prol, AA 4:341–2 [Kant 2002:132], emphasis added

Further, similar problems face the metaphysical two-aspect reading as they did the well-known methodological two-aspect reading (see e.g. Allison 1983; cf. Robinson 1994 for a critique)—which sees a consideration of things in themselves as a consideration of things in abstraction from the conditions under which they can be considered objects of knowledge, that is, as appearances—by regarding the distinction between appearances and things in themselves in terms of disjunctive kinds of property of the same underlying thing.

In conclusion, I believe appearances cannot really *be numerically the same as* things in themselves or that an appearance A is numerically the same thing as a thing in itself T because (1) appearances are merely the effects of deeper grounds, or, accidents of underlying substances,[13] and (2) fundamental appearance properties such as space and time are on Kant's account, by definition, not properties *of* things in themselves, even if they were to be seen as merely the relational or extrinsic or subject-relativized properties of things in themselves (and since all appearances are contained in space and time, *no* appearance properties can be properties of things in themselves). Moreover, if space and time and appearance properties were to be seen as properties of things in themselves, even if only as their extrinsic or relational or subject-relativized properties, the pressing question remains—despite it being logically possible that various attributes can be attributes of the same substance—how two *exclusionary* types of property, namely *non-spatial* intrinsic properties and *spatial* extrinsic properties, could be said to be properties of *one and the same* (numerically identical) underlying thing. Such a view is at any rate difficult to square with Kant's emphatic claim that space and time are not properties of things in themselves.

6.2 Reinhold's Representationalism

I want to zero in on the Kantian idea that, whilst things in themselves must logically be presupposed as the unconditioned or more fundamental ground underlying appearances and things are not reducible to their representations, (1) objects as appearances are not properties *of* things in themselves, and (2) things in themselves or the thing in itself cannot *properly* be represented or even thought. To do this, I turn to one of the earliest defenders and champions of the Kantian philosophy, Karl Leonhard Reinhold, who published his so-called *Letters on the Kantian Philosophy* in instalments in *Der Teutsche Merkur* in 1786 and 1787, with which he came to public prominence and which helped him get the post of professor of Kantian philosophy in Jena, and his first relatively orthodoxly Kantian monograph *Versuch einer neuen Theorie des menschlichen Vorstellungsvermögens* (henceforth *Versuch* for short) in 1789. My interest here concerns the latter work. Reinhold's *Versuch* can be read as a commentary of sorts on Kant's Critical philosophy, although Reinhold specifically fashioned the book as an attempt to give the Critical philosophy a more secure, systematic foundation than the *Critique of Pure Reason* itself provided. I am here interested neither in the extent to which Reinhold's interpretation of Kant is correct or even adequately represents Kant's thought in all of its aspects, nor whether Reinhold's attempt to present a systematic philosophy based on a rigorous deduction from a single principle—his strong foundationalism—stands up to scrutiny.[14] I am here solely interested in some of Reinhold's positive insights, in his first major work,[15] concerning elements of his representationalism that may shed light on Kant's idealism, specifically, the relation between appearances (as objects of knowledge) and things in themselves. I read the early Reinhold of the *Versuch* as confirming the Kantian view that objects as appearances are not properties *of* things in themselves (*ad* 1) and that we are radically ignorant of things in themselves, in the sense that we can neither know things in themselves, through the senses, nor intellectually grasp things in themselves through the understanding alone (*ad* 2). Reinhold reads the principle of apperception in a most radical way. It seems, at first blush, as if on his account we could not even represent things in themselves, making his account vulnerable to the flaws of Fichte's later reading of apperception (which we saw in Chapter 4).

Reinhold's main line of reasoning is that the Critical programme can be presented in an analytically more thorough manner if we start from a clearer premise, namely the very possibility of *representation*. The idea is not that representation is the most basic notion from which all further analysis should proceed just *because* anything that we can have knowledge of must be able at least to be represented. That would be so trivial as to be practically meaningless. Reinhold's representationalism might be interpreted as if it advanced simply a psychological principle of representation stating that since our human psychological make-up is such that we process impressions by way of representations, the notion of representation should be seen as the fundamental assumption upon which philosophical analysis of anything more complex is based.[16] But reading the *Versuch* makes it abundantly clear that Reinhold is not at all interested in psychological or indeed typically metaphysical questions concerning the origin of representations, whether it be empirical or not, but rather *in what* representation consists, what it *means* to represent. The point of the enquiry is an epistemological one, not a metaphysical (ontological) one.

> Here it is not a question of how representation *arises*, but in *what it consists*; it is not a matter of the *origin* but merely of the *nature* [*Beschaffenheit*] of the capacity for representation, not *where* the capacity for representation gets its components *from*, but what components it possesses; not how the capacity for representation can be explained genetically, but what is meant by capacity for representation [*was man denn unter Vorstellungsvermögen zu verstehen habe*].
>
> Versuch 2:237, my underlining

Unlike previous philosophers (before Kant), whether they be materialists or what he calls spiritualists (or more broadly, idealists or dualists), Reinhold is not interested in the question of whether representations are ultimately to be located in a simple soul-substance or are merely the effects of causal impingements and reducible to sense impressions in 'organic bodies' (*Versuch* 2:214). He does not deny though that representations may be attributes of a simple soul-substance, or may ultimately be derived from sense impressions, the outcome of some 'organizational capacity' (*Versuch* 2:213). (Reinhold systematically associates the term *Organisation* with bodily arrangement; see *Versuch* 2:216.) Reinhold points to the necessary external and internal conditions of representations: e.g. parents are the necessary *external* conditions of a human being, mind and body are his necessary *internal* conditions (*Versuch* 2:217). A necessary internal condition for a representation would be to have a functioning brain, a mind (*Gemüt*) that does the representing.

But these are not the conditions which make a representation a *representation* of some specific content, having a meaning. The central question—and this makes Reinhold a quintessentially Critical thinker in the wake of Kant's revolution in metaphysics—is a transcendental one, namely, what does it *mean* to have a representation of some x?[17] To explicate the meaning of representation, Reinhold sets out to analyse what he calls the *bloßes Vorstellungsvermögen* in contrast to *Vorstellungskraft*. The latter term connotes more the capacity for representation as a power of the soul-substance, as the rationalists attempted to determine it. In keeping with Kant's subjective turn in metaphysics, Reinhold wants to focus purely on the representing *subject*, specifically the element of the formal productive capacity (*hervorbringendes Vermögen*) or activity (*Tätigkeit*) in representation (*Versuch* 2:272, 273-7 [§20]), which operates in conjunction with a receptivity for objective matter (*Versuch* 2:271, 299), regardless of the question whether this subject is a simple substance or just the outcome of some material organizational power. Reinhold's analysis is fundamentally based on what he later, in his *Beyträge*, comes to call the *Satz des Bewußtseins*, which—as formulated in the *Versuch*—states that

> [o]ne can agree, necessitated by *consciousness*, that to representation there belongs a representing subject and a represented object which must *both* be *distinguished* from the *representation* to which they belong.
>
> *Versuch* 2:217, §7; cf. 2:315, §38

The principle that is expressed here says that in consciousness one is necessarily conscious of the fact that an occurrent representation implies that, anticipating Wilfrid Sellars's distinction (Sellars 1992:32, 36), there is something represent*ed* and something or someone doing the represent*ing*, in other words, there is a distinction between the *subject* and *object* of representing, which is made *in* and *through* consciousness, that is, *by* the agent of representing.[18] The differentiation between subject and object, between representing and represented, is a differentiation of which one is necessarily aware in consciousness, *when* one represents. Now Reinhold is interested in the purely internal or transcendental conditions of representation; in other words, the analysis concerns the *bloßes Vorstellungsvermögen* only, what Reinhold calls the *Vorstellungsvermögen in engster Bedeutung* (*Versuch* 2:232–3, §12).[19] Hence, he is interested in the meaning of the distinction itself between representing and represented made in and through consciousness, that is, in and through the pure capacity for representation, rather than the status of the subject or object of representation in and of themselves.

Again, questions about the ultimate (ontological) nature of the representing subject and the represented object or thing are not at issue, which concern merely the strictly speaking external (non-transcendental) conditions of both the agent of representing and represented object. The ground for this emphasis lies in the fact that whatever questions about the nature of the subject and object as things of some kind may arise, such questions *already assume* the *Vorstellungsvermögen* as the fundamental ground of any such inquiry, and hence can be questions of secondary philosophical interest only in the transcendental analysis of our representational capacity.[20] Before we can meaningfully ask what the concept of a 'thing' means, we must first clarify the meaning and fundamental status of the term 'representation', that is, the *Vorstellung im strengsten Sinne*, as genus, since 'concept' is a species of representation (*Versuch* 2:238–9, 242). Representation is foundational since it is that through which any possible object is *understood* as being related to the subject that represents the object. The focus on representation thus reveals the fundamental and necessary *reflexivity* underlying our knowledge; it explains what it really means for one to make knowledge claims about objects, and how the form of our claims and the objects themselves are intimately related at the level of representation itself.

6.3 Reinhold's Representationalism and the Thing in Itself

An important consequence of this fundamentally representationalist approach to metaphysical issues, such as the possible knowledge of things or objects, is some form of idealism: our knowledge of objects outside us is restricted to what we represent them as, namely, as *represented* as distinct from us. Reinhold argues:

> We know the objects outside of us and even the representing in us *only through the representations* that we have of them and that we ourselves must distinguish from them. The represented things outside of us and our souls are not the representations themselves, which we have of them, and our consciousness must make every effort to make it quite impossible to *substitute* the *represented* for the *mere representation* [*bloße Vorstellung*] and the latter for the *representing*.
>
> Versuch 2:223

And a few lines down, he asserts that

> one can know something about all these things [i.e. the representing being or the soul and the objects outside the soul] *only through the representations* that one has of them, but which one [also] oneself must differentiate from them.
>
> Versuch 2:224

Reinhold might be taken to present here what is basically a short argument to idealism, namely, the representability thesis implies the restriction or unknowability thesis: whatever is not representable is therefore unknowable.[21] But, despite appearances to the contrary, I believe this is not what Reinhold means to say.

It is important to note that, in the first passage, first, from the context (see e.g. *Versuch* 2:208–9) it is clear that Reinhold means the object outside of us as signifying the thing as it is 'in itself', namely, as it exists apart from our representation, and, secondly, he says that we should not conflate the things that we represent (whether they be outer things or our souls) with their representation— we must keep the things that we represent separate from their representation, though, to be sure, we do not *know* anything about them other than *through* their representation; so by implication anything that is not representable is also not knowable.

My view is that one should not read this as saying that as *simply* a matter of definition,[22] anything that is 'in itself' is 'not representable', and since anything that is 'not representable' is 'unknowable', a thing in itself is *eo ipso* unknowable (Reinhold does think that unrepresentability analytically entails unknowability, but this seems unproblematic, since knowing is a species of representing[23]). Reinhold has arguments for the position that he has on the restriction or unknowability thesis: as we shall see below, a thing in itself *as* properly a thing *in itself*, namely, as a thing *qua* thing (Reinhold employs the term *Sache* to refer to mind-external objects), and thus not *as* a representation (i.e. a representing), is necessarily separate from or outside the representation (representing), and so not something represented. It is not that *in-itselfness* simply implies unrepresentability just because it is not represented, but rather, given what we understand by a thing, *thingness* (*qua* in-itself existence) means *not-being-due-to-a-representing*, which implies *not-being-a-represented*, which in turn implies unrepresentability; so unrepresentability follows from *not-being-due-to-a-representing*. The *in-itselfness* also implies an element of unconditionality or fundamentality that *eo ipso* cannot be represented by us, for all we are able to represent is represented *conditionally*.[24] (The conditionality here is just the analytic truth that something *x* is constrained by the conditions for representation if it is to be represented at all.) Of course, a thing existing outside or external to representation *can* be represented (is representable), but only *on condition of* it being modified *in* representation, by being made into a represent*ed*, for, as per the above argument, it is not representable *qua* thing-in-itself, in its unconditionedness, in its absolute nature.[25] Its unconditionedness prevents it from being represented *qua* unconditioned. Only represent*eds* correspond strictly speaking to being-representable. Thus, to put it succinctly, a thing in itself *is* representable, but only *as represented*, not *as thing in itself*.

This can be expressed in terms of the Sellarsian distinction between, on the one hand, 'existing in itself' as 'existing *simpliciter*' and, on the other, 'existing *as represented*', or existing 'as idea (content) or representable'. For Reinhold, a thing in itself would be, in Sellars's terms, a 'non-representing *qua* existing *simpliciter*', and a thing in itself *as modified* in representation would be, in Sellars's terminology, a 'represented non-representing *qua* represented' (Sellars 1992:36, 38). It is exactly Reinhold's point, not just to formally contrast 'existing in itself' and 'existing as representable', but in fact to assert that *a thing* that exists *in itself* cannot, *as so existing*, exist *as representable*, and that only a represent*ed*, a determinate object, exists in a representing (cf. A374–5n).

We should see the above analysis against the backdrop of the fact that Reinhold's idealism is an idealism of the explicitly non-reductive kind, not a type of phenomenalism that denies the mind- or representation-independent existence of the *things* that are represented, just as Kant does not deny the mind-independent existence of things in themselves whose appearances we experience. Reinhold specifically mentions the objection (from 'our empiricist') that he (i.e. Reinhold) admits the actuality (*Wirklichkeit*) of representations, whilst denying it of the things themselves (*Sachen*), an objection which he rebuts by saying that his

> non-committal . . . is not a dogmatic doubt and [that he, i.e. Reinhold] in no way makes claims about the distinction between soul and body or indeed the actuality of things outside us.
>
> *Versuch* 2:225

And further, more emphatically:

> I am refraining from all assertion until my readers and I have reached agreement about principles, after which it will then be shown that I ascribe merely *ideal* actuality to the so-called *things* [*Sachen*] just as little as I ascribe *real actuality*[26] to *representations*, as the misunderstood writer of the Critique of Reason has so often been accused of doing.
>
> Versuch 2:225; cf. 2:229

Reinhold's position thus does not imply a reductive idealism—for the existence and representation of things in themselves (*Sachen*) are not conflated. Neither is it the case, though, that there is a strict identity or correspondence between, on the one hand, the thing in itself outside representation and the represented, on the other, in the same way as there is a conceptual, analytical connection between representation and represented. In other words, while thing in itself and representation should indeed not be conflated, this does not mean that we are able to represent the thing in itself as it is, *as such, apart from* its being represented. This is often assumed in contemporary direct-realist interpretations of Kant, such as that of Langton (1998), who believes that representations are merely the means *through* which things (in themselves) are represented, even if only their appearance, extrinsic, or relational properties, the properties that are mind-dependent or relativized to the epistemic subject. This suggests that the thing in itself, even if only its appearance, extrinsic, or relational properties, is the *direct* object of my representation. And, as we shall see, this is not the case, according to Reinhold (and I would argue, for Kant too[27]).

Reinhold proceeds to distinguish (in *Versuch*, §15) as one of the inner or *essential* conditions of a representation, the 'matter' (*Stoff*) of a representation, by which he means the matter *in* a representation, the 'proper matter' of a representation (*Versuch* 2:244; cf. A20/B34). This 'matter' directly refers to that which is represented as distinct from consciousness, namely, the object (*Gegenstand*). Reinhold distinguishes between subjective and objective matter, and it is this latter objective matter which makes that a representation relates to an actually existing object (*Versuch* 2:245, 249, 265, 295–7). The matter of a representation is the determinate effect of the object's affecting our sense organs. The object as such always remains the same, unchanging mind-independent object (*Versuch* 2:245). It is the matter of a representation of the object which gets modified in accordance with any further specification of the *representation* of the object. The 'matter' of a representation is what makes a representation a *repræsentatio*, in the truest sense of the term,[28] of something other than consciousness *in* consciousness, namely, a conscious content that refers to a mind-external represent*ed* (a thing) which is *re*-presented[29] in consciousness. Even so-called 'empty' representations, representations that represent something that in reality does not exist or obtain (in Reinhold's words, has no 'real actuality'), have a material content—*any* representation has representational content, or a representational *object*, otherwise they would be representations that do not represent, which is contradictory (*Versuch* 2:246–7). So a representation always has a representational object, an object that is differentiated from the representation, or a represent*ed*, even if this represented is not an object really existing outside the representation. However, only 'objective' matter refers to an actually existing mind-external object or thing (*Versuch* 2:295), which is *re-presented* in representation in terms of the *matter* of representation. (In the case of a represented that does not exist outside the representation, Reinhold speaks of 'subjective' matter.)

The second essential inner condition of a representation is its 'form'. Whereas matter is that which makes that the represented object 'belongs' to the representation (*Versuch* 2:249), form is what relates the representation to the *subject* of representation (the representing), what makes that the representation 'belongs' to the mind (the representing capacity). Form is what in fact first makes out of the manifold of the matter a genuine representation (*Versuch* 2:290); only the conjunction of form, which makes a unity out of the manifold, and the receptivity for matter constitutes a representation *sensu stricto*.[30] Matter as such, without form, is not yet a representation in the strict sense (something that is *representational* content, i.e. referring to an object, whether real or imagined). The matter of a representation can acquire form '*only* in the mind [*Gemüt*] and only through the capacity for representation' (*Versuch* 2:249). As Reinhold later in Book III of the *Versuch* delineates, the quintessential forms of a representation are, more specifically, both the Kantian forms of sensibility, space and time, and the categories as the forms under which an object can be thought. Importantly, the form of a representation is not determined by the represented, the object, but by the *subject* of representing. For this reason,

> no represented, no object [*Gegenstand*] can be represented in its form that is independent of the form of representation, [i.e.] as it is in itself, but can occur only, modified through the form of representation, in consciousness.
>
> *Versuch* 2:252

Similarly, Reinhold writes:

> The object [*Gegenstand*] that is differentiated from the representation can therefore only occur in consciousness, i.e. be *represented*, under the *form of*

representation, which the matter corresponding to it [i.e. to the object] had to take on in the mind. And hence, it could by no means be represented as *thing in itself*, i.e. under that form which it would have outside of all representation, would be denoted through the mere matter of representation, and would have to be differentiated from the form of representation.

Versuch 2:257

The representation of an object in its own proper form independently of the form of representation, or the so-called *thing in itself*, contradicts the concept of a representation in general [*Vorstellung überhaupt*]; that is, no thing in itself can be represented.

Versuch 2:256, §17 heading

Hence, what we represent of the represented object, which exists mind-independently, is not the object *an sich* (the thing in itself), but how (*wie*) it is represented in consciousness, necessarily by means of the form of representation. This is crucial and explains Reinhold's fundamentally representationalist position: there is nothing reductively idealist about this position, but it shows that a representation of an object *ex hypothesi* implies that an object cannot be represented *an sich*, for this would mean, contradictorily, to represent it in abstraction from representing it (cf. *Versuch* 2:254); moreover, it would presuppose that the unconditionedness of a thing can indeed be represented. The object an sich is only *re*-presented—Reinhold employs the term *vertreten* (*Versuch* 2:246)—in the representation by means of the matter (*Stoff*) that it effects in the mind, i.e. the sensations that are prompted as a result of the object's affecting the mind externally. The object is not *re*-presented *an sich*, but only as 'modified through the form of representation' (*Versuch* 2:252), which is analytic because the object *as re-presented* is fully dependent on, or must conform to, the necessary conditions under which alone it is represented, namely the form(s) of representation. The form that the *Ding an sich* has in itself is essentially different from the form it acquires when it is represented in consciousness: as *Ding an sich*, as an unconditioned, it lacks the 'form of representation', so how can it be *represented* as *an sich*, whilst *intrinsically* lacking the form of representation under which alone it can be represented? Reinhold therefore believes that *representing* the thing in itself *as in itself* amounts to a contradiction, as we saw in the last of the above quotations.

It seems to me that the objection that Frederick Beiser raises to Reinhold's reasoning here is not compelling. Beiser writes:

[I]t does not follow that in conforming to the form the content can no longer represent the object in itself; for 'to conform to the form' here means only that the content enters into consciousness; and merely to enter into consciousness does not prevent the content from representing the object in itself. As pure consciousness in general, the form of a representation does not necessarily change any of the determinate features of its content.

1987:258

It is important to note Reinhold's point that by entering into pure consciousness, the content of a representation, which is the determinate result of the affection by the thing in itself, is changed *at least* insofar as it takes on the form of representation, a form which *ex hypothesi* it could not yet have had before it took on the form, that is, before it was represented. (Indeed, Beiser notes this too, but he then says that in so arguing Reinhold illegitimately presupposes the active role of the subject, thus undermining his attempt to base the deduction on the pure notion of a representation; I do not think that Beiser has a point here, for, as Reinhold argues, representation itself already implies subjective activity merely in terms of a representation being a *representing*, which refers to the subject of representation, as much as it implies a represent*ed*, which refers to the object of representation.) Therefore, whatever 'determinate' features the content, and by implication the thing in itself to which the material content directly refers, may still have as represented, under the form of representation the content has changed into *re*-presented content. The element of being-represented is an added feature that it did not have before. Reinhold is of course not saying that *re*-presenting content means to alter the content *completely*, for all of its features. He means to say that if a content, and hence a thing in itself, is *re*-presented under the form of representation, it is *ipso facto* not represented as *an sich*—that is, with all of its (empirical) features, including possible forms, *but without the form of representation*—but only *as* represented, under the form of representation, with all of its empirical features. To use Reinhold's own example, i.e. 'a statue whose material is white Salzburg marble', the fact that being made (changed) into a statue (its form), does not alter the material being white marble, but it does change the piece of marble (the matter) at least insofar as the piece of white marble is moulded into the form of a statue. The statue is white and made of marble purely in respect of its *matter*, whereas it being a statue is an essential feature the white and marble object has only in respect of its form as statue. As Reinhold says, 'certain predicates apply to representation only in respect of its form, others only in respect of its matter' (*Versuch* 2:248–9).

It is important to note that the restriction of the way that the thing in itself is *re*-presented in consciousness or representation, namely solely as modified, is not so much because of the fact that *merely* the forms of our sensibility, and not the forms of our conception per se, constrain our knowledge of things—that is, because space and time are not properties of things in themselves—as that it has to do with the transcendental conditions under which we are able to *re*-present the mind-external object, the thing in itself, at all. These transcendental conditions concern the forms of our conceptual capacity as much as the forms of sensibility, for they concern more fundamentally the way we *re*-present mind-external objects in consciousness. In other words, for Reinhold our very conception of things as objects is already affected by idealism, namely, an idealism of the Copernican sort that argues that things must conform to *both* our forms of conception and our forms of intuition in order for knowledge, indeed *representation*, of objects to be possible (cf. Bxvii–xviii; see Chapter 2).

Reinhold makes an important observation in reaction to a possible objection that surely we do have a *conception* of a thing in itself, an objection that also Kantian commentators who take Kant to be a direct realist, are apt to make. He points out that this objection plays on the ambiguity between having the *concept* of a *Ding an sich überhaupt* and having a representation of the thing in itself as a determinate object, a *Sache* (*Versuch* 2:258). Reinhold writes:

> That concept [of the thing in itself in general] is admittedly also a representation, but a representation whose object is not the thing in itself as *thing* [*Sache*], but rather as the mere intellectual concept of an *object* in general [*Gegenstandes überhaupt*].[31] This representation of a merely *logical* entity is confused in that objection with the representation of a *thing* [*Sache*]. For those who advocate the representability of things in themselves believe it is possible to grant to and save for our understanding a *knowledge of things* [*Sachkenntnis*] only by construing representation of the thing in it itself as representation of some *thing* [*Sache*], [i.e.] representation of that object that is outside the mind to which the matter and form of representation belong. What I call the concept of the thing in itself, the possibility and origin of which are to be elaborated in the theory of the cognitive capacity, is the representation of an object *in general*, which is not a representation; [i.e. it is] not a *determinate, individual, existent* thing.
>
> Versuch 2:258–9

What Reinhold rejects is the possibility of having a representation of a thing in itself as a representation of a 'determinate, individual, existent thing', a real thing (*Sache*), which by implication is not a representation—because it is a thing *an sich*, an unconditioned—whilst still claiming that it has the form of a representation, which gives the represented its determinacy (and confers objectivity *strictius dicta* on it, as we shall see further below), but has this form *independently* of the subject of consciousness, which first gives it this form. The mistaken assumption here, according to Reinhold, is that one takes the thing in itself to have the form of objective determinacy *an sich*, outside of its representation, that it can have only by virtue of the form of representation, but not *an sich*. The assumption thus rests on a misconception of what it means to have a *representation* of a thing in itself, and on the presumed identity between the form of representation, which determines objectivity, and any form that the *Ding an sich* itself might have independently of the form of representation. In other words, one cannot have one's cake and eat it—both to have a *representation* of the thing in itself and represent it *an sich*, as it is independently of its being represented. One could put this differently by saying that on Reinhold's view representation is by definition extrinsic, implying at least two relata in an external relation, namely an agent of representing and a represented. By contrast, with regard to the *an sich* nature of a thing, its intrinsicality defines its inwardness (*Ansichsein*), apart from any possible external relations whereby intrinsicality and extrinsicality are considered absolutely distinct and irreducible; on this account, inwardness excludes the possibility of representability unless one formulates a Hegelian type account of how the extrinsicality of representations supervenes, or more precisely, inwardly latches onto the inwardness of a thing in itself.

Notice again that Reinhold does not deny the existence of things in themselves, for they *are* the represented objects insofar as they are *not represented*, lacking the feature of 'being-represented' (*Versuch* 2:259). More precisely, a thing in itself is

> that something which must ground, outside the representation, the mere matter [*bloßen Stoffe*] of a representation, but of which—since its representative [*Repräsentant*], the matter, must take on the form of representation—nothing of what were to belong to it independently of this form, would be able to be represented, except the negation of the form of representation, that is, that which cannot be attributed any other predicate, except that it is not a representation.
>
> *Versuch* 2:259

What is capable of being represented of a thing in itself, is its 'representative' (*Repräsentant*) in representation only, namely, the matter (*Stoff*) in representation which refers to the underlying thing in itself, based on an affective relation to the mind in which the representation occurs.[32] Were we to positively determine the thing in itself, we would have to *re*-present the thing in itself, and as such the thing would necessarily take on the form of representation that is wholly due to the subject or mind—and so change into something represented. Apart from its *re*-presentation, a thing in itself is not capable of being represented as a thing

(*Sache*), but is thought '*merely* as a *concept* of something which is not capable of being represented' (*Versuch* 2:260, emphasis added). With this latter specification, it appears that Reinhold regards the representation of a thing in itself as a representation of something that lacks all predicates, that is, a representation of a 'bare subject without all its predicates' (*Versuch* 2:260; cf. 390, 254), similar to Kant's conception of the transcendental object (A109). However, Reinhold may be taken to hold the view that the thing in itself *qua* thing in itself—that is, as not represented—has all the qualities (*Beschaffenheiten*) that it has, distinctly from and independently of the form of representation. This seems to be confirmed by what Reinhold says two pages further down [a] and a few pages earlier [b]:

> [a] The *representable* predicates are then not predicates of things in themselves, but predicates of things which have taken on the form of representation, which does not belong to the things in themselves.
>
> *Versuch* 2:262, emphasis in original

> [b] All its [the thing's] positive predicates, insofar as they are representable, must have taken on the form of representation through the matter corresponding to them in the representation, and this form cannot pertain to them in themselves. The thing in itself and its properties [*Beschaffenheiten*] distinct from the form of representation are not only not impossible, but even something *indispensable* for mere representation, because no mere representation is conceivable without a matter, and no matter [is conceivable] without something outside the representation which does not have the form of representation, that is, without the thing in itself.
>
> *Versuch* 2:259–60, my underlining

It is important to stress the fact—and this reinforces the unbridgeable gap between the representation of an object and the thing in itself, which cannot be represented as such—that, for Reinhold, the matter in a representation only becomes a proper representative (*Repräsentant*) of the object, when the matter *re*-presents the object *to* the subject, in consciousness, which occurs in that the representation refers to both subject and object (*Versuch* 2:320). A representation only truly represents in consciousness. Or, more specifically, I have a representation of something if and only if *I* represent something to myself, signifying self-consciousness. 'A representation which *I do not* have and which represents *nothing to me* is not a representation' (*Versuch* 2:320–1). What I take Reinhold to mean here is that a representation is genuinely a representation of an object only when I am conscious of it (and not that he is making an existential claim about representations).[33] Only consciousness generates a *determinate* representation of an object. The matter of a representation in an intuition already constitutes an immediate relation to an object, but this relation is still implicit, not made explicit to and in consciousness (cf. *Versuch* 2:332–5). With consciousness of the object, the object is not only distinguished from the representation, but also *represented* as distinct from it (cf. *Versuch* 2:367). And this constitutes knowledge of the object:

> I call the object that is distinguished from mere representation and represented (conceived of) in its quality as object the object *determined in consciousness*, and I call the being-related of the representation to the object determined in consciousness *knowledge* in general.
>
> Versuch 2:330–1

As Reinhold further notes, the notion of a 'determinate object' is ambiguous—and here we come back to the ambiguity mentioned earlier regarding the predicates represented of a thing in itself, and the qualities that a thing in itself has, apart from its being represented. The notion 'determinate object' either denotes the thing in itself, which outside the subject of consciousness 'subsists quite independently of the capacity for representation in itself on account of its properties and qualities' (*Versuch* 2:331). Or, it signifies the object that is determined in consciousness. (There is also a third meaning, namely, the matter in a representation is the result of a *determinate affection* from the side of the object [*Versuch* 2:331–2], but we can leave this aside here.) However, it seems that Reinhold denies the possibility of a determinate object as thing in itself, independently of the subject of representation— but again, there remains an ambiguity about having a *representation* of a thing in itself and its determinate properties and, on the other hand, the thing in itself with all its properties as it would be independently of representing it. Reinhold points out that the traditional conception of *Gegenstand* is the totality (*Inbegriff*) of properties and qualities, that is, a 'whole of connected determinations, an individual (*Individuum*)' (*Versuch* 2:401). The connectedness of characteristics, which make up the concept of object, thus defined, is established by the combination of the manifold in intuition. Like Kant, Reinhold considers the unity of the manifold that ensues as a result of this combination an *objective* unity, and it is this unity that defines the concept of object. The objective unity in the manifold is the unity under which the object is first *thought* or *conceived of*. The combination of the manifold in an intuition is the origin (*Entstehungsgrund*) of the representation of an object *as object*, and the object is as such 'nothing but the unity of the represented manifold' (*Versuch* 2:401–2). This is all very much in line with Kant's own conception of objective unity as defining an object (cf. B137).

Importantly, for Reinhold the very conception of an object (a *Gegenstand überhaupt*), defined as a connectedness of determinations, strictly rests on the combination of the manifold in intuition, in consciousness. An object is first an object when the 'predicate of objective unity, of the unity of the manifold represented in a representation, is attributed to something [*einem Etwas*]' (*Versuch* 2:402–3). This unity is due to the spontaneous combining activity of the understanding (the form of representation) and not yet given with the objective matter that rests on the affective determination by the external object (*Ding außer uns*). This means that objective unity does not belong to the thing in itself, *insofar as the thing is a thing in itself*. This has implications for the way we putatively think about any thing in itself:

> It [i.e. the unity of the understanding] is therefore also only the form of the object insofar as it is *conceivable* [*denkbar*], not the form of the *thing in itself*, which till now was usually confused with the merely *conceivable* [*denkbar*] thing (the intelligible [*dem Intellektuellen*]) to the detriment of philosophy. <u>Even the understanding is not capable of conceiving [*denken*] the object as *thing in itself*, but is able to conceive it only under that form which is determined *a priori* according to its nature as the representation (the concept) proper to it, i.e. as the objective unity produced through the combination of intuitional characteristics</u>. ... The *thing in itself* is that outside us to which corresponds the mere matter of our representation alone without its form; something to which, therefore, no form of our representation—neither an intuition nor a concept— may be related and that consequently <u>cannot be intuited nor thought</u>.
>
> *Versuch* 2:403, my underlining

Unlike what the rationalists believed, including the pre-Critical Kant (e.g. in the *Inaugural Dissertation*), according to Reinhold (and the Critical Kant) we do not have an intellectual grasp of the thing in itself and its intrinsic properties, when we abstract away from appearances, which are constrained by the conditions of sensibility. We are capable of *thinking* an object only under the form which first constitutes an objective unity, through combination of the manifold of representations in an intuition. Apart from this objective unity, we cannot even think the thing in itself as a thing proper (*Sache*), for that would mean, contradictorily, to represent a thing in itself as an object for the understanding alone without representing it in accordance with the form under which I can first conceive of an object at all, namely the form of objective unity that combines a manifold in intuition. Having a putative purely intellectual grasp of the thing in itself is already constrained by the conceptual forms of representation, that is, the form of objective unity that first constitutes what it is to conceive, by means of the understanding, of an object at all; so in fact *representing* a thing in itself as a thing proper in abstraction from these constraints purely by means of the understanding is an impossibility. Reinhold thus makes an important distinction between *thinking* an object, which together with intuition is one of the constitutive components of having *knowledge* of an object, and *putatively thinking* a thing in itself *qua* thing in itself (as a *Sache*), that is, *an sich*, in abstraction from the forms of representation. This, as we saw already earlier, is a conceptual impossibility.

The only thing in itself that we are capable of representing *qua* thing in itself is the mere *notion* of a thing in itself (with its possible intrinsic properties);[34] or else the thing in itself should be modified *in* representation in accordance with the constraints of sensibility and conceptuality so as to provide us with a genuine representation of an object for knowledge. Reinhold writes:

> If anyone takes the thing in itself to be nothing but the objective unity itself ..., for him the thing in itself will indeed be conceivable but not as a thing [*Sache*] distinct from its representation and independent of his faculty of representation, but, on the contrary, as a mere concept, which can be more than a mere concept only if it relates to an intuition in which a matter [*ein Stoff*] is determined through its being affected [*durchs Affiziertseins*]. That outside the representation to which this matter corresponds is rightly called the object [*Gegenstand*], but it can only thereby be represented as something different from the intuition insofar as the form in the sole terms of which an object is conceivable, [i.e.] the objective unity, is related to it—not therefore as *thing in itself*, but as thing conceived under the most general form of a concept.
>
> *Versuch* 2:403–4

6.4 Kant, Reinhold, and the Radical Reading of the Ignorance Thesis

For Reinhold, the predicate 'objective unity' cannot be attributed to the thing in itself *qua* thing in itself, just as little as the property of spatiotemporality is a property that belongs to things in themselves (*Versuch* 2:392). Given that Reinhold understands by the concept of object the connectedness of determinations predicated of something, this means that the totality or whole of properties that belong to an object can be attributed to the object only insofar as this concerns the object of representation, defined by the unity that the understanding brings to the manifold of sensible matter in an intuition. For Reinhold, then, it appears that apart from the constraints of representation (both conceptual and sensible), there is no representation of a thing in itself in any positive sense, namely, as an individual that has all of its properties, though he does not deny the existence of the thing in itself (with all *its* properties) outside representation. We can only have a *notion* (*Begriff*) of the thing in itself in abstraction from representation, as it subsists in itself independently of representation.

This seems thoroughly in line with Kant's own conception of the thing in itself. For Kant, too, the object of knowledge is first constituted by the joint cooperation of our conceptual capacity and the forms of sensibility (space and time) that establishes the possible knowledge of a mind-external sensible object. The conceivability of an object that goes beyond the bounds of sense is logically possible (cf. A96, Bxxvi note), but this does not translate to the thinkability of things in themselves as noumenal *things*. This comports with Reinhold's view that

> the domain of the knowable, which does not extend beyond sensibility, is not yet the domain of the thinkable, much less the domain of things in themselves, which we are incapable of representing, and which must be clearly distinguished from both [of the former].
>
> *Versuch* 2:394

For example, we have a conception of God and his properties as e.g. the highest being, who is omniscient, omnipotent etc., but by no means do we conceptually determine God as a really existing thing in itself, as an object (*Sache*) exclusively for the understanding; from the purely theoretical point of view, 'God' is just a logically consistent concept that we intelligibly entertain, not a noumenal being of whom we have an intellectually determinate grasp. It is an oddly common view among commentators to hold that in abstraction from appearances we can, purely by means of the understanding, have a thorough grasp, even if only intellectually, of the thing in itself and its intrinsic properties.[35] But, for both Reinhold and Kant, we are radically ignorant of the thing in itself's nature *as a thing in itself*, meaning that we neither know *nor think* it as a *Sache* that exists for itself.[36]

However, there is prima facie an important difference between Reinhold's conception of the thing in itself and Kant's. For Reinhold, as we saw, it appears that the whole of an individual's determinations is just a function of the objective unity that the understanding puts into the manifold of sensible matter in a representation of an object. This means that we cannot conceive positively of *a thing in itself* with all its possible determinations, as an individual, even if only as *ens rationis*³⁷ (although, as I pointed out, there are passages in the *Versuch* that seem to tell otherwise). This is unlike Kant's view, who, in the chapter in the *Critique* on the Transcendental Ideal (A571ff./B599ff.), argues quite clearly that the thoroughly determined individual defines the thing in itself, but whose ontological determinacy or the totality of all whose possible predicates (what elsewhere I call o-determination)³⁸ we cannot positively determine by means of the necessary conceptual and intuitional forms of knowledge, that is, by means of what jointly amounts to epistemic determination (what I call ε-determination).³⁹ The positive ε-determinations concern the totality of possible objects in possible experience only (A581–3/B609–11).

For Reinhold, prima facie at least, the concept of thing in itself seems an abstraction from all the predicates an object can have by means of ε-determination, and to concern only the bare subject of predication (*Versuch* 2:254, 260–1), not a thoroughly complete individual in Kant's sense.⁴⁰ Although this would appear to reveal a consistent adherence on Reinhold's part to the radical ignorance thesis, which heeds the absolute distinction between what can count as an object of representation (both conceptual and sensible) and what would be a putative thing in itself as a *Sache* in abstraction from representation, it also poses a problem for Reinhold in that the ε-determination of the object, which is first received in terms of the still indeterminate matter in representation, does not seem to be related in any significant way to the ontological determinacy of the affecting thing in itself other than being affected by it insofar as its material aspect is concerned. In fact, Reinhold appears to deny any kind of correspondence or equivalence between the determination by the affecting thing in itself and the determinate object, which is purely a function of the understanding (cf. *Versuch* 2:240, 252, 254). Moreover, labelling the concept of a thing in itself as *merely* a bare subject of predication stands in tension with granting the independent *existence* of a thing in itself in abstraction from representation.

By contrast, for Kant, although ε-determination does not map one-to-one onto o-determination (hence, a standard correspondence theory of truth is rejected by Kant as well as Reinhold), o-determination *defines* the thing in itself as a thoroughly determined thing, *qua* thing (what Kant, and Reinhold, call *Sache*). The apparent problem for Kant, though, is how the absolute discrepancy between ε-determination and o-determination can be explained if ε-determinations must be seen as part of a thing's o-determination. It would appear logical to think that any partial series of actual determinations belongs to the set of all possible determinations, and a fortiori that the set of *all possible* ε-determinations would map onto o-determination, given that the latter defines complete ontological determinacy, i.e. the totality of a thing's possible predicates. But Kant appears to deny, in the chapter on the Ideal, that the determinations of objects of possible experience are simply *aggregates* of the *ens realissimum*, the all of reality, which instead *grounds* empirical reality in its totality (A579/B607)— and this only makes sense, given his firm denial that e.g. spatiotemporal properties of a phenomenal object could ever be considered properties of an underlying thing in itself.[41] In other words, not even *all* of a thing's *possible* ε-determinations map onto its putative o-determination, for the realm of possible experience does not correspond, one-to-one, to the underlying noumenal reality of things in themselves that is the metaphysical ground of the phenomenal world.[42] So, it seems that, like Reinhold, Kant just denies any strict equivalence or isomorphic correspondence between the world of objects as appearances and its objective determinacy, on the one hand, and the unconditioned noumenal reality of things in themselves and its o-determination, on the other. The main difference between Kant and Reinhold concerns the latter's lack of clarity with regard to the definition of a thing in itself as an ontologically determinate individual.

In conclusion, appearances, including the form under which appearances are representations of outer objects, that is, of things as existing mind-independently, cannot be considered properties *of* things in themselves, as that would mean that what can only be represented, and first be constituted, under the representational forms of sensibility and conceptuality (space, time, categories), namely, an object, is or subsists at the same time independently of or apart from those forms, namely, as thing in itself, which is contradictory. As Reinhold says (*Versuch* 2:403–4), objective unity is not a predicate that can be attributed to things in themselves as such, that is, without being *re*-presented, and so modified, in consciousness. Metaphysical dualists respond to this objection by saying that appearances are to be considered the mind-*dependent* or extrinsic or relational properties *of* things in themselves, but this reading faces the unsurmountable problem of how to explain Kant's (and Reinhold's) representationalist view that appearances *are just* representations, and more importantly also how mind-dependency is supposed to be linked to the unconditioned spontaneous *subjective activity* that is irreducible to metaphysical dispositions, a central plank of the Critical philosophy. There is thus an unbridgeable gulf between the object as determined by and in consciousness and the thing in itself, which as such, as Reinhold rightfully argued, cannot be *properly* represented, even thought, but whose *independent* existence must nonetheless be admitted, contrary to what the later German Idealists believed.

7

Apperception and Representational Content: Fichte, Hegel, and Pippin

7.1 Introduction

If by conceptualism is roughly understood the thesis that all that can be represented is amenable to being brought under concepts and thus susceptible of judgemental or rational organization for it to have any normative meaning, there is little doubt that Hegel can be called the quintessential conceptualist since, for Hegel, it can be held, anything that is representable is in principle intelligible—or, 'there is nothing in principle unintelligible' (Pippin 2015a:168). The traditional picture that most contemporary philosophers have of Hegel is certainly that of an extreme conceptual or even an ontological *idealist*, who believes, respectively, that everything that is real *must* be able to be thought or is just constituted by what can be thought; or put more radically, that everything in the world is just a product of mental states or acts, or even more implausibly and mysteriously, that everything simply emanated from some cosmic mind. Scores of text passages in Hegel's corpus could be quoted that, out of context, at least appear to show Hegel's strong conceptualism about the possibility of representational content, or even about the very possibility of having sensations, which, if only inchoately, contain already a rational capacity or the seeds for their being understood rationally (e.g. in the famous chapter on Sense Certainty in the *Phenomenology of Spirit*).

A crucial aspect of Hegel's conceptualism—and one that I shall concentrate on here—is that he also explicitly says, both in early work such as *Faith and Knowledge* and in his magnum opus the *Science of Logic*, that it is inspired by Kant's form of conceptualism, particularly its emphasis on the central constitutive role of subjectivity. This would seem to mean that if we take Hegel at his word when he says that, in a certain respect, he builds on Kant, and assuming Hegel's strong conceptualism (in its more plausible variant), it is prima facie ruled out that Kant himself can be read as a nonconceptualist if by the latter is meant the thesis that, at least, not all that can be represented *must* be brought under concepts,[1] or put in the terms that Kant uses, that not all intuitions must be brought under concepts in order for representations or intuitions *to be* what they are (whatever they are or represent). Or, Kant is indeed a nonconceptualist and Hegel is fundamentally mistaken about Kant's conceptualism. In reality, the contrasts are not as stark as this disjunction suggests. Hegel's relation to Kant is rather complex. This is already indicated by Hegel's frequent qualifications of his Kantianism, that is, that in his view Kant's conceptualism or idealism is not yet the right kind of, or is an inadequate, conceptualism or idealism and must be amended. And the caricatures of Hegel that I mentioned at the outset are of course just that: Hegel's own positive story is much more nuanced and complicated, and also philosophically valuable, than the traditional view of it has us believe. But to keep my account here relatively straightforward, I shall focus on Hegelian criticisms of Kant, specifically those advanced by Robert Pippin since his seminal book *Hegel's Idealism* (Pippin 1989), and examine to what extent these criticisms are, at least to some extent, misguided or misleading, and shall leave a more favourable delineation of Hegel's revisionist Kantianism for the following chapters.[2] I shall also here largely leave out issues of idealism, so as not to complicate matters, although of course Hegel's form of conceptualism is very much intertwined with his so-called absolute idealism (see further Chapter 8).

In this chapter, I am specifically interested in how, following Hegel's critique of Kant in the aforementioned works, recent Hegelians have interpreted Kant's claims in the Transcendental Deduction of the categories in the *Critique*, in particular the claim that there is a synthetic a priori connection between the intuition of objects and their conceptualization; or, to put it in the famous words of Kant, that intuition and concepts must be conjoined to enable knowledge, otherwise intuitions remain blind and concepts empty (A51–2/B75–6). Hegelians think that in the Deduction Kant effectively 'compromise[s]' (Sedgwick 1993:275)[3] the distinction he stipulates at A51/B75, that he 'waver[s] on the strict separability of concept and intuition' (Pippin 2015b:74). For if the argument of the Deduction, in particular in its B-version, is that the categories are not only the necessary conditions under which I *think* objects, by virtue of applying concepts, but also the necessary conditions under which *anything is first given in sensibility*, the fixed separation of concepts and intuitions seems incompatible with the very aim and conclusion of the Deduction. The way this argument is framed is based on a phrase that Kant uses in the important introductory section of the so-called 'second step' of the B-Deduction (§21), where he says that in the sequel … it will be shown *from the way in which the empirical intuition is given in sensibility* that its unity can be none other than the one the category prescribes to the manifold of a given intuition in general according to the preceding §20.

B144–5, emphasis added

As one of the most prominent Hegelians who has written extensively on Hegel's Kantianism, Pippin takes this phrase as an indication that Kant's separation of intuition and concept, when read in the context of the argument of the Deduction, is not as strict as it seems. Similarly, the distinction between receptivity, as the form of sensibility, and spontaneity is rendered problematic if it is the case that Kant argues that the spontaneity of the understanding 'determine[s] sensibility inwardly' (Pippin 1989:28–9).

In the following, I want to examine these charges by looking more closely at Pippin's reading of the Deduction. Pippin believes the orthodox Kant cannot be retained if we want to extract something of philosophical value from the Deduction; he wants to focus on 'the Kant that can speak to us' (Pippin 2015b:75).[4] Heeding Hegel's so-called immanent criticism of Kant (Sedgwick 1993:273) shows us a Kantianism beyond the strictures of the orthodox Kant: a Kantian conceptualism shorn of the remaining nonconceptualist tendencies, which are in fact antithetical to the spirit of the Critical revolution. I believe, however, that we must retain the orthodox Kant, including its nonconceptualist tendencies, in order not to succumb to an intemperate conceptualism, the sort of which, rightly or wrongly, solicited the caricatures of Hegel I mentioned at the beginning.

In Sections 7.2 and 7.3, I address some more general issues relating to the separability of concept and intuition. Subsequently, in Section 7.4, I relate the problems underlying Pippin's conceptualist reading of separability to a key section (§26) in the second half of the B-Deduction, where, in a notorious but pivotal footnote, it seems that Pippin thinks Kant is wavering most clearly on the strict separability of concept and intuition, as well as on the distinction between spontaneity and receptivity. I think that the textual and philosophical evidence rather points to the necessity of a nonconceptualist remainder that is compatible with Kant's overall conceptualist aims.

7.2 Distinguishability and Inseparability

Pippin wants to exorcize a picture of Kant's argument about the cooperation between the capacities for intuitions and concepts that takes that cooperation to consist in an application of concepts *to* an already given manifold in intuition, so that the received intuition is exogenous to the conceptual activity, or that any judgement is based on what was first a mere nonconceptual representation. Secondly, Pippin argues that the relation to objects is not '"secured" *by* receptivity, by the deliverances of sensibility, *alone*' (2015a:168). Only the conjoining of concepts and intuitions fixes the relation to objects; hence, concepts and intuitions are inseparable so far as the relation to an object is concerned. The nonconceptualist thesis that intuitions have a separable role to play in establishing knowledge might indeed be seen as entertaining the idea that concepts are applied to intuitions exogenously, namely, to already more or less determinate given particulars (see e.g. Allais 2009:391). Moreover, nonconceptualists might indeed appear to be committed to the view that intuition already 'secures' a relation to the object even before categorially governed determination, in an actual judgement, further determines the given object *as* having certain properties (see e.g. Allais 2009:384). Kant does of course argue that an intuition *gives* us the object immediately (A320/B377, Prol, AA 4:281, A68/B93), but at the same time, according to Kant, the 'relation … to an object' (B137), which is a 'determinate relation', is solely a function of judging, so what secures the relation to an object in the strict sense—*in addition* to the (equally) necessary *immediate* relation provided by the intuition (which is a relation in the weaker, non-explicit or indeterminate sense)[5]—is a judging. Securing the connection with the object is therefore achieved in virtue of the act of judging, not through receptivity (intuition). This is what Pippin says is expressed by the Hegelian claim that 'it is only because our uptake of the sensory world is already conceptually articulated that these deliverances [of sensibility] can assume a justificatory role', and thus that 'thought's relation to … objects cannot be secured or *even intuitionally* pinned down, by the deliverances of sensibility alone' (Pippin 2015a:168, emphasis added). I agree with Pippin here insofar as nonconceptualists tend to see, wrongly, intuition as functioning wholly separately from a priori concepts in securing reference to particulars. The relation that intuitions have to objects, as Kant indeed suggests they do (A19/B33), is an immediate one, where the *relata*, object and intuition, are entirely undifferentiated; this relation is only first determined *as* a relation in the strict sense (as Kant uses the term *Beziehung* at B137, as a 'determinate relation')—namely, determined as a relation between two *differentiable* items, a subject of intuition and the object of intuition—by the determining act of the understanding.

The nonconceptualist reading of intuition as separably providing the relation to an object is also problematic in the sense that on that reading it is difficult to fathom how Kant can be taken to have established a synthetic *a priori connection between* concepts, more precisely, the categories, and intuitions. A post hoc application of categories to pre-given intuitions is not a priori, but simply a posteriori—quite the contrary of what Kant is aiming for in his analysis of the possibility of knowledge of objects.[6] The nonconceptualist reading cannot explain the way in which the understanding and sensibility *do cooperate* so that knowledge arises out of this combined effort. We would not be able to explain how the categories are in fact not just the necessary (and sufficient) conditions of our thought of an object, but also the necessary conditions of the intuition of objects. In this light, Pippin seems right to stress the *inseparability* of conceptuality and intuitions. The inseparability of conceptuality and intuitions is most clearly shown by Kant's *Leitfaden*, which says that

> the same function that gives unity to the different representations *in a judgment* also gives unity to the mere synthesis of different representations *in an intuition*, which, expressed generally, is called the pure concept of understanding. The same understanding, therefore, and indeed by means of the very same actions through which it brings the logical form of a judgment into concepts by means of the analytical unity, also brings a transcendental content into its representations by means of the synthetic unity of the manifold in intuition in general, on account of which they are called pure concepts of the understanding that pertain to objects *a priori*.
>
> A79/B104–5

As Kant writes here, it is not only that representations are united so as to form concepts, serviceable in judgements, by a unifying function of the understanding, that is, by certain 'actions' of the understanding, but these same 'actions' also unify manifolds of representations in *intuition*, and hence are called categories that pertain to objects given in sensibility in an a priori manner. These 'actions' connect concepts and intuition at the fundamental level. It is one and the same set of actions that *originally and simultaneously* form concepts that serve as predicates in judgement *and* unite intuitional representations that are the correlate of perceived objects. In this way, Kant here, in the run-up to the Transcendental Deduction, indicates a guiding thread to finding the *synthetic a priori* connection between intuitions of objects and concepts, whose function or set of functions (the same 'actions') *ex hypothesi* cannot be shared out *between* concepts and intuitions: the synthetic a priori connection, provided by a unifying action of the understanding, is rather the original intermediary or 'third thing', as Kant calls it elsewhere (A155/B194), which binds concept and intuition. Thus, the roles that concept and intuition play *in* this synthetic a priori connection that is due to *one* function (or *one* set of functions, i.e. the combined categorial forms of synthesis) cannot be *separated* into distinct 'components that belong severally to sensibility and understanding' (McDowell 2009:124), on pain of inviting an infinite regress that would ensue as a result of asking which even more originary function would bind the separate components.[7]

However, notwithstanding the valid reasons for not allowing room for a notion of nonconceptual content that is separably contributory to knowledge, there are some apparent problems with Pippin's belief that the 'strict *putative* separability between the sensory deliverance of a manifold of appearances and the conceptual conditions of unity really is *not* a possibility'. He sees showing this impossibility as 'the goal of the deduction' (Pippin 2015b:71), and at the same time this goal, namely, the ultimate inseparability of intuition and concept, is incompatible with Kant's own 'fixed', a priori formal separation between the two components. In a typical Hegelian move, Pippin thus urges Kant's readers to go beyond Kant's own formulations, whilst heeding the innermost principles of his thought, be mindful of the 'spirit' of Kant, and not be bound by the letter. Pippin writes:

> If it turns out, as it begins to seem in the second-edition deduction, to be impossible to consider the intuited manifold 'purely' and as a separable component of any knowledge claim, if 'what presents themselves to the senses' must be considered always already conceptually articulated and that conceptual articulation cannot be considered an immediately *given* aspect of the manifold as such, then *any a priori claim about the fixed, necessary conditions of receptivity and thereby strong objectivity in experience … cannot be made in the terms originally proposed by Kant*. In Hegelian terms, this means there cannot be a fixed, a priori determinable separation between the subject of experience on one side and some formal consideration of all possible deliverances of sensibility on the other; or, more familiarly, the subject and the object side of this equation are far too intertwined to allow one to say that what the subject side requires from the object side can never be contravened by any deliverances from the object side.
>
> Pippin 2015b:72–3, emphasis added[8]

Pippin here refers to the conclusion of the B-Deduction, namely §26, specifically the notorious note to B160, where indeed it seems that, as Pippin puts it, the categories 'determine sensibility inwardly' (1989:28), seemingly undermining the strictness of the separability of at least spontaneity and receptivity because it is here that they appear to intertwine inextricably. It would appear though that seeing the goal of the Deduction the way Pippin does conflates two different kinds of enabling condition, which Kant keeps clearly separate even in that difficult footnote, that is, the conditions for 'merely' intuiting something in space (the conditions of sensibility) and the conditions of representing something *determinate* in space, respectively, and relatedly, two different ways of construing the argument of the conclusion—the latter point concerns the modality of Kant's argument. I briefly discuss the footnote, and the conclusion of the B-Deduction, in Section 7.4.

However, less ambivalently, Kant does appear to insist quite explicitly on the separability (or distinguishability[9]) of concept and intuition in a famous passage at A51/B75. This is a crucial passage that conceptualists and nonconceptualists alike cite as evidence for their respective readings:

> Neither of these properties [sensibility and understanding] is to be preferred to the other. Without sensibility no object would be given to us, and without understanding none would be thought. Thoughts without content are empty, intuitions without concepts are blind. It is thus just as necessary to make the mind's concepts sensible (i.e., to add an object to them in intuition) as it is to make its intuitions understandable (i.e., to bring them under concepts). Further, these two faculties or capacities cannot exchange their functions. The understanding is not capable of intuiting anything, and the senses are not capable of thinking anything. Only from their unification can cognition arise. But on this account one must not mix up their roles, rather one has great cause to separate [*abzusondern*] them carefully from each other and distinguish [*unterscheiden*] them.
>
> A51–2/B75–6

Pippin says the passage has 'a dialectical and somewhat unstable form', for '*both* distinctness *and* necessary intertwining (inseparability in any claim to knowledge) are emphasized' (2005a:25). At any rate, according to Pippin, Kant does not mean to say here 'that we are first subject to blind intuitions which can be said to become "informing" and "guiding" intuitions "after" concepts are applied to them' (Pippin 2013:102). The argument about the possibility of objective experience as grounded in the cooperation between intuition and concepts should not be understood as if there were 'a move or transition of any sort *from* a perceptual uptake [construed as being in a state with nonconceptual content] *to* a judgmental state of conceptual content [understood as a result of a separable cognitive function]' (Pippin 2005a:29).[10] I agree that would indeed be contrary to Kant's aim to explain the possibility of synthetic *a priori* knowledge. The idea of nonconceptual content that informs our cognition, and *becomes* specifically intentional, or comes to have objective purport, *after* concepts have been applied to it, has the appearance of being a posteriori, rather than a priori, as noted earlier. Thus, 'there are no blind intuitions, waiting to be conceptualized'. 'Kant means to be rejecting the idea of nonconceptual content, not specifying its initial blindness. Blind intuitions are no more determinate intuitions than dead eyes are eyes', says Pippin (2013:102). For this reason, Pippin points out the '"blurring" of the strictness of the distinct roles [concept and intuition] should play in cognition ... not ... its elimination' (2005a:30). The issue is to refute a 'strict *separation* claim', not indistinguishability per se, according to Pippin.[11]

But it is unclear to me what the difference between separability and distinguishability is supposed to mean exactly, the more so because Kant seems to identify 'separating' (*absondern*) with 'distinguishing' (*unterscheiden*) concept and intuition. What does it mean to say that Kant cannot uphold a 'strict separation claim' concerning concept and intuition? Kant clearly says that they must be differentiated, cannot be confused, that is, cannot exchange their functions, *whilst* they must also be conjoined for cognition to arise. It is unclear what is meant by strictness and what the problem with it amounts to. Does it mean that, although concept and intuition are formally distinguishable—since, of course, an intuition is a singular representation, whereas a concept is always a general or universal representation, and so by definition they are irreducible to each other (A320/B376-7)—they are not really distinct or separate because in reality, that is, in cognition, the understanding as the conceptual capacity and sensibility as the capacity for having intuitions *must* always cooperate?

Pippin's reading suggests that, notwithstanding their irreducible defining characteristics, there is a necessary entailment between intuition and concept, that is, that intuitions *always* entail conceptualization. However, the reciprocity between the manifold in intuition and conceptuality—the activity of the apperceiving 'I'—holds only *insofar as* this 'I' indeed apperceives, for herself, the manifold that is before her. To this extent and this extent only, intuition and concept are indeed inseparable. This, I contend, is indicated by an implicit conditional contained in Kant's remark that 'only from their unification can cognition arise', that is, the conditional that *if there should be cognition, then concept and intuition are unified*. The cooperation of which Kant speaks obtains not because conceptuality is always already, as it turns out, necessarily contained in intuition, but because of the bi-conditional claim that *if and only if* intuition should yield cognition, then it is necessarily connected with concepts. This connection happens just because the subject *takes* the manifold in intuition as her own (this is often also stressed by Pippin). This shows that intuition is not *necessarily* conjoined with concepts *simpliciter*, that is, absolutely. Kant does not deviate from the strict separation of concept and intuition, as both have very distinct and distinctive roles to play in their cooperation to yield knowledge, and because intuitions *need* not be unified with concepts in all cases (cf. A90–1/B123). Intuitions are not intrinsically disposed to being brought under concepts; this is why in fact Kant needs a deduction to show that, despite their irreducible natures, they must be considered conjoined in the specific case of objective knowledge. But there is no 'blurring', no 'lessening' or 'weakening' of the strictness of the separability (or distinguishability), and the strictness of the separability of concept and intuition is not incompatible with their necessary cooperation in the case of knowledge.

There is also a problem with Pippin's admission that there is indeed a 'notional separability between intuitional and conceptual elements in experience—albeit one entertained in order to be denied' (Pippin 2015b:67, also 71, 73), referring to an oft-discussed passage in §14 of the Deduction at A89–91/B122–3, where Kant suggests the possibility of separability, which conceptualists argue is eventually, when we reach the conclusion of the Deduction, ruled out. Pippin does not think reference to this passage by nonconceptualists is warranted, as it does not settle the issue of whether it is possible to intuit *an object* independently of concepts. In Pippin's view, Kant is not here endorsing the viewpoint that there could be nonconceptual content, but talks 'rather only about the nonconceptual, *formal* aspects of any *relation* to an object', and these intuitional features can of course not 'be attributed to the results of the understanding's determination' (Pippin 2015a:165). Notwithstanding Pippin's rightful observation that, at A89–91/B122–3, there is no suggestion of the possibility of 'a *cognitively* significant pre-conceptual experience of an *object*' (2015a:165, emphasis added), I think that he misses Kant's conclusion that, independently of concepts, 'appearances would nonetheless offer objects to our intuition' (A91/B123), even if this would only yield a 'blind play of representations' (A112) with no objective validity. In earlier work (Schulting 2015, 2017a), I have argued in detail why the strongly conceptualist reading of this passage, which denies the possibility of intuitions that exist independently of the categories, must be dismissed on textual grounds alone.

There is an implicit conceptualist bias in Pippin's analysis, both of A51/B75 and A89–91/B122–3, in the very manner that he analyses the relation between intuition and concept: namely, intuition presumably can only be relevantly considered from a conceptualizing perspective, so must already be conceptual in some sense, and can therefore not really be considered, formally, in separation from concepts—but this just begs the question against Kant's strict separation between intuition and concepts.

7.3 The Short Argument to Inseparability

One of the reasons why Pippin thinks that the strict separability cannot be upheld harks back to an argument that Hegel adopts from Fichte, and which is often employed by Hegelians to refute Kant's restriction thesis, that is, the idealist thesis that we cannot know things in themselves (see e.g. Sedgwick 1993:276–8). In relation to the argument of the Deduction and abstracting from issues concerning idealism, the idea is that the categories are not just

> mere subjective requirements of thought imposed on the 'matter' of sensible intuition because the very possibility of *determinate conceptual content* at all, even in the intuitional presence of the world to consciousness, requires both categorical and intuitional conditions.
> Pippin 2015b:71, emphasis added

Apart from an ambiguity here in the italicized phrase (which I address later, in Section 7.4, in relation to the conclusion of the B-Deduction), Pippin means to say that there could not be intuitional content that has any cognitive relevance if it were not already conceptually laden. This is made clearer by what he asserts next:

> There could be 'nothing' contrary to these conditions because such a putative exception could not even be a content of thought; it would be 'less than a dream'.
> Pippin 2015b:71

In a footnote, he adds that such 'a putative exception could *not* be, ultimately, a content of thought because it could not be self-ascribable by an apperceptive subject continuous in all its experiences' (Pippin 2015b:71n.25). The implication is that Kant insufficiently appreciates the intertwinement of concept and content, where in a discursive logic such as that of Kant concepts as mere forms of unity (analytic universals) rely on exogenous material content for their objective validity. But his own argument in the Deduction, presumably, shows that whereas concepts that have objective validity do indeed rely on externally, independently given content, that content must in its turn be apprehended and conceptually recognized *by an apperceptive subject* as that content; so external content can count as external content only from the perspective of the subject apprehending it as a necessary complement in her act of cognition. In other words, the externally, independently given content only counts as such *just because* a subject apprehends it as her own. *Outside* the perspective of the apprehending subject, the external content fulfils no cognitive role, and could in fact be said to come down to nothing, at any rate 'less than a dream'. With that last phrase, Pippin refers to a passage in the A-Deduction, where significantly it says:

> The possibility, even the necessity of these categories rests on the relation that the entire sensibility, and with it also all possible appearances, have to the original apperception, in which everything is necessarily in agreement with the conditions of the thoroughgoing unity of self-consciousness, i.e., must stand under universal functions of synthesis, namely of the synthesis in accordance with concepts, as that in which alone apperception can demonstrate *a priori* its thoroughgoing and necessary identity. Thus the concept of a cause is nothing other than a synthesis ... *in accordance with concepts*; and without that sort of unity, which has its rule *a priori*, and which subjects the appearances to itself, thoroughgoing and universal, hence necessary unity of consciousness would not be encountered in the manifold perceptions. But these would then belong to no experience, and would consequently be without an object, and would be nothing but a blind play of representations, i.e., less than a dream.
>
> A111–12

Kant's argument here is—and we shall have cause to return briefly to this passage in Section 7.4, when we come to discuss B160—that without the categories no necessary unity would be encountered in the manifold of appearances, which would then not amount to *experience*, and would be without a relation to an object. Without the categories, grounded in the identity of the apperceiving subject, representations would thus have no objective representational content; they would be just a 'blind play of representations'.

The Fichtean heritage of the above Hegelian reasoning regarding inseparability, which is a short-argument version of Kant's longer argument leaving out the categories as the constitutive elements of the objective content, is nicely put by Sally Sedgwick:

> Any content taken to be independently given is in fact no more than a product of the 'I think's' act of self-limitation—of positing in addition to the 'I', the 'not-I'. *Any* content for thought is the product of the self's a priori determinations, even if that content is supposed to represent what is external to or independent of the self.
>
> Sedgwick 1993:276

The Fichtean point is that, however much there is something that is not the self, namely sense content, even if independently given (Sedgwick 2012), such content does not have cognitive relevance except by way of the self's knowing or determining it as *her* content, by way of the self's self-determination (where determination must *also* be taken literally as a negation).[12] Thus, as Sedgwick says, 'there can be no thought-content for us which is independent of [formal] determinations' (1993:276), indeed, 'all content available to consciousness is necessarily subject to the determinations of form, and . . . therefore [we] have no access—not even in *thought*—to what may lie outside those determinations' (1992:158).[13] In his *Versuch zu einer neuen Darstellung zur Wissenschaftslehre* from 1797/98, Fichte has explicit recourse to Kant in support of refuting the at the time widely held belief that his *Wissenschaftslehre* is not authentically Kantian, and offers his own interpretation of Kantian themes, which are relevant to the present topic. With reference to B136, where Kant says that 'all the manifold of intuition stand under conditions of the original synthetic unity of apperception', Fichte writes the following:

> That something intuited is *thought* is possible only under the condition that the possibility of the original unity of apperception can exist thereby, and, I infer further—since according to Kant the intuition is also possible only by being thought and understood [*begriffen*], while according to him <u>intuition without concept is blind, that is, is nothing at all</u>—therefore the intuition itself stands under the conditions of the possibility of thinking, not only thought in an immediate fashion, but by virtue of the latter also the intuiting conditioned by it, hence *all consciousness*, stands under the conditions of the original unity of apperception.
>
> GA, I,4:227–8, trans. mine, my underlining

It is thus, according to Fichte, not just that thought content stands under the principle of apperception, but *any* intuitional content.

Pippin takes this to imply that the a priori identity between subject and object—an identity that lies at the heart of Kant's thought of the original-synthetic unity of apperception as a principle, not just of *representation* of objects, but also of the *objects* themselves, a claim most clearly advanced at B138 (cf. Pippin 2015b:71, 2005a:32)[14]—must be more radically interpreted than Kant himself seems to allow. That is to say, in Pippin's view the fixed separation between concepts and intuition is incompatible with Kant's truest insight into the original identity of the subject and object of thought. Hence, the Hegelian overtures of shifting the separability of concept and intuition to *within* the domain of the conceptual: any difference is determinable only from within identity, and so is *relative* rather than *absolute* or *fixed*, or, in Hegel's original terms, Kant's original-synthetic unity is an 'identity of identity and difference';[15] this means that the difference or distinction between concept and intuition comes to the fore only within the theoretical *a priori* perspective, from the conceptual point of view.

But I think that this conclusion is too hasty—not least because it seems to be saying that, contradictorily and question-beggingly, the position of nonconceptualism is only first possible if one assumes the truth of conceptualism! The Fichtean line of reasoning is at least ambiguous about the precise kind of conditions we are talking about in the claim that there is an entailment relation between sense content and the self's conceptual determinations. Two different arguments can be discerned, namely, on the one hand arguing that

(A) Any (sensible) content for thought is a product of thought's self-limitation or determination;

and, on the other hand, that

(B) Any (sensible) content is a product of thought's self-limitation or determination.

Fichte, and following him Hegel and the Hegelians, seems to slide from 'any content *for thought*' to 'any content'. Argument A contains a claim about what is epistemologically necessary for any content to be a thought content, namely, that it should be a product of the self's own determination—in good Kantian: that it should be 'apperceivable' by a self. In argument B, there is an implicit claim about the constitutive condition of content *tout court*, namely, that it only *exists* as a product of thought's self-determination.[16] Where self-determination is understood as saying that sensible content is determined as the not-self, or what is other than thought, it is trivially true—from a Critical perspective, at least— that any content that is *for thought* is the product of thought's self-determination, namely, insofar as the content is *thought about as* not-being-thought, or being other-than-thought. This should be understood in the sense that, as Pippin says, 'the distinction between what we take to be the case and what is the case is *one we make*, in response to what we learn about the world, not an intrusion from outside that happens to us, whatever that could mean' (2015a:164). In other words, any content *for us*, that is, relevant to us, is a content *we* make relevant for ourselves. There is of course no question of us, as rational agents, literally producing our own sense content—rather, the *distinction* between the content and ourselves, and so *its* relevance to us, is one we make, not the content *an sich*. But it is of course not trivially true that just any content is the product of thought's self-determination if such content is not content *for thought*, for it is trivially true that content that is *not thought about* is not a product of thought's self-determination.[17]

Pippin obviously realizes that there could, in principle at least, as a possibility entertained, be content ('putative content') that is not the product of thought, but, as we saw earlier, such content would, according to Pippin, be 'less than a dream', since it would 'not be self-ascribable by an apperceptive subject continuous in all its experiences' (2015b:71n.25).[18] I agree to the extent that such content would not be relevant to us, and so *ex hypothesi* it would not be content determined by us. But I think we should be careful not to infer from the unthinkability of 'putative content' that contravenes the conditions under which that content is thought—which, again, is a trivial truth—that *that* content could not *exist* (in some mind, albeit not *for a self aware of her mind's contents*), regardless of strict epistemic relevance.

Notice that I am of course not here charging Pippin with conflating the existence of a particular intuition *x* with the condition of *x* being conceptualized. Indeed, Pippin argues that 'X cannot be representationally significant except as Y'ed' does not imply 'There are no X's; there is only Y'ing' (2005a:27n.8). This points to his insistence that inseparability does not mean indistinguishability, to avoid any neo-Leibnizian style reductive conceptualism. That intuitions must be conceptualized in order for knowledge to arise does of course not mean that intuitions are just confused concepts, that intuitions and concepts cannot really be distinguished. But by employing the terminology 'representationally significant', Pippin fudges the difference between representing by means of an intuition, as one species of representation, and representing by means of a concept, as another species of representation (cf. the *Stufenleiter* at A320/B376–7), whilst thus suggesting that *any* representing entails conceptualization. A lot hinges on what 'representationally significant' is supposed to convey. If it means that a brute, say, cannot have a representation, in *any* significant sense (to him, even if in a very limited way), of an object that is a house without employing the concept 'house'—an object which anyone familiar with houses would normally recognize as 'a dwelling established for men' (Log, AA 9:33)—then the requirement that 'X cannot be representationally significant except as Y'ed' seems too strong, where by Y we understand 'conceptualized'. For clearly Kant suggests (in the passage at issue in the Jäsche Logic) that there are two real possibilities: either one represents the house by way of intuition *only* (*bloße Anschauung*), as the brute does, or one represents the house by way of *both* intuition and concept (*Anschauung und Begriff zugleich*) (Log, AA 9:33). The brute's seeing (intuiting) the house without knowing that he sees a house because he is not acquainted with the concept 'house' is not 'representationally' *insignificant* in the sense that he does not represent at all—in fact, Kant calls the brute's seeing a form of cognition (*Erkenntniß*). His seeing the house by means of intuition alone would only not be 'representationally' significant in the sense of seeing the house by way of *both* intuition and concept inseparably (*zugleich*), namely, 'determinately'. The distinction between these two ways of being 'representationally significant' is fudged by the Hegelian.

Of course, Pippin could rejoin that the example of the brute does not at all provide a convincing ground for denying the inseparability thesis, for the brute could very well be incapable of assigning the right property or *empirical* concept ('house') to what he intuits, while nonetheless the view can be endorsed that the brute's intuitional representations must at any rate be taken to instantiate *pure* concepts, the categories, in order even to be able to intuit the object that he sees. This would then still suggest that intuition and *pure* concepts (which is what Kant effectively means at A51–2/B75–6, not empirical concepts) are inseparable, and that thus *anything* that is 'representationally significant' presupposes conceptualization in the specific Kantian sense of being subsumed under the categories. But I believe that the Jäsche example at any rate shows that a kind of representation (intuiting) is possible that does not require an occurrent conceptualization (in the sense of applying empirical concepts).

I think that Pippin's qualification that neither Hegel nor Fichte aim to '*eliminate* the idea of a "not-self"' and that 'in Fichte there is always a "shock" delivered *to* the I's self-positing' is a welcome one. But his emphasis on the fact that '*what comes to count as* a determinate not-self, experienced as such for the self, is always a matter of conceptual determination' and that 'the distinction between self and not-self is … one always resulting from a theoretical view of the self-world relation' (1993:291, emphasis added)[19] might appear to downplay the essential distinction between epistemological and existential type claims, that is, the difference between claims A and B as explicated above, or at least to silently sanction a slide from the one claim to the other.[20] And, as we shall see in the next section, it appears that Pippin does need the stronger (implicitly) existential claim B, when considering Kant's central claim in §26 of the B-Deduction, that the very 'way in which the empirical intuition is given in sensibility' (B144) is necessarily in accord with categorial determination—a lot here depends on how one interprets 'empirical intuition'.[21] I take it Pippin does not want to read this claim as amounting to the triviality of A, but wants a stronger claim which encompasses 'anything given in sensibility', not just 'any objects given in sensibility', precisely because so much hangs on the fact that the apperception principle is, as Pippin rightly emphasizes, not just a subjective principle of representability or analytic thought, but an objective, constitutive principle that *first establishes* what it is to conceive of an 'object' and thereby fixes the relation to an object (see e.g. Pippin 1993:293, 2015b:71–2)—so objects cannot just be assumed to be *already given in sensibility*, so that the categories are subsequently *merely* applied to these. But we must tread carefully here. I address this important issue in the next section, when discussing Kant's foremost important argument in the Deduction, namely, the apparent conclusion that the categories 'determine sensibility inwardly' (Pippin 1989:28).

7.4 Inseparability and the Conclusion of the B-Deduction, Specifically, the B160 Note

Pippin argues that Hegel concurs with Kant that there is a necessary cooperation between the capacities for intuitions and concepts, and that there *are* such distinguishable aspects of cognition,[22] but also that

> he is objecting to a 'mechanical' opposition in favor of an 'organic' role for the imagination in understanding the relation between intuition and concept, and that he is enthusiastically applauding those passages in the second-edition deduction where Kant, by Hegel's lights, follows the logic of his own argument and begins to understand that the concept–intuition distinction is not strictly congruent with the distinction between spontaneity and receptivity, that there is an 'active' and even conceptual element in the sensible uptake of the world (a claim which, again, hardly disputes that there is any such uptake).
>
> 2005a:28

As Pippin says, 'Hegel wishes to stress *more*, make more out of, the organic unity or organic inseparability of such elements than Kant' (2005a:28).[23] The cooperation between intuition and concept happens by means of the productive imagination—as Kant argues in §24 of the B-Deduction—which is the 'effect of the understanding on sensibility' (B152). The imagination is the faculty which enables sensibility to be conceptually determined by the understanding by means of the categories. Hegel understands this in such a way that the imagination is in fact the mediating factor between intuition and concept, such that intuition and concept, or sensibility and the understanding, can only retroactively, from a formal 'understanding' perspective, be considered separately. Hegel accuses Kant of hypostatizing this formal 'understanding' perspective, which makes the synthetic a priori, original unity look like a mechanical opposition between intuition and concept. Their apparent separateness is in fact merely an *abstraction from* their original 'organic' unity that Hegel says they have in the imagination.[24]

Hence Pippin's claim that concept and intuition are formally 'distinguishable', namely, as formal elements in what is 'organically' united, but not in fact separable.

This original 'organic' unity of the imagination plays a significant role in the conclusion (the 'second step') of Kant's argument in the B-Deduction, where he labels it the *synthesis speciosa* (B151), to distinguish it from the intellectual synthesis, which merely concerns the organization of representations on the conceptual level. *Synthesis speciosa* is veritably concerned with sensible images of objects, which have a direct connection, via empirical intuition, to actual spatiotemporal objects in experience. Already in the A-Deduction, Kant indicates that the imagination's 'action exercised immediately upon perceptions' is apprehension, but in the B-Deduction it is even more clearly stated that the productive imagination as active in sensibility is the synthesis of apprehension (B160-1). Crucially, Hegel interprets the productive imagination therefore as the very 'principle of ... sensibility' itself (GuW, GW 4:327 [Hegel 1977:70]). This might seem confirmed by Kant's own argument in the earlier quoted passage at A111-12, where he says that 'the entire sensibility, and with it also *all possible appearances*' (emphasis added), is bound by the categories, which are the 'universal functions of synthesis'. It is therefore not unreasonable to claim that the imagination, which is the synthesis at issue here, and instantiates the categories in sensibility, is indeed the very 'principle' of sensibility. Pippin writes that, for Kant,

> 'from the side of givenness, sensibility' as it were, ... there could not be such deliverances not subject to the unity made possible by categories. We have a way of representing the domain of the immediately, sensibly given as such (because it has a pure form accessible as a pure intuition, a distinct representation) and so ... [1] the categories not only prescribe the unity required for objective purport at all *to* any manifold, but also [2] that any *manifold*, given especially its temporal aspects, *requires* categorical unity <u>if it is to provide any possible content for thought</u>.
>
> 2005a:33, my underlining

Pippin means the second clause [2] to be an additional claim, but really, the condition contained at the end of the clause makes the second clause just repeat what was said in [1]: the categories are required for any manifold that has objective purport or objectively valid representational content. The categories are not required for a manifold just to be that manifold, in contrast to what in earlier work Pippin did explicitly assert, namely, that 'nothing given *in* intuition can fail to be subject to the categories' (1989:29), 'there can be no intuitions not subject to the categories' (1989:30) and, most emphatically, 'the content of any intuited manifold must be subject to the categories just to *be* an element of a spatiotemporal manifold in the first place' (1989:31).[25] Unlike what Pippin seems to be suggesting in these passages, the categories are not required for an intuition *to be* an intuition. Pippin can on this basis therefore not claim that 'there could not be such deliverances not subject to the unity made possible by categories' (2005a:33). He could rejoin to this that Kant might be thought to say as much, when he writes that 'all synthesis, through which *even perception itself becomes possible*, stands under the categories' (B161, emphasis added), quoted by Pippin (2005a:33). Or in an earlier passage, at B160, also quoted by Pippin (1989:28), where Kant writes that 'everything that may ever come before our senses must stand under the laws that arise *a priori* from the understanding alone'. But this must be seen in the context of the claim made earlier in the same paragraph, which says that what 'is to be explained' in §26 is

> the possibility of cognizing *a priori through categories* whatever objects *may come before our senses*, not as far as the form of their intuition but rather as far as the laws of their combination are concerned.
>
> B159, my underlining

The passage at B161 is indeed a more ambivalent one, but it depends on how one reads Kant's notion of 'perception'.[26] From the context of the 'second step' of the B-Deduction, it should be clear that what is at issue is the unity or combination in intuition that is due to the determination by virtue of *synthesis speciosa*. This is also already made clear in the above-quoted passage in §21, where Kant says that 'in the sequel (§26), it will be shown from the way in which the empirical intuition is given in sensibility that *its unity* can be none other than the one the category prescribes to the manifold of a given intuition in general' (B144–5, emphasis added). So the *unity* of empirical intuition is concerned, and not just intuition or mere sensibility.[27]

But Pippin refers to the notorious footnote to B160 as more evidence for a Hegelian alteration of Kant's official thoughts about the separability of concept and intuition 'towards a version more in keeping with Kant's spirit' (2005a:34). It is here that he believes

> that thought is not merely presented with[,] and then applied to and restricted by, a thoroughly nonconceptual sensory manifold. The manifold is already conceptually articulated; concepts are engaged in our 'sensory uptake' of the world, and the separation claim *and* the strategy it grounds *and* the mind-world picture it assumes must now all be qualified, even re-thought.
>
> Pippin 2005a:34, my underlining

The reason for this belief is that Kant seems to be saying that what previously—in the Transcendental Aesthetic—was considered sensibility's own *sui generis* unity turns out to be the result of the understanding's determination of sensibility. Pippin believes that the crucial claim in the footnote is that 'the issue for [Kant] is not only ... how intuitions, as given, are conceptualized', but also 'that conforming to the *intuitional* constraints of sensibility itself requires a minimal conceptualization' (1989:30). This 'minimal conceptualization' concerns the unity of spatiotemporal manifolds, without which we could not even *receive* these manifolds. This is reason for Hegel (and Pippin) to say that the strict distinction between the understanding's spontaneity and sensibility's receptivity, and a fortiori the strict distinction between the form of intuition, namely its unity, and conceptuality as that which provides this unity, can no longer be upheld (cf. GuW, GW 4:327ff.).

But if we read the note carefully (and Christian Onof and I have done this *in extenso* in Onof & Schulting 2015), then it becomes clear that the separation between intuition and concepts remains as it is—this is reflected by Kant's distinction, in the footnote, between 'form of intuition', which 'merely gives the manifold', and 'formal intuition', which 'gives unity of the representation', under the guidance of the imagination, by means of an act of the understanding that determines sensibility. While imagination *determines* the manifold in sensibility, it is not suddenly the principle of sensibility *simpliciter*, as Hegel alleges, nor is the imagination the common denominator of sensibility and understanding, where supposedly the imagination is the higher principle in comparison to the *discursive* principle of the understanding, or an 'organic unity' that holds understanding and sensibility together. It would mean that imagination is the principle of space and time; but there are a series of problems with such a reading that go against the core of Kant's doctrine in the Aesthetic, which are addressed in Onof & Schulting (2015) but for which I have no space here to rehearse.[28] It is clear that Hegel wants to read it the way he does, but his claim (and Pippin's endorsement thereof) that his reading is an immanent one that is in keeping with the spirit of Kant's thoughts can hardly be vindicated.[29] Kant's 'formal intuition' is an intuited object as determined by the understanding, so indeed not any longer *merely* an intuition (an indeterminate appearance) but a determinate object, that is, the result of a conceptual determination of the mere intuitional manifold (by means of the categories). This does not, however, sublate the *strictness* of the distinction between intuition and concept—a *mere* manifold is still just an intuition—nor does it imply that intuitions per se *must* be conceptually determined.[30]

Pippin seems to play 'dualistically inclined' interpretations of Kant's distinction between intuition and concept, endorsed by nonconceptualists, off against 'holistically inclined' readings, such as his own. Dualists think that intuitions by themselves already refer to objects and constitute intentionality, while holists emphasize the fact that 'representationally significant intuited content at all' (Pippin 2005a:36n.27) is solely due to the unifying function of the understanding (as demonstrated by the *Leitfaden* passage). Pippin is right to criticize the nonconceptualists on this score. But it is important to acknowledge—based on Kant's own clear distinction in the footnote between 'form of intuition', *giving the mere manifold*, and 'formal intuition'—that, on the one hand, *determinate* intuitions are indeed not separable from the unifying function of the understanding, and that intuitions by themselves have no *cognitively significant* content if by that is meant a content that represents the object of intuition *as* object, but also that, on the other hand, *mere* intuitions are perfectly separable from concepts and a fortiori from judgements, since not being cognitively relevant they do not presuppose categories nor do they have an inbuilt tendency towards judgement.

Only insofar as intuitions (or perceptions) are to be seen as determinate (unified) intuitions (or perceptions), as an indispensable and inseparable part of a determinate cognition of objects, *must* intuitions (or perceptions) themselves be taken to be affected[31] by the understanding. This means that it is not true to say that the conclusion of the Deduction is that, *necessarily*, intuitions or perceptions are conceptualized or are susceptible to conceptual or categorial determination, or judgemental organization. There is nothing in intuitions or perceptions per se that makes them susceptible to conceptual or categorial determination such that they are or become perceptions of external (or internal) objects. Kant's argument does not show this, but it would also be odd if it did, since that would mean that he could have spared himself all the effort of the second half of the B-Deduction and rested content with the principle of apperception explicated in the first half, if interpreted (wrongly, as it happens) as a principle of sheer representation, which holds that every representation is subject to the principle of being *thought*. (In actuality, as we saw earlier, Pippin himself does not believe that the 'first step' of the B-Deduction is sufficient to prove that objects actually instantiate the subjective forms of thought, but his apparent belief that in the 'second step' Kant proves that *any* representational content is subject to the categories stands in tension with this.)[32] Such an argument—that perceptions show a susceptibility to being affected by the understanding—also could not explain why Kant would worry about how to differentiate genuine objectively valid representations from merely subjectively valid representations.

We should keep in mind that the intimate connection between perceptions (intuitions) and the understanding in the case of genuine empirical knowledge is seen *from the perspective of the understanding*, the view from the cognizing subject, which is a transcendental or sideways-on perspective (*intentio obliqua* instead of *intentio recta*). The transcendental perspective does not allow us to locate the internal ground of the connection in the perceptions themselves as if they showed some inner disposition to being conceptualized or had an inbuilt tendency towards judgement, a conation to being determined categorially, as Béatrice Longuenesse (1998) argues.[33] The determination of perceptions—and this was clearly and rightly seen by Fichte, and later Hegel—is of course a determination that is wholly due to the understanding, and also wholly internal to the understanding, that is, the self-conscious 'I'. But Fichte's mistake was thereby to reduce the very givenness of perceptions, of what is external to thought, to merely being an aspect of thought's self-determination, one of the formal *relata* in the conceptual differentiations of self-determining reason.

7.5 Concluding Remarks

Hegelian conceptualists are wont to relativize the immediacy and absolute externality of sense content. They do not deny that it is required, and they do not deny that it is, in some sense, irreducible to thought; they are not neo-Leibnizians. The phrase 'in some sense' is the operative issue here. Of course, the absolute distinction between sense content and thought that Kant emphasizes is not such that it poses a problem for, as it were, bridging the gap between them. The solution for bridging the apparent gap between them, which Kant proposes in the Deduction, is not a solution aimed at *relativizing* the absolute distinction (let alone collapsing it), thus in fact *denying* that there is any gap to be bridged (cf. Pippin 2015b:72). Rather, the solution is provided in terms of offering a unique and irreducible perspective from the side of the cognizing subject; that is, insofar as the goal is to explain the possibility of knowledge, which is the premise of the analysis in the Deduction, and insofar as *mere* conceptuality cannot of itself provide the modal constraint for such knowledge—namely, the connection with *real, existing* objects—the apperceiving subject of understanding must be seen as *taking up sensible content as a cognitively relevant constraint on our conceptuality*. To this extent and to this extent only is sensible content to be seen as a content that is not itself given *in* thought but still determined *by thought* as a content given to it, and so it is only relatively distinct from thought or conceptuality—'relatively', because external content is defined as external only to the extent that the apperceiving subject of understanding takes up such content *as her own*, that is, *internalizes* it, and in this way 'determines sensibility inwardly', as Pippin puts it. This does not in the least relativize the absolute distinction between sensibility and conceptuality as such; it only relativizes that distinction insofar as from the cooperation between sensibility and understanding knowledge should arise, which is guaranteed by the subjective act of apperception.

Hegelians and Kantians can agree on these core issues to the extent that the possibility of knowledge is concerned. But it appears that the Hegelians want to deny that this leaves Kant's strict distinction between sensibility and the understanding intact. They do not see any warrant for keeping this distinction as an absolute one (see especially the reasoning in Pippin 2015b:72–4). The problem with this failure to understand Kant's distinction is, as I see it, twofold.

First, it confuses the epistemic and constitutive levels: sense content is *intelligible* only on condition that it is grasped or determined by an act of understanding, but it is not *constituted* by such an act. This becomes clear when we look at the way in which the understanding determines space, and how the unity of space is said by Kant to presuppose a synthesis (B160n.). This latter requirement does not reduce space, or indeed its *sui generis* unity, to a function of the synthesis of the understanding, by way of the imagination, as (some) Kantian as well as Hegelian conceptualists would like to believe. Space and time are not products of the understanding. Only determinate spaces and determinate times or time intervals are products of the understanding, by way of the imagination.

Second, it ignores the counterfactual possibility of cognitive failure or indeed the real possibility (for human beings) of subcognitive intuitional coping with one's environment.[34] Kant allows for this possibility, even though it is not the focus of his argument in the Deduction. But the correlation between, on the one hand, the intimate epistemological relation between sense content and conceptuality and, on the other, the fact that sense content is intelligible only by means of conceptuality should have given pause to Kantian as well as Hegelian conceptualists: if it is the case that sense content is *intelligible only* within the perspective of conceptuality, the perspective of the apperceiving subject, then this does not entail that there could not *be* sensible content that is not made intelligible within that perspective. Surely there is the real possibility of sensible or representational content that is not (although it could be) taken up by some apperceiving subject of understanding, for example, the sensible content that some non-apperceiving representer *X*, Kant's brute, say, has when he sees the house without knowing (apperceiving) what he sees, or, the sensible content that a properly functioning apperception-equipped adult human being, but one with a penchant for dark moods, has when (and only when), for example, he is staring wearily out the window after having read about Levinas's *il y a*.

8

On the Kinship of Kant's and Hegel's Metaphysical Logics[1]

8.1 'Logic Thus Coincides With Metaphysics'

In this chapter I want to look at some aspects of Robert Pippin's recent essay 'Hegel on Logic as Metaphysics' (Pippin 2017), which concern in particular Hegel's relation to Kant, elements of which were already discussed in the last chapter. In that essay, Pippin advances compelling arguments for seeing Hegel's logic as a metaphysics which takes objects, in some sense, to be a product and content of thought (W, 5:30). An earlier version of this chapter was published as Schulting (2016b), which referred to the German version of the article entitled 'Logik und Metaphysik: Hegels "Reich der Schatten"' (Pippin 2016), which was published before the English version in a collection of Pippin's German essays.[2] That German title refers to a passage in Hegel's *Greater Logic*, where Hegel compares the science of logic to 'the realm of shadows':

> The system of logic is the realm of shadows, the world of simple essentialities [*Wesenheiten*], freed of all sensuous concretion. To study this science, to dwell and to labor in this realm of shadows, is the absolute culture and discipline of consciousness. Its task is one which is remote from the intuitions and the goals of the senses, remote from feelings and from the world of merely fancied representation [*bloß gemeinten Vorstellungswelt*]. Considered from its negative side, this task consists in holding off the accidentality of ratiocinative thought and the arbitrariness in the choice to accept one ground as valid rather than its opposite.
>
> W 5:55 [Hegel 2010b:37]

Pippin concentrates on Hegel's statement, in §24 of the *Encyclopædia Logic*, that '[*l*]*ogic* thus coincides with *metaphysics*, i.e. the science of *things* captured in *thoughts* that have counted as expressing *the essentialities of things*' (Enz §24, W 8:81 [Hegel 2010a:58]). The central theme of the essay is that the science of logic *is* a metaphysics, albeit of a special kind.

Ever since I started studying his *Hegel's Idealism* and *Idealism as Modernism* in the mid-1990s (Pippin 1989 and 1997a respectively), I have been in general agreement with much of what Pippin writes, at least as far as Hegel is concerned. Pippin's *general* approach to Hegel's metaphysical logic is, it seems to me, the only viable one, interpretatively as well as philosophically. I beg to differ however with respect to some of the details in relation to Kant, which I shall be focusing on here.

Pippin is well-known for espousing a 'Kantian' reading of Hegel's philosophy. He reads Hegel as taking Kant's 'Idee einer apriorischen Spezifikation von Inhalt allein durch das "Denken"' as a starting point, albeit without Kant's 'distinkte, abtrennbare Formen der Rezeptivität' (2016:188/2017:217). However, as Pippin points out in the introduction to *Die Aktualität des Deutschen Idealismus*—the volume in which Pippin (2016) appeared—readers and commentators have often mistaken this for holding the view that, like Kant's idealism, Hegel's idealism is a form of subjectivist idealism, or, in other words, that by linking Hegel intimately to Kant Pippin plays down the realist ('ontological') aspects of Hegel's thought. This assumption is based on a mistaken idea about the subjectivity that is so central to both Hegel's and Kant's thought, but also about the purport of realism in Hegel. This last aspect will be the topic of Chapter 9.

I agree with Pippin that Hegel's notion of the 'absolute' has got nothing to do with it being a thing or some sort of entity, or a substance (let alone the Christian God), and that it would be entirely wrong-headed to read Hegel as if he simply returned to or continued (or even built upon) a pre-Kantian rationalist metaphysics, which is interested in determining things and their properties intrinsically apart from how they are necessarily determined in and by *thought*. As Pippin says, Hegel must be placed 'firmly in the post-Kantian world' (2016:165/2017:200). The subjective, reflexive element of Hegel's metaphysics is incontrovertible and centrally important—compare the way that Hegel sometimes speaks of the 'activity' (*Tätigkeit*) of the 'universal' (*Allgemeine*); Pippin also points to the employment of the adjective 'conscious' (*gewußter*) in a passage in the *Science of Logic* where Hegel writes about truth as self-consciousness:

> As *science*, truth is pure self-consciousness as it develops itself and has the shape of the self, so that *that which exists in and for itself is the conscious [gewußter] concept and the concept as such is that which exists in and for itself.*
> W 5:43 [Hegel 2010b:29]

Hegel's logic of concepts is not a conceptual realism, but emphasizes the active, subjective aspect of conceptuality, much as Kant's analytic of concepts is focused on an analysis of the capacity of the understanding, rather than a mere analysis of given concepts (cf. A65/B90). Concepts themselves do not make assertions; it is the thinking subject who makes assertions, in judging about objects and the world. In other words, as Pippin rightly says, concepts '*behaupten* nicht für sich selbst, was sie sind' (2016:169), and hence we need to be able to establish the extent to which *self-consciousness* 'drives' the logic of concepts. But on the other hand, as Pippin wants to make it clear, his reading of Hegel does not make of him merely a category theorist as if Hegel's logic were concerned with the *mere* rules of intelligibility only or some kind of conceptualist coherentism that risks spinning in a void (to use a McDowellian coinage), i.e. merely *our* rules of understanding something, and not with *Wirklichkeit* or Being itself.

There is, to be sure, one crucial aspect of Hegel, according to Pippin, that departs from Kant, and this is conveyed by the fact that, as Pippin argues, Hegel follows Aristotle in the principle 'Zu sein heißt, auf bestimmte Weise verständlich zu sein' (2016:17/cf. 2017:213), thus asserting the identity of Being and intelligibility; this means that metaphysics is the study of the categorial structure of what is, but at the same time what it means to *say* about something what it is (cf. Enz §21).[3] The focus in Hegel's metaphysics is squarely on the 'in principle' transparency of Being itself to reason, to our understanding (broadly conceived), a general assumption not shared by Kant's philosophy. Being can be known because it is in principle articulable in thought (2016:189n.52). Pippin says: 'Wer auf das Sein mit der Frage der Intelligibilität blickt, dem blickt es intelligibel entgegen' (2016:18).

But this means that we cannot consider Being and thought apart as if Being were somehow that which is completely external to and distinct from thought. If we put it in the terms of that against which a type of philosophy that is currently en vogue argues, Hegel is a thoroughgoing 'correlationalist' in that talk about reality that were supposedly antecedent or prior to reason, and hence external to it, is *ipso facto* nonsensical. In this, Hegel is a thoroughbred Kantian: even if there is a reality *actually* beyond any particular judgement or belief I entertain—and who would deny that there is an external reality, something *de facto outside* of our reasoning? (e.g. the words I'm now typing on my MacBook Air, and more radically, the far side of the moon, the physically real past that anteceded humanity and thus human reason in a historical sense, 'what it is like to be a bat', etc.)—in an a priori sense no *possible* reality is completely outside the scope of reason, just as for Kant what belongs to the domain of *possible* experience is determined by the functions of thought: nothing outside the scope of those functions *can* be experienced, and indeed can exist in the strict sense of determinate existence—namely, be *said* to exist or, indeed, be said to have existed.

This differentiation is important: it marks the difference between a realist (speculative or not) perspective on Being and a transcendental one. Hegel is definitely a transcendental philosopher, just like Kant.[4] Hegel broadens the Kantian transcendental perspective, which focuses on possible experience of empirical objects determinable by mathematico-physical laws, to all possible objects of human experience without distinction, not just those that are governed by mathematico-physical laws. This means that within a Hegelian transcendental perspective, we can talk sensibly about whatever is relevant in the context of whichever aspect of human experience (be it sensible objects, history, moral life, legal institutions, art, religion, etc.). No object, no aspect of Being, is *in principle* excluded from being articulable, or made intelligible, in the terms of (human) reason, that is, conceptually—everything can intelligibly be accounted for, even if only negatively, e.g. by describing why we *cannot* know what it is like to be a bat, or what it would literally have been like in ancestral times. And something is *an und für sich* only if it can indeed be made intelligible in thought; when something cannot be made intelligible in thought, it remains 'a mere indeterminate and indistinguishable being' (2016:171/2017:208). This is the way in which Being and reason must be seen as inextricably connected. The identity of Being and thought must be seen from this transcendental perspective, not in terms of metaphysical substances and their relations and properties in abstraction from reason. It would be a grandiose mistake to read Hegel's metaphysics as if it were concerned with a straightforward pre-Kantian realism or ontology.

Does that mean that reality is reduced to a form of subjective idealism, to how things are *merely for us*? Of course not. There is nothing relativistic or reductionistic about Pippin's approach:

> Dies heißt nicht, zu behaupten, dass der Gegenstand nur als ein denkend aufgefasster Gegenstand existiert oder dass das Denken, von dem seine Bestimmtheit abhängt, als eine subjektiv-mentale Episode verstanden werden sollte.
>
> 2016:170

But this was already not the case for Kant, albeit that Kant restricted this intelligibility somewhat more narrowly than Hegel to possible *empirical* experience strictly speaking. It just shows that we can be confident about the intelligibility of whatever is real that presents itself to us.

8.2 General Logic and Transcendental Logic

Pippin rightly stresses the fact that Hegel's logic concerns the making intelligible of *things*, not just of *our understanding of* things. He points to a distinction Adrian Moore (2012) has made, a distinction between (and I'm using Pippin's useful German renditions that appropriately refer to the understanding) *das Verständlichmachen des Verstehens* (Moore has 'the making sense of sense') and *das Verständlichmachen von Dingen* ('the making sense of things') (2016:174/ 2017:209), which Pippin argues are necessarily connected: the one cannot obtain without the other. In other words, the constitutive conditions for understanding understanding, or for how we *think* at all, are the *same* conditions that are constitutive of the understanding about objects, how we think *about objects*. This is a crucial, and centrally Kantian, point, which Pippin argues is taken up by Hegel, albeit in altered form. The making sense of the understanding or sense cannot be separated from the making sense of things, in the way they are, and this is precisely what is meant by Hegel when he says that logic is a metaphysics, that 'that which exists in and for itself is the conscious concept'. When making intelligible our ways of understanding things, we have not just made intelligible the way we, human beings, understand things, but rather how things *are*, namely such that they are seen to be intelligible.

The difference with Kant, supposedly, is that Kant seems, in the eyes of the Hegelian, to claim that we know only what can be made understandable *to us*, within the spatiotemporal domain that is species-specific to human experience. Pippin (and Hegel) want the identity between the two sets of conditions—making sense of understanding and making sense of things—to go deeper, and to do away with Kant's 'angeblich übermäßig subjektivistischen Ansatz' (2016:172): it rather concerns a real identity between thought and Being, from the incontrovertible perspective of thought, the concept (the *gewusster Begriff*), without the constraint of *human* spatiotemporal experience. Notice that, of course, we can abstract from the relation to objects or the world and just consider the conditions of mere understandability, and purely concentrate on logical matters of making sense. But the point is that this is an abstraction (and general logic is an abstraction) from the transcendental-logical vantage point from which objects and the world can be understood.

Pippin here appeals to Kant's distinction between a general logic and a transcendental logic, the latter of which alone can consider the relation to an *object* of thought, as something outside of thought, and the former merely expounds on the laws or rules governing relations between concepts, inferences, and judgements. Hegel is interested in the relation between the 'absolutely universal forms of sense [*Verständlichkeit*]' and 'a consideration of any possible thought of objects' (2016:175/2017:210). As with Kant, the logical form has an immediate influence on how we should understand the possibility of objective intentionality or object reference in thought. Kant's novel idea that the very forms of judgement are the categories, insofar as they relate to objects, is one that Hegel fundamentally shares. But Pippin thinks that Kant did not go far enough in affirming the identity between the forms of thought and the categories of objective knowledge or experience (cf. 2016:176). He maintains that the relation between general logic, which governs the rules of the forms of judgement or thought in general, and transcendental logic, which is about the forms of knowledge about objects, is far more intimate than Kant cares to admit (2016:177).

It appears that Pippin believes that the metaphysical deduction in and of itself already shows, or, suitably emended, should show that intimacy between the forms of thought and things. The distinction that Kant makes between general logic and transcendental logic is not as sharp as one may think, says Pippin. It is certainly not the case that general logic should be understood as a form to which content is being *added* (2016:177). If this is indeed meant as a criticism towards Kant, I think that it shows a few misunderstandings with respect to how Kant regards the relation between the metaphysical and transcendental deductions, and secondly, I should like to suggest that Kant's own understanding of that relation is much closer to Pippin's own presumptively corrected view of Kant's take on it or, at any rate, of the 'standard' Kantian reading (see Chapter 9).

(1) The distinction between general logic and transcendental logic does not map onto the distinction between the metaphysical deduction and the transcendental deduction; Kant only retroactively labels the sections that are considered to be part of the metaphysical deduction a metaphysical deduction (in B159, at the start of §26 of the Transcendental Deduction). This suggests that the metaphysical deduction is just a part of the overall project of a deduction of the categories, not something that can be uncoupled from it and fully assessed on its own. (Of course, one can decide to limit one's analysis to it, as e.g. the work of Wolff [1995] has shown is a worthwhile endeavour; but to be able to appreciate fully the extent and role of the metaphysical deduction one should include an account of the transcendental deduction.) As I have pointed out elsewhere (Schulting 2018b), the account in the metaphysical deduction fully belongs within the purview of transcendental logic, specifically the account concerning the *Leitfaden* (which has Pippin's particular interest), to the extent even that the

so-called table of judgement is as much a *transcendental* table, or a consideration of *transcendental* logic, as is the table of categories (see A97–8). Further, Kant indeed says at B159: 'In the *metaphysical deduction* the origin of the *a priori* categories in general was established through their complete coincidence with the universal logical functions of thinking, ...' If this is the central argument of the metaphysical deduction, and the categories are the forms of possible experience of objects, then the metaphysical deduction cannot be concerned just with *general* logic.

(2) Relatedly, Pippin seems to confuse the distinction between general and transcendental logic with the distinction between the forms of thought and the categories. I return to this aspect further below.

(3) For Kant, content is not simply *added*. His argument in the Deduction is concerned with the determination of content from within the subject's perspective, entirely and wholly internally. After all, the central issue is to explain the synthetic *a priori*. In no sense is there an a posteriori addition of content to form insofar as *determinate* content is concerned. What is at issue is showing, from a transcendental perspective, how the intrinsic link between forms of thought and things (objects) is formed, from the perspective of thought and thought only (given of course sensory content, but that would also not be denied by Hegel).

It is difficult to see how, on Hegel's account, the connection between the functions of thought and the categories can be seen as '*more* an interrelation', *more* intimate (*inniger*) (Pippin 2016:77/2017:211) than it already is in Kant's account. Kant claims indeed that the functions of thought *are* the categories insofar as they concern the relation to an object, or their objective validity. Kant writes at B143:

> The *categories* are nothing other than these very functions for judging, insofar as the manifold of a given intuition is determined with regard to them.

The 'insofar' (*so fern*) here does not so much denote a limiting condition, which would still suggest some sort of discrepancy between the functions of thought strictly speaking and the categories, as that it indicates the outward perspective *from* thought itself. As Pippin himself says, considerations of mere general logic are, also for Kant, an *abstraction* from transcendental logic. Transcendental logic is not an addendum to general logic, which is *inhaltslos* insofar as it has an unrestricted domain and not bound to a specific type or set of objects, or a distinct logic that *merely* concerns the examination of our understanding of objects. As Kant says, the 'synthetic unity of apperception', the quintessential marker of transcendental logic, 'is the highest point to which one must affix all use of the understanding, *even the whole of logic, and after it, transcendental philosophy*' (B134n., emphasis added). As Pippin points out—but he means this as a correction of a certain reading of Kant—transcendental logic reveals that *thought itself* is already intrinsically objectively valid; the transcendental deduction shows this, most clearly in the B-Deduction, where in the so-called 'first step' the very form of an object—an object in general, which is the concept of object that is instantiated in *any* object, spatiotemporal or not—is argued to be dependent on the synthetic unity of apperception, the principle that constitutes consciousness of the object (and the object of consciousness) as much as it constitutes self-consciousness.

Of course, Kant limits this objective validity, namely, to the extent that our knowledge is about empirical, spatiotemporal objects only. But nothing gets *added* to the intimacy between form of thought and the categories in this case. In the 'second step' of the B-Deduction, the intimacy between the functions of thought (or of judging) and the categories is shown to apply, in virtue of the figurative synthesis, to objects of sensibility too. Often the view is held by Kant commentators that the figurative synthesis is distinct from the intellectual synthesis, but I think this is a mistake. Though they are formally distinguishable, the figurative synthesis or the productive imagination is nothing but the *understanding's* effect on sensibility (B151–2), and since the understanding is the intellectual synthesis in abstraction from its effect on sensibility, the figurative synthesis is in fact the set of functions of thought insofar as they apply, as categories, to an actual, empirical object; in other words, the intimacy at the intellectual level equally applies to the level of sensibility, insofar as the categories are said to apply to it.[5]

The deep intimacy between understanding and imagination, or indeed their identity (in the non-trivial, transcendentally meaningful sense that Pippin rightly foregrounds), is made clear in e.g. B164:

> Now that which connects the manifold of sensible intuition is imagination, which depends on understanding for the unity of [the manifold's] intellectual synthesis and on sensibility for the manifoldness of apprehension.

I have interpolated 'the manifold's', where in the English text it says 'its', which might give the impression that it refers back to the imagination. But reading it in that last way does not make sense: it is not as if the intellectual synthesis *of the imagination* were at issue (what would that be?). Although the German *ihrer* can, grammatically speaking, refer to *Einbildungskraft*, it should be read as referring to

Anschauung; this also makes interpretative sense since the point of the passage is that the manifold in intuition is dependent on the understanding for its intellectual synthesis, which is carried out by the imagination with respect to the sensible intuition, and it is dependent on sensibility for its *manifoldness* of apprehension. (The Meiklejohn translation aptly, though somewhat freely, translates it as follows: 'Now that which conjoins the manifold of sensuous intuition is imagination, a mental act to which the understanding contributes unity of intellectual synthesis, and sensibility, manifoldness of apprehension.')

The imagination is truly the intermediary between sensibility and understanding—and Hegel had seen this clearly already early on, in *Faith and Knowledge*—but in order to be that intermediary it cannot be *distinct from either* understanding or sensibility; it must have both qualities, and somehow be identical to *both* understanding and sensibility in a certain respect, to be that true *a priori* intermediary. How can something be an intermediary of two entirely *different* things and still, in some sense, be *identical* to both of them? Such is accomplished by what Kant calls the productive imagination or the original-synthetic unity: an original unity that holds together what are opposites, understanding and sensibility. This is the deep identity between thought and object that Hegel, too, has in mind, and to which Pippin points—I think that Hegel is wrong though, or at least the early Hegel of *Faith and Knowledge*, to prise apart the imagination and the understanding by seeing the understanding as just a derivative form of the original synthetic unity that is the imagination; rather, as is made clear by the passages at B164 and B151, the *understanding itself* is the imagination in terms of the former's effect on sensibility; the imagination is how the *understanding* affects sensibility.[6]

8.3 Inseparability and Transcendental Content

Clearly, then, it is not just Hegel, but Kant himself who sees a deep intimacy between understanding and imagination insofar as the affection of sensibility, and thus the knowledge of objects, is concerned. The intimacy is even deeper on the purely intellectual level (i.e. in the 'first step' of the B-Deduction argument), where, just as Pippin argues, there is an *identity* between thought and object, more precisely, between the unity of apperception and the concept of an object. Some Kantians may baulk at this reading of the Deduction, but they are just mistaken to see a gap between the argument for self-consciousness and the objective unity of consciousness that defines an object or to believe that Kant's argument for the necessary application of the categories for our experience does not imply that the categories are in fact instantiated in the objects of our experience. These objections are based on (typically realist/naturalist) misunderstandings of the central point of the Deduction.[7]

Pippin is of course right to reject what he calls the 'two-step picture' of Kant's argument in the Deduction (2016:179/2017:212), according to which we first receive sensible content, and only after which we apply concepts (he refers to an 'Aufprägung der begrifflichen Form' [2016:15]) to sensible content.[8] But although some nonconceptualists may read it this way, I think no Kantian would read the *central* positive argument of the Deduction in this manner, as it would immediately raise the question as to how sensibility and the understanding *are in effect* a priori related if the understanding is only subsequently seen to apply concepts to a prior given content for any given cognitive judgement (Kant's use of terms like *Anwendung* at B149 do invite though this interpretation). Such an interpretation just fails to explain how sensible content and concepts are in fact a priori connected, so that cognition of objects is made possible by means of it.

So the content that is a priori bound with conceptual form is not some a posteriori content added to form afterwards. When Kant says that general logic is without content or that it abstracts from all content, he means of course the *transcendental* content that relates concepts to objects outside them, i.e. real objects. Kant writes:

> [G]eneral logic abstracts from all content of cognition [*allem Inhalt der Erkenntnis*], and expects that representations will be given to it from elsewhere, wherever this may be, in order for it to transform them into concepts analytically. Transcendental logic, on the contrary, has a manifold of sensibility *that lies before it a priori*, which the transcendental aesthetic has offered to it, in order to provide the pure concepts of the understanding with a matter, without which they would be without any content, thus completely empty.
>
> A76–7/B102, emphasis added

Compare the passage at B78/A54:

> As general logic it abstracts from all contents of the cognition of the understanding and of the difference of its objects, and has to do with nothing but the mere form of thinking.

Transcendental content, however, is not empirical *logical* content, namely such content of which judgements consist (the contingent logical content of any arbitrary judgement; cf. B142), and neither is it *sensible* content, namely the content of empirical intuitions (i.e. sensations). Rather, transcendental content is the combined set of the categories that make up the synthetic a priori unity of representations, defining an object, and also defining a judgement, for a judgement qua judgement is 'nothing other than the way to bring given cognitions to the *objective* unity of apperception' (B142). It is this content that needs to be 'added' to the general form of the way in which concepts are related (analytically), and from which general logic abstracts. Pippin would, I think, concur here. But of course there is not just this a priori *intellectual* element: it needs to be connected with sensible content somehow, and here Pippin appears to diverge. However, it is important to stress the fact that, for Kant, the way that sensible content is connected with the synthetic a priori intellectual aspect, the objective unity of apperception, is still wholly *a priori*. Hence, Kant says in the above quoted passage that transcendental logic has 'a manifold of sensibility' lying 'before it a priori'. That content is what he calls *pure* intuition, so it is not as if the sensible matter is offered to concepts a posteriori, or that concepts are a posteriori applied to pre-given sensible matter, i.e. *sensations* as such. The connection between concepts and their transcendental content, that is, between concepts and pure intuition as the necessary form of sensations, lies at the a priori level, namely, it occurs by means of the synthetic unity of apperception that determines sensibility inwardly (to use Pippin's wording [1989]), that is, by way of the figurative synthesis of the productive imagination. Transcendental content is not constituted by a literally external relation to something outside conceptual form, or by literally apprehending sensations one by one.

Content is therefore not in any way 'added' externally to conceptual form. But does this mean that Kant's distinctions are unwarranted or at least misleading? Pippin says that

> if this idea of some possible independent contribution from sensibility is dubious, either as a reading of Kant or in itself (if the two sources of knowledge are notionally distinct, but inseparable), then the general/transcendental logic distinction, which depends on this understanding of 'contentless' versus 'having content' or 'being provided with content exogenously' would have to be rethought as well.
>
> 2016:179/2017:212–13

I do not think this is right. First, as I have argued, the contribution by sensibility is not independent, also not for Kant, which is what Pippin implies. As Kant says, transcendental logic has the sensible manifold lying before it *a priori*, namely in the way that the transcendental aesthetic has offered it, hence in the form of a *pure* intuition: the connection with sensible content is with the necessary *form* of this content. The 'contentlessness' of pure general logic concerns the *abstraction* from thought's transcendental relation to objects. Transcendental logic is precisely not contentless because it relates to (sensible) objects, but not because it relates to them *externally*, as Pippin here suggests is how Kant is often read. I'd say that critiquing *this* Kant comes down to attacking a straw man.

The distinction between general and transcendental logic is meant to convey the idea that purely by means of an analysis of concepts and their interrelations, one does not get a connection with an object; it is in that sense that concepts are without content. To obtain that relation with an object, one must make a distinction between general logic, which looks merely analytically at conceptual relations—or truth-functional relations between propositions, as Pippin refers them as (2016:181)—and transcendental logic, which incorporates a connection to objects. But that has nothing to do with the presumed idea that content is supplied from the outside, 'being provided with content exogenously' (Pippin 2017:213). The only thing that comes from outside is the sensory material itself, *qua* sensory material; but Hegel would hardly deny that this indeed comes from outside thought (because it *is not* thought). The determination of this sensory content comes from 'inside', i.e. it is due to the spontaneity of the understanding, of thought itself (B151–2).

Pippin is right to criticize a reading of Kant's Deduction that takes there to be a nonconceptual content that (1) is in and of itself objectively valid and (2) is built upon by means of subsequent acts of judgement (or understanding), such as for example Robert Hanna (2008) believes. Such readings do not make sense in the Kantian context, where it is precisely the goal of the Deduction to demonstrate how it is possible that we can determine, *a priori*, how thought content and sensory content hook up *inwardly*, which justifies our conceptual claims about empirical objects. If the contribution by sensible content, more precisely, 'transcendental content', were really supplied 'from the outside', one would be none the wiser from any argument in the Deduction that supposedly showed how we are justified in making claims about objects, how pure concepts are justifiably (necessarily) employed *in* any judgement that says that some *a* is F. If it were true that such content is supplied from the outside, Kant could not have shown the fundamental intimacy between the pure concepts and empirical knowledge of objects, precisely the goal of the Deduction. But the adjective 'transcendental' in 'transcendental content', which is mentioned in the *Leitfaden* passage (B104–5/A79) already shows that this cannot be the case: it concerns content that *a priori* relates the pure concepts to objects outside concepts (whether empirical or imagined, such as mathematical objects). The transcendental content of which Kant speaks is the synthetic *a priori* element that secures this relation. A series of passages from the *Critique* show that this relation and the content at issue is produced entirely a priori, and so 'inwardly', in other words, *in* sensibility insofar as the manifold of sensations is apprehended by the understanding:

> [T]hat by means of which we cognize that and how certain representations (intuitions or concepts) *are applied entirely a priori*, or are possible (i.e., the possibility of cognition or its use a priori) [is called transcendental].
>
> B80–1/A56, emphasis added

> Transcendental logic, *since it is limited to a determinate content, namely that of pure a priori cognitions alone*, cannot imitate general logic in this division.
>
> A131/B170, emphasis added

> But the peculiar thing about transcendental philosophy is this: that in addition to the rule (or rather the general condition for rules), which is given in the pure concept of the understanding, *it can at the same time indicate a priori the case to which the rules ought to be applied*.
>
> B174/B135, emphasis added

> [T]he synthesis alone is that which properly collects the elements for cognitions and unifies them *into a certain content*.
>
> A77–8/B103, emphasis added

Sometimes Kant seems to say that *experience* gives us the matter to which pure concepts can be applied, e.g. at B87–8/A63: '[E]xperience ... itself alone can give us the matter (objects) to which those pure concepts of the understanding can be applied.' But this should by no means be read as if the categories were literally 'being provided with content exogenously'. In this passage, Kant makes more of a global argument about the fact that logic in and of itself cannot provide us with a connection to objects; for that we need to take recourse to experience. But how this is to proceed will have to be explained in the body of the Analytic of Concepts, in the sections that follow this particular passage in the introductory section of the Analytic.

Pippin's point that Kant's general logic is not to be conflated with a contemporary notion of a formal logic that considers truth values is well taken, but in my view this does not warrant conflating general logic with transcendental logic (Pippin writes that no 'strenge Trennung von allgemeiner und transzendentaler Logik statt[findet]' [2016:181]). Pippin argues that logic, for Kant (as for Hegel), concerns intelligibility (*Verständlichkeit*). But I believe, Kant's remarks about general logic do seem to say that this intelligibility should be seen merely in terms of how concepts are analytically related (and, by implication, how judgements in inferences etc. are analytically related). Even though this is not formal in the contemporary sense, those relations which general logic, in Kant's sense, considers are purely formal in the sense of abstracting from the content of cognition of objects, and so it considers questions of logical validity, governed merely by the rules of logic (primarily the principle of non-contradiction and the principle of excluded middle). Perhaps the point that Pippin wants to make is that general logic and transcendental logic are not two distinct logics in terms of separably 'operable' or 'operative' in any judgement. Transcendental logic is a specification of the possibility of logic as a theory of understandability (in Pippin's sense), while general logic abstracts from this specification, but is governed by it nonetheless. This would be in agreement with Kant's understanding of the relation between general and transcendental logic (see again the earlier quoted footnote to B133–4).[9]

Pippin appears to confuse the distinction between general logic and transcendental logic with the distinction between the forms of thought and the categories. That the very distinction between the forms of thought and the categories is only formal and that in an actual judgement the forms of thoughts *are* in fact the categories, and thus show the identity of the form of thought and the categories, does not warrant conflating general and transcendental logic. In fact, only making the distinction between general logic and transcendental logic enables one to appreciate this point about the intimate relation between the forms of thought and the categories. General logic (in Kant's sense) does not make (and does not *need* to make) the distinction between it and transcendental logic, and so does not see that the forms of thought *are* intrinsically objectively valid—have extensional content, and refer to substances and their properties— and so have cognitive content that goes beyond the *logical* content of conceptual relations (i.e. intensional content) (cf. Pippin 2016:184).

Precisely the distinction between general and transcendental logic thus enables us to appreciate the fact that discursive logic, employed in judgements, in and of itself provides relation to an object, to *cognitive content* strictly speaking. Only *transcendental* logic makes this clear. Another way to make this point is to say that transcendental logic is a distinctive and distinct *perspective* on logic, which alone exhibits the objective validity of our thought forms, or in other words, that the latter *are* the categories. So in a way, as I suggested above, one may agree with Pippin in saying that there are not so much two distinct *kinds* of logic, which are operative independently of and or even concurrently with each other; rather, there are two different, distinguishable perspectives, for which there are two distinguishable types of account—a *general* and a *transcendental* logic—of the one logic that is paradigmatic for human thinking, namely an Aristotelian-based discursive logic.

Pippin is of course right to say that the Transcendental Deduction needs to prove that concepts apply to intuitions of objects, in order to finally prove that categories are instantiated in the objects of our judgements (2016:184). It seems though that Pippin dismisses the need for such a *transcendental* deduction— elsewhere (Pippin 2014), he says that all we need is an updated *metaphysical* deduction. This is unsurprising if we realize that Pippin's Hegelian reading of Kant wants to do away with any reliance on *a priori* or *pure* intuition, as absolutely distinguishable from concepts (though he would still need the first part of the B-Deduction[10]). But Pippin's claim (2016:184) that Kant himself points to a blurring of the distinction between intuition and concepts does not seem warranted at all by the passages he quotes (most importantly, the *Leitfaden* passage). Moreover, the dismissal of pure intuition notwithstanding, Hegel's point is much closer to Kant's view than Pippin acknowledges. Pippin writes the following:

> [W]enn Hegel zu erklären versucht, was *er*—im Gegensatz zu Kant—tut, indem er 'Inhalt in die Logik einführt', macht er deutlich, dass er weder von der Vielzahl empirischen Inhalts, der angeschauten Mannigfaltigkeit, spricht noch lediglich von gedanklichem Inhalt im Sinne des logischen Gehalts—etwa der Subjekt-Prädikat-Form. Stattdessen sagt er etwas, das zwar näherer Erläuterung bedarf, das aber die ... Idee ... aufruft, dass die Kategorien den 'Rahmen' der Bedeutung jeder möglichen Bezugnahme auf Gegenstände bilden.
>
>> 'Mit dieser Einführung des Inhalts in die logische Betrachtung sind es nicht die *Dinge*, sondern die *Sache*, der *Begriff* der Dinge, welcher Gegenstand wird.'
>
> 2016:185, quoting Hegel, my underlining

But this is precisely, not in opposition to Kant, but in conformity with Kant's own claim, namely, an object is defined as that in whose concept a manifold of representations has been unified (B137), and *this* is the transcendental content introduced into our concepts, which makes our pure concepts objectively valid, that is, binds purely logical form to empirical content (cf. A103–5). Pippin himself quotes the formulation at B137 as Kant's own 'Hegelian' expression for the same view (2016:182n.39).

8.4 No Need for a Transcendental Deduction?

Of course, Pippin wants to argue, following Hegel, that a logic of the intelligibility of things does not stop at empirical spatiotemporal objects as such; unlike for Kant, there are no bounds of sense (cf. 2016:189n.53). Instead, Hegel's analysis is aimed at 'Formen des Denkens von Gegenständen, *von Gegenständen, die als verstehbar aufgefasst werden*', *in general*. That means that the forms of thinking objects, of conceiving of them *as intelligible in principle*, 'konstituieren alles das, was Gegenstände sein können'. They are the forms of objects, '*und zwar ohne Kants Einschränkung "nur für uns"*, denn er beruft sich in seiner Formulierung dieser Behauptung nicht auf nicht-begriffliche Formen der Sinnlichkeit' (2016:183, emphasis added). Quite clearly, then, Pippin argues, for Hegel, 'Kants Berufung auf die Form des Außerbegrifflichen als eines weiteren, beitragenden Faktors [ist] irreführend und überflüssig' (2016:183).

Kant must indeed show that sensible, spatially located objects in fact conform to the categories; there is no a priori guarantee that they do. This is the reason why a *transcendental* deduction of the categories is needed. Pippin rejects that this is necessary, that is, he rejects a reliance of the categories on nonconceptual intuitions for the objective validity of the categories; hence he rejects the need for a *transcendental* deduction. In a sense, the additional constraint that Kant adds, namely, the necessary schematization of the pure concepts to sensible intuitions is arbitrary, and not required by the argument about the identity between apperception and the concept of an object in general. Pippin's point can be taken to refer to Kant's distinction between the *thought* of objects and the *cognition* (or *knowledge*, i.e. *Erkenntnis*) of objects (B146), a distinction that parallels the so-called 'first and second steps' of the B-Deduction, and which concerns the distinction between objects *qua* conceived and objects of sensible experience (spatiotemporal objects). And here it seems that indeed, if one shears off the possible pure intuition of spatiotemporal objects, one can still have the conception of an object in general, which comports with the set of categories that first make up that a priori concept. It seems that Pippin has such a conception of object in mind for any judgement, an object as it is to be understood *in general*, and outside of whose perspective there just is no intelligible object; their concept or conceivability is all the intelligibility objects could have. Kant would agree that outside the concept of an object in general there indeed is *no* intelligible object.

For Kant, however, categories first have genuine objective validity in a judgement only if and when they are applied to sensible objects, requiring their intuition, one way or the other. Of course, they still have *meaning* even apart from that application, but they do not refer to objects strictly speaking. In abstraction from their application, categories just have intensional meaning. It does not seem possible to employ categories other than in judgements about objects, which means to apply them to those spatiotemporal objects about which we judge. Pippin's Hegel, who conceives of the categories as those concepts which 'den "Rahmen" der Bedeutung jeder möglichen Bezugnahme auf Gegenstände bilden' (2016:185), does not, it seems to me, go beyond Kant's mere formal conception of an object (the categories forming the concept of an object in general, beyond which there is no possible conception of an object strictly speaking)—and perhaps Pippin concurs. However, Hegel wants to talk about 'die Vernunft dessen, *was ist*' (cited at 2016:185), but it is difficult to see how Hegel can assume that reason as such can provide us the reference to real objects, to what *is*, without reliance on the relation to pure intuition. Notwithstanding the fact that, as Hegel frequently claims, the Concept produces its own *Wirklichkeit*—by which Hegel intends to disabuse us of the idea that our knowledge claims were about *external* reality, or reality out there, *apart from* our conception of it—he needs to be able to differentiate between merely imagined objects—like ghosts or cherubim, say (cf. A96)—and real ones, even if we do not define reality strictly in terms of empirical-physical reality (the latter a persistent complaint from Hegelians against Kant).

Pippin (cf. 2016:185n.43) is of course right that intuition does not *add* anything to the conceptual content of an object, otherwise it would not be the same object to which I applied a concept and of which I had an intuition. But that does not mean the intuition of the object is not needed for the concept to refer to some particular that is actually existent. The reference is not fixed by means of an *external* determination (whatever that might be), but still the relation between concept and an intuition needs to be specified in order for the reference to an actual object to be fixed. The concept cannot in and of itself fix this reference. Obviously, Hegel does not mean that the actuality of the object is reduced to or produced by the concept; just its *objectivity*, or *intelligibility* as an object is wholly dependent on the concept; it is the *concept* of a thing or object that is object or product of thought (as activity; see Pippin 2016:186). This is actually quite similar to what Kant wants to say, albeit that any epistemic role for any form of sensible intuition, which is presupposed by the discursive logic that Kant espouses (B145), seems to have no equivalent in Hegel: even apart from the question of application to spatiotemporal objects, Hegel's concepts do not require *any* manifold of representations in an *intuition* at all or any combination of such a manifold; all there is, it seems, is a coherent arrangement of relations among concepts only. But even apart from this peculiarity, there is a distinction, however, between saying that the categories together constitute what it means to refer to an object, namely by means of what Kant calls the transcendental object, outside which there is nothing to compare it with (A104), and the actual instantiation of that concept in a really existing object; and this marks the crucial difference with Kant's conception of the possible knowledge of an object. Kant writes:

> Hence the categories require, beyond the pure concept of the understanding, *determinations of their application to sensibility in general (schema), and without these are not concepts through which an object can be cognized* [*erkannt*] and distinguished from others, but only so many ways of thinking of an object for possible intuitions and of giving it its significance [*Bedeutung*] in accordance with some function of the understanding (under the requisite conditions), i.e., of defining it; they themselves cannot therefore be defined. . . . . The pure categories, however, are nothing other than the representations of things in general insofar as the manifold of their intuition must be thought through one or another of these logical functions . . . .
>
> A245, emphasis added

8.5 Absolute Identity of Subject and Object

For Kant nor Hegel is there discontinuity between conceptuality and sensibility. Hegel reads this more absolutely than Kant though. For Kant, there is still the possibility that some subcognitive forms of sensibility—animal sensibility, the way infants experience, subcognitive coping or cognitive abnormalities in adult behaviour[11]—do not comport with our standard conceptual forms of making intelligible. More importantly, Kant's perspective is more modest and analytically stringent than Hegel's: it seems that Hegel has more confidence in the 'in principle' intelligibility of *Being* per se, whereas for Kant Being is intelligible *only insofar* as the cognizing subject *takes* it to be intelligible, with the additional constraint of our knowledge necessarily being conditioned on it having to be related to sensible objects for our acquaintance with objects to count as knowledge. Pippin seems to say that for Hegel too there is an identity between the object *being* intelligible and *my taking* it to be so, effectively the same as what Kant asserts (minus the additional sensibility constraint).

But I venture to say that Hegel's claim is slightly different than Kant's. From a strictly Kantian perspective, the identity is one constituted by the subject *taking* the object to *be* in certain ways, which by the same token restricts that identity to the subject's perspective without this leading to relativism about knowledge. Hegel seems to be saying that Being *lets* itself be known in virtue of our conceptuality, rather than that its intelligibility is dependent on our merely *taking* it so. This is reflected by what I earlier quoted Pippin as saying: 'Wer auf das Sein mit der Frage der Intelligibilität blickt, dem blickt es intelligibel entgegen' (2016:18). The identity between object and subject—which constitutes intelligibility in the way that this identity is 'apperceivable', so to speak—is one that is reflective of Being itself, not *just* of our perspective on it. This is why, in *Faith and Knowledge*, Hegel criticizes Kant for first proposing this identity between subject and object, established by means of the original synthetic unity of apperception, and subsequently weakening this insight into what Hegel calls 'absolute identity' by assigning this original unity merely to the human understanding, which Hegel sees as rather derivative of that unity.[12]

In the *Science of Logic*, Hegel further develops this insight into the absolute identity of subject and object, whereby 'absolute' should be read as expressive of a lifting (*aufheben*) of Kant's restriction to what the *understanding* understands and as instead simply asserting Being's own intelligibility, because the Kantian restriction shows to be an arbitrary one (at least, within the Hegelian conceptual scheme). More precisely, the absolute identity constitutes the synthetic a priori unity that is manifested in the reciprocally determining relations between contrasting pairs of pure concepts, starting with Being and Nothing, that is, in the way each contrasting concept is shown to be a priori and reciprocally related with its putative opposite and hence to any successive concept that a priori combines, synthesizes, two supposedly contrasting concepts. The a priori synthesis between any two contrasting concepts shows both their identity and their contrast; this a priori synthesis is in turn united with a subsequent contrasting concept that is equally a priori synthetically united with the preceding synthesis. The 'a priori' aspect is just indicative of the fact that this can all be made clear purely by attending to the logical implications of concepts. (This is a complex story, which I cannot tell here.) Since Hegel starts with the most immediate and basic concepts, there is no reason, inherent to the dialectical logic of showing the synthetic a priori relation between pure concepts, to assume that there is anything left, at the end of the complete conceptual analysis, that remains absolutely *outside* that analysis to which the combined set of pure concepts would have to be applied in order for these pure concepts to be instantiated in Being itself, so to speak.

By contrast, Kant's own analysis of the synthetic a priori is constrained by the fundamental assumption that objectively valid knowledge can be knowledge of empirical (that is, mathematical-physically determinable) objects only. This is of course a legitimate assumption—and Kant's premise is indeed the existence of such objects, as well as the science that studies these objects—but one may argue that Hegel is right to say that this perspective is rather limited or that, in a sense, it is philosophically dissatisfying, since such an analysis presupposes too much; i.e. it assumes as unproblematic the existence of mathematical-physical knowledge or science *as paradigmatic of* possible knowledge. Why would religious knowledge or historical knowledge, say, be *less* knowledge than mathematical-physical knowledge? This has of course nothing to do with expanding the scope of what can be *empirically* known, that is, going beyond the bounds of sense, but everything with keeping the domain of possible human experience as wide and *diverse* as possible. What I believe Hegel is claiming is that no specific criterion, such as a priori forms of intuition, let alone empirical criteria, should be taken as an a priori constraint on what is *philosophically* and thus conceptually intelligible, on what is within the bounds of reason—and arguably, even Kant sought to examine the possibility of the intelligibility of phenomena that are not within the bounds of sensibility (cf. his accounts of morality, aesthetic judgement and religion). Needless to say that Hegel does not mean hereby to claim that we do not need empirical intuitions in those cases where perceptions of *empirical* (logico-mathematically determinable) objects are involved.

But the problem remains that Hegel assumes that there *is no* distinction between pure concepts (categories) and *pure* intuitions (space and time), that space and time are just types of concept or categories, like Being, *Dasein*, infinity etc. This would appear to mean that Hegel is not able to specify *how* the pure concepts are instantiated in *given spatiotemporal particulars*, but just *that* space and time are pure concepts that are necessary for the intelligibility of any particular object, as much as other pure concepts are. In and of itself, this is not a problem; Hegel just has a *different* conceptual methodology in approaching the problem of the intelligibility of Being than Kant's more specific methodology, when it comes to the analysis of the intelligibility of percepts. Hegel's perspective might, in this sense, be more global (less specific). In another sense the Hegelian more systematically conceptual approach is philosophically more parsimonious in that it does not have the burden of initially presuming, in the lead-up to the Deduction proper, that there is a 'gap' between intuitions and concepts, which in the conclusion is then to be seen as bridged. As Pippin's discussion shows, one might be tempted to say that there is no gap to be bridged in the first place (2016:302). Though I think it is a mistake, as an interpretation, to approach Kant's Deduction in this way, it seems apt to see Hegel's own approach to the issues for which Kant offers a solution in this 'gap-denying' manner: for Hegel, there simply is no gap that needs bridging, given his denial of a sharp distinction between pure concepts and pure intuitions, and given the systematic and consistently immanent deduction of the pure concepts, which, once one has reached the end point of the dialectic in the absolute idea, does not require any application, schematization or demonstration of the instantiation of concepts in objects or intuitions of objects. Although for Kant too it is the case that there is no gap between the pure concepts and sensibility, via pure intuition, Hegel's insistence on the absolute identity of subject and object more overtly highlights the intrinsic intelligibility of things, indeed of Being itself.

8.6 Concluding Remarks

To make this last point without insisting too much on the differences between Kant's and Hegel's approaches, we should be focusing on the central premise of both Kant's and Hegel's metaphysics. Their vision of metaphysics is principally concerned with showing that the categories are, *by their nature*, categories of the objects, *as* we encounter them in actuality (in Being, in more Hegelian speak), and that since—and this is the revolutionary Kantian claim, which Hegel fully endorses—the categories are *nothing but functions of thought*, insofar as these are directed at objects, objects and our *judgements* about them reduce to each other. This should be taken in as radical a sense as it sounds: there is no fundamental discrepancy, or 'gap', between the object and my judgement that would, in principle, prevent me from knowing the object as *it is* (*qua* determinate object). There is no good reason to believe such could be the case, and every reason to be confident that reason has the capacity, in principle at least, to know reality.[13] There exists a deep intimacy between thought and objects. Of course, I could be wrong about some empirical property of an object *a*, but I could never be wrong about the necessary categorial forms of the object *a* about which I judge, correctly or incorrectly, that it is F, say.

Any putative opposition between subject and object, between a concept of an object and an intuited empirical (spatiotemporal) object, obtains only in the formal analysis of the presupposed constitutive elements of objectively valid judgement, i.e. in the Deduction itself (this *formal* opposition is reflected in the so-called 'two step' procedure of the B-Deduction); this is the business of transcendental philosophy, an analysis of what is originally synthetically combined. In an *actual* judgement or experience, I judge about the object such as it presents itself, as concrete object, to me empirically—the way it presents itself objectively strictly correlates with the objective unity of my apperception that defines judgement, but only *within* the subjective perspective of apperception. There is no gap here: my apperception is a 'reflection' of the very objectivity of the actual object that I thereby perceive. Kant's analysis in the Deduction is an abstraction of the constitutive elements of what actually takes place integrally, and these constitutive parts should not be taken factually (as if these parts were localizable in space and time). With Hegel the abstract analysis of the dialectical logic turns out somewhat more favourable, that is, the way that the constitutive parts manifest themselves gradually, in the course of the logic, as 'logically' implicative admits less of misapprehending this as requiring a further instantiation in the *real* world. For with the thoroughgoing deduction of the concepts all relevant determinations of the object will *have already been* given with my *concept* of the object. To persist in asking the question of the application of concepts to a *real* object is pure abstract gesticulation; it is to misconceive of what logic, in Hegel's sense—namely as a metaphysics—actually *means*.

In some sense, then, one might say that the aforementioned Hegelian-Aristotelian idea, which Pippin quotes, namely that 'Zu sein heißt, auf bestimmte Weise verständlich zu sein' is also signalled by Kant's definition of an object as a unity of my representations, as Pippin also suggests, albeit that, given Kant's interest in an analysis of the *how* of the possible instantiation of particulars in Euclidean space, but more importantly his different systematic methodology,[14] Kant has certain qualms about extending this, his own, fundamental insight about objectivity to the realm of Being *simpliciter*.

9
Hegel, Transcendental Philosophy, and the Myth of Realism

9.1 Introduction: Hegel's Supposed Naturalism

One of the ostensible aspects of Hegel's idealism that captivates the attention of naturalists is the idea that nature or reality is not reducible to what subjects make of nature or reality, but is rather that into which the cognitive agent or subject is herself integrated. The subject is as much *part* of nature as it has *knowledge of* nature, and as such it is constrained and determined by it. Hegel is often read as if he abandoned the transcendental perspective that Kant inaugurated in philosophy, whereby nature or reality, insofar as the physical realm of spatiotemporal objects is concerned, depends for its objectivity wholly on the transcendental subject. Hegel, it is thought, rejects such a subjective, transcendental idealism in favour of an idealism that is actually a fully-fledged realism in all but name, a realism *sans phrase* which makes substantial claims about the fundamental structure of reality itself and that encompasses knowledge about how things in themselves are constituted. Unlike Kant, Hegel is considered a thoroughbred naturalist about things and their existence.

To give a very recent example: Paul Giladi (2017) for all his acuity in succinctly enumerating the criticisms that Hegel raises against Kant as they are standardly conceived, keeps perpetuating the Hegelian myth—a myth that originates in Hegel himself, in his less felicitous statements on Kant (Giladi appropriately quotes *Encyclopædia*, §§ 41z and 42z)—that Kant's transcendental or formal idealism fatally suffers from a psychological subjectivism, a charge that I explicitly sought to counter in my book *Kant's Radical Subjectivism*.[1] This is the myth that—and this is how Giladi himself puts it—'the *structure*, *order*, and *unity* of empirical reality are all derived from *us* and that thought and being are fundamentally separate from one another', and that apparently *because* the objectively structuring categories are *applied by us*, they are not, or at least not *ipso facto*, really instantiated by the things themselves, in being itself so to speak, and thus not *truly* objectivating, but in the end *merely* subjective.

Giladi says that '[f]or Hegel, what Kant should not have argued was that the necessity and universality provided by conceptual form that constitutes the formal unity and order of empirical reality is not inherent to the world itself', that 'on Kant's account, the objectivity of representation provided by the pure concepts is not a full-blooded objectivity, i.e. the objectivity is in some sense artificial and contingent', that 'the categories confer on objects the formal characteristics of objectivity (such as causality, substantiality, etc.), but leave us cut off from things in themselves', and that 'it is because the formal characteristics of ordinary objects and the formal structure of empirical reality are derived from us that the Kantian account of the objectivity of representation, for Hegel, is not a full-blooded one'. In other words, the objectivity of *our* categorially structuring, on Kant's account, is 'not *genuinely objective*'.

This seems, at first blush, a correct picture of how *Hegel portrays* Kant's idealism—not, to be sure, of *Kant's own* view of his idealism, as I pointed out in some detail in my book *Kant's Radical Subjectivism*. But even with respect to Hegel's portrayal of Kant's idealism there are a couple of mistaken assumptions here that persist among Hegelians discussing Kant's philosophy, and that create the continuing misunderstanding of the core of Kant's Copernican thought; and I am also not so sure if this way of framing Hegel's criticisms captures what Hegel has in mind with his own brand of idealism (and an *idealism* is certainly what Hegel has in mind). Most conspicuously, their criticism of Kant in this regard trades on an ambiguity about the notion of 'objectivity'. The language that Giladi employs is emblematic of this misrepresentation: we are supposedly 'subjecting the world to our filtering' and it is in this way that we claim to acquire knowledge about the world, which comes at an 'epistemological cost'. Worse, our discursive cognition of reality is 'some kind of *viol cognitif*, where reality is forced to *conform* to concepts', wrongly suggesting—a brilliant trouvaille though that turn of phrase is!—that our discursive way of knowing *perverts* reality, rather than that it accurately captures it. If the objectivity were indeed established in virtue of such 'subjecting' or 'filtering' or 'cognitive violating', the alleged objectivity would not amount to real knowledge *of* the world as it is, *objectively*, and the charge of subjectivism would be most apt.

Most remarkably, Giladi even suggests that the knowledge established by the categories, on account of Kant's theory, *is nothing but* 'self-knowledge', suggesting that Kant's account of knowledge reveals a form of 'solipsism'. This is a most radical critique of Kant's thought about what constitutes objectivity, one that I think goes much further than Hegel's own critique. Giladi differentiates the form of solipsism he attributes to Kant from 'metaphysical', 'epistemological' and 'methodological' solipsism, but given how damaging the charge of solipsism is, I do not see how his version could be differentiated from 'epistemological' solipsism, namely that 'we can only know the contents or our mental states', basically saddling Kant with a form of Berkeleianism (i.e. a bad phenomenalism, in contrast to the phenomenalism that I attribute to Kant, which is specifically *not* an ontological phenomenalism that says that the objects of our cognition are just the sensations that we have).[2]

I think Giladi's reading of Kant's theory of the conceptual constraints of objectivity, i.e. the categories, *and* his own reading of what Hegel's critique of Kant in this respect is supposed to be about, are both mistaken.

First, Kant's category theory is not at all subjective in the bad sense—which in Schulting (2017a) I differentiated from subjective in the good, Critical, sense, namely the 'radically' subjectivist variant—and so least of all 'solipsist' in whatever sense. There is a way though in which Kant's idealism might still be seen as unnecessarily restrictive, seen from a more Hegelian perspective (see the comments on John McDowell below).[3]

Secondly, Giladi's proposal for reading Hegel's metaphilosophical critique strikes me as thoroughly anti-Copernican, suggesting that Hegel harks back to a pre-Kantian metaphysics, which sees our forms of thought as conforming to the objects, rather than the objects as a priori conforming to our thought forms as it is on the Copernican hypothesis (see Chapter 2). To believe that Hegel does hark back to a pre-Kantian metaphysics is of course an interpretative option, but I do not think that Giladi means it that way. Often there is a lot of hedging, among so-called ontological or metaphysical interpretations of Hegel's philosophy, about what it really means to say that Hegel is a post-Kantian philosopher. Often it is mere lip service to say that Hegel builds on Kant, or is as much a *critical* philosopher as Kant is. My impression is that it is not really understood why Hegel himself alludes so often to, and frequently explicitly mentions, the importance of Kant's revolution in thought for his own system of thought; numerous attempts are made to play down the importance of passages in e.g. the *Science of Logic* that clearly indicate the influence of Kant, even in its most 'subjectivist' form (and, as may be clear, I take these subjectivist-sounding passages in the positive, radical sense), on Hegel's own thought. This is a long story of course, which I cannot even begin to address in the short space of a chapter.

9.2 Category Theory and Epistemological Relativism

First, concerning Kant's category theory and the scepticism or epistemological relativism that it supposedly entails, I believe it would be mistaken to think like so many Hegelians that on account of Kant's theory that knowledge (in Kant's sense of *Erkenntnis*) is established in virtue of category application we must remain sceptical about whether, if the categories are applied by us to our experience of objects, the categories are actually instantiated in the objects themselves, that is, that the objects themselves exemplify the categories that we need to apply in order for us to be able to experience objects. An oft-heard Hegelian complaint—a criticism too frequently also shared by many Kant scholars (see Schulting 2018a, d)—is that Kant's absolutization of subjectivity—seeing subjective form as external to content—does not reach nature as such, that is, it does not reach objective or common reality, the 'absolute', or the 'really real' (Hegel, GuW, 4:325), committing Kant to a kind of scepticism or at least some form of relativist epistemology. Hegel might be taken here to mean by objects things in themselves (in Kant's sense) and not objects of experience, but this is not always clear, neither with Hegel nor with Hegelians. Sometimes, Hegelians—but also Hegel himself, to be fair—seem to think that Kant just means that the categories apply to how we *experience* objects or nature, and not to nature or the objects in nature qua their existence *as* nature or objects. But, clearly, without the categories there would not *be* nature or objects, in Kant's view (cf. A126f.). This indicates that the categories are not just the necessary conditions of *experience* of nature and object, but are equally and at the same time constitutive of them as being nature and object. Sally Sedgwick, for one, appears to deny, in her important recent book *Hegel's Critique of Kant*, that the categories are sufficient for the objectivity of the content of our cognition. She writes:

> [F]rom the necessity of the categories in unifying the given manifold into a thinkable content, it does not follow that the categories ... conform to the independently given sense content (the matter of experience) itself. It is one thing to claim ... that we need a priori concepts in order to think or judge some sense content; it is quite another to claim ... that our concepts can be demonstrated to reflect the nature of that independently given sense content. To claim the latter, according to Kant, would be to overreach the limits of what we can know.
>
> Sedgwick 2012:87n.16; cf. 2012:89, 92, 94, 95n.28

But to say that the categorial form of cognition cannot 'reveal the reality of that content itself' (Sedgwick 2012:87f.) because allegedly form is merely subjective, surely reflects a misunderstanding of the goal of Kant's deduction of the categories, which is precisely to demonstrate how the categories apply to the sense content given in intuitions which directly refer to actually existing objects that affect our senses, and so apply not just to our *experience* of, or *judgement* about, objects, but also to the objects of our experience or judging, to sense content itself. The categories are the necessary *and* (formally[4]) sufficient conditions for both experience and objects. There is nothing outside of these conditions, *cum* the givenness of sense content, which could give us *more* objectivity.

Certainly, there are still things in themselves, which *as such* are independent of those conditions. Kant's radical subjectivism constitutes an idealism with respect to the object as being in some sense dependent on our judging, but this is not the idealism of Berkeley, say, which denies the mind-independent existence of things in themselves. Kant's radical subjectivism ensures that we can explain the intimate correspondence between knowledge and object as a function of our own capacity to judge, namely the objective unity of apperception, and that at the same time things insofar as their existence is concerned are not reduced to being a function of our representations. Whereas Kant's subjectivism is thus characterized by both a metaphysical and epistemological element—metaphysical because not only the knowledge or experience of an object but also the known object itself is a function of transcendental apperception—the thing in itself retains its existential independence.

This in no way renders our knowledge of objective reality only relative because supposedly it would not reach the things in themselves. Such a conclusion ignores the fact that the object determined by the judging subject is the appearance of the thing itself, *for* that judging subject. Although the judging subject does not know the thing as such, i.e. *in itself*, he does know the thing in the way in which it appears to him as an object. In point of fact, the fact that the subject does not know the thing as a thing in itself, namely as it is independently of judgement, follows logically from the fact that knowledge of something is not possible apart from the necessary conditions under which such knowledge is first possible: For how can I *judge* of something that it is so and so *independently of judgment*?[5] But what should be clear is that there is no suggestion that the judgement is not about the thing that has an independent *in itself* existence.

Things are therefore knowable if and only if they are subject to the necessary conditions for knowledge, and they are subject to those conditions only when they appear to us (are something *for* us), not as things in themselves.

Knowledge of objects is thus possible only if the necessary a priori conditions for knowledge of objects are met; outside of those necessary a priori conditions knowledge is *ex hypothesi* not possible. This means that things in themselves, that is, things as they are *independently* of the conditions under which alone they (as objects) can be known, cannot be known as such (as things in themselves) under the conditions under which alone objects can be known. (To be sure, this is the *conclusion* of the 'long' argument for the necessary conditions of knowledge that is provided in the Transcendental Deduction, these necessary conditions being the twelve categories and the pure forms of space and time. Things in themselves do not meet these conditions of knowledge, and this is to be expected from assuming the Copernican hypothesis that says that knowledge of the possibility conditions of objects is possible only on condition that objects conform to our forms of intuition and understanding, rather than that our understanding and intuition conform to the way things are in themselves.)

As already suggested, the criticism raised against the supposed mere subjectivity of Kant's categories, as external to objective reality, is further ambiguous about whether the objective reality of empirical objects, i.e. the whole of nature, is meant, or the noumenal realm of things in themselves, which is not knowable and exists independently of the determining mind. It is hardly plausible to argue that Hegel thinks that we do know that *noumenal* realm (in the sense Kant means). But if it is the whole of empirical nature that Hegel believes the Kantian categories are external to (and there are sometimes indications that he thinks this), then it is clear he misconstrues Kant. In that case, the Hegelian critique of Kantian idealism as a merely subjective idealism, which denies us knowledge of reality itself, is misguided. In other words, either Hegel is completely mistaken about Kant or he means something entirely different than either claiming that we do know the *noumenal* realm after all or believing that on Kant's account nature cannot be known. Hegelians like Sedgwick, and it seems Giladi, believe that Kant should have argued that the categorial structures are not just subjective form but also the intrinsic form of being itself (of things in themselves). Sedgwick even talks about a 'two-way determination', in the sense that not only does the mind, in virtue of the categories, determine nature, being, or reality, but also nature, being or reality themselves in their turn determine the mind, in other words, that 'concept and content are *reciprocally* determining' (2012:68). I think this is much too simple a way of reading Hegel's critique of Kant, because it fails to capture the reason why Hegel sees himself as an *idealist*, and it makes Hegel's self-professed Kantianism entirely unintelligible.[6]

9.3 Is Hegel's Metaphysics Pre-Kantian?

More radically even than Sedgwick's thesis of the two-way determination of content and form, mind and world, Giladi (2017) believes that Hegel's view is that the structure and unity of the world are intrinsic to it and that it is then our capacity for thinking which can observe *this* structure and unity. Giladi writes:

> Our cognitive activity, according to Hegel, does not consist in being the sources of the unity in objects and does not consist in us being the sources of the unity of the world as a whole. Rather, what this activity consists of is our ability to detect the intrinsic unity of objects themselves and the intrinsic unity of the world as a whole (cf. *Encyclopædia*, §381 …). In other words, for Hegel, our discursive cognitive architecture, from the standpoint of dialectical Reason rather than nomothetic Understanding, is constituted in such a way that it enables the determinations of thought to reveal themselves as we refine our cognitive practices through inquiry. The activity of making sense of things through *Begriffe* does not seize the things they are directed at.

If I understand Giladi correctly, according to Hegel, the structure and unity of things *reveal* themselves to our capacity for reason—but apparently not to the understanding; it is not clear why not, and what, according to Giladi's picture of Hegel's view, makes that our reasoning capacity is superior to the capacity of our understanding. At any rate, to think that *we* construct the unity of objects is to 'misconstrue our own cognitive activity', says Giladi. For him, '[o]ur cognitive activity, according to Hegel, involves developing insights into how the world incorporates structures that can only be *uncovered* by thought' (emphasis added). It seems, on this reading, that the world contains dispositional properties that are discoverable by our reasoning capacity, suggesting some innate similarity between the structure of the world and the structure of our minds, or, reason. This appears to mean that Hegel upturns the very Copernican perspective which stipulates that we regard things as conforming to *our* forms of intuition and understanding, to reason. Our cognitive activity, on Giladi's reading of Hegel, merely consists in registering those structures of being that make themselves available for thought (note the term 'uncovered' used by Giladi, suggesting an a posteriori uptake). I am not sure if this does not hark back to a problematic pre-Kantian metaphysics, but I am certain that it is not in any way in alignment with the parameters set by the Critical philosophy. It is of course an interpretative possibility to read Hegel in this way, and I'm sure many examples in past literature can be found which propound similar views. But I am also unconvinced that it is a good interpretation of Hegel, and in fact I believe such a reading is directly contradicted by numerous passages in the Logic; this comports with my view that Hegel should be read in a way that does align with the parameters of the Critical philosophy.

By contrast, Stephen Houlgate, for one, thinks Hegel does indeed return to a pre-Kantian style rationalism: 'Hegel certainly reverts to the position of pre-Kantian metaphysics by claiming that pure logic can know being after all' (Houlgate 2018:104). In Houlgate's view, logic is also 'the direct thought, or intellectual intuition, of being and thus a metaphysics in a pre-Kantian rationalist sense.' But note that Houlgate does not mean to say that this constitutes a direct thought of what 'lies beyond thought', but rather of *thought* itself as pure being itself (2018:113). There is an identity between thought and being from the word go, even though this identity is still wholly indeterminate at the start of the Logic. Houlgate's view on this point is quite subtle and worth pursuing, but it is clear that he wants to differentiate his ontological reading here from Pippin's conceptualist take on the issue, by claiming that being is in some sense basic and irreducible to thought whilst also identical to it. This explains his view that Hegel is a pre-Kantian rationalist in the sense that thought maps onto being as what is properly basic.[7]

9.4 Metaphilosophy, Realism, and the Nature of Absolute Idealism

Hegel's chief worry about Kant's metaphilosophical stance is that it holds on to a type of philosophy that is unphilosophical in the sense that—in Hegel's view naturally—it is beholden to extra-philosophical constraints, such as in the case of Kant's theory of cognition the fact that our knowledge is bound by the senses: knowledge is really possible only because our concepts are constrained by sensible input in virtue of pure intuition. Hegel's complaint is that Kant's procedure is not sufficiently a priori, and hence it is not sufficiently philosophical, *speculative*, if you will, as a direct consequence of this reliance on sensibility.[8]

At crucial points in his account Kant recoils, Hegel believes, from thinking through the consequences of the assumptions that underpin his theory, most importantly the central place of empirical experience. As a result of this, Kant squanders the potential of absolute idealism—of 'genuine philosophy' as Hegel sees it, which is oriented towards 'the Absolute' rather than towards human experience—that Hegel detects in other central pillars of Kantian thinking, especially in the Deduction: foremost the productive synthesis of the imagination, which he interprets as that which binds concept and representational content at the fundamental level; in other words, a properly philosophical notion that Kant in the end downgrades to being just a function of the understanding, or even equates with the understanding (which, to be sure, is a correct *interpretation* of Kant).

The problem for Hegel is Kant's starting point, which issues from the blind assumption of discursive logic (i.e. Aristotelian logic), and the adoption of a representationalist language: 'a fixed Ego-point' (GuW, GW 4:332 [Hegel 1977:77]), a merely formal 'I', seeks to combine with material content it cannot provide itself. The problem here is the dualist starting assumption, which once assumed cannot be overcome—the formal and finite understanding becomes 'the stake of the absolute antithesis' (*der Pfahl des absoluten Gegensatzes*) (GuW, GW 4:323 [Hegel 1977:65]). This is of course a characteristic of Kant's way of thinking that in itself seems unproblematic: Kant's approach is not in principle internally inconsistent, given his basic metaphilosophical assumptions.

Hegel though makes it seem as if Kant's dualistic viewpoint *is* internally inconsistent or, more precisely, inconsistent with the essential characteristics of his Copernican thought, more in particular, the notion of the synthetic a priori. Hegel says that if our cognition rests fundamentally on an a priori synthesis, 'it surely contains determinateness and differentiation [*Unterschied*] *within* itself' (WL, GW 12:23 [Hegel 2010b:520], emphasis added). Determinateness is not provided by the sensible manifold—which delivers the material that is a necessary condition for real possibility—but is rather a function of thought itself. Hegel's point here is that even though the material *content*, empirical intuition or the manifold of sensations, is obviously not provided by thought, the fact that content is needed, and that content is the *other* of form (of the form of thought) is something that is wholly determinable and determined by thought and thought alone. There is nothing outside thought that is a determining factor in determining the material content. In other words, determinateness is not something *outside* thought/form nor even *between* thought/form and matter/content, by way of a 'two-way' determination such as Sedgwick and apparently Giladi propose, but is fully and completely *internal* to thought's own form, which is the form of the synthetic a priori (matter is just the determinable). This is Kant's own belief (see e.g. B151–2), so why, Hegel reasons, does Kant persist in being a dualist with respect to idealist form and material content?

In Hegel's view, Kant's philosophy shows a '"reflective" bias' (Schulting 2017a:348), and as said he chooses a particular type of logic (discursive), resulting in the kind of idealism that he adopts, and a preference for focusing on possible *empirical* knowledge. Connected with this is the fact that, as McDowell has aptly described it in his paper 'Hegel's Idealism as Radicalization of Kant' (McDowell 2009), in Kant spatiotemporality 'remains a sort of brute fact about us' (2009:76), which for Hegel is clearly an assumption that should not be playing a defining role in one's philosophical 'construction'. As McDowell puts it, not without a hint of drama:

> Transcendental idealism, which is just this insistence that the apparent spatiality and temporality of our world derive from the way our sensibility is formed, stands revealed as subjective idealism. *And the rot spreads*.... [I]t appears that in the context of the transcendental ideality of space and time, the very idea of the objects as they are given to our senses has to be seen as reflecting a subjective imposition.... Kant's whole construction is dragged down, by the transcendental idealism about space and time that is at its foundation, into being a subjective idealism.
>
> 2009:76–8, emphasis added

Though there is some controversy among Kant scholars about the connection between Kant's transcendental logic, more particularly the argument in the Deduction, and his doctrine of transcendental idealism, I think McDowell is mistaken about the fact that Kant's 'whole construction is dragged down' by the transcendental idealism about the *general* spatiotemporality of the objects we can know. For this doctrine is integral to Kant's discursive logic, which requires input from outside, and is thus in line with the principle of determination by which it is typified, insofar as it prevents us from knowing things as they are in themselves, i.e. as they cannot be *further* determined (things in themselves namely are fully determined, having all of their possible properties), and given the further characteristics of space and time that conflict with the simplicity as well as the complete determinacy of things in themselves.[9]

But he is of course right that Kant just accepts the thesis that Euclidean-based spatiotemporality is a brute fact about *our* experience of objects—and one may claim that that is not as such a basic *philosophical* principle that one *must* accept. In that sense McDowell is somewhat justified in saying that in order to rescue Kant's insights we should 'discard ... the frame' of transcendental idealism about spatiotemporality if, of course, we want to go along with the Hegelian line of approach—and to be sure nothing internal to Kant's logic says Kantians *must* accede to the Hegelian critique, contrary to what Hegel and Hegelians such as McDowell want us to believe. This means that the Kantian insights that Hegel does appraise positively—such as chiefly the notion of an original-synthetic unity of apperception—will morph into a different philosophical strategy, if that is the proper word, tackling philosophical problems differently, but still from a broadly Kantian perspective. This broadly Kantian perspective comprises the central idea that it is the capacity for thought (or reason) itself that determines what is objectively valid, not sensible input, nor any other exogenous ground or source or properly basic fact, nor reality itself, that provides the justification or warrant for our knowledge.

But it also means to emphasize and supplement the Kantian insight that we cannot, but also need not, go beyond our representations to seek the ground of the real possibility of our concepts. That is to say, in the Hegelian perspective it is no longer needed to rely, as Kant does for his Deduction argument, on *pure* intuition that provides our concepts with real possibility. Pure intuition does not lend any more warrant to our conceptual claims than is already provided by the determinative capacity of our judgement, given of course sensible input (Hegel does not deny that for some cognitive claims based on empirical evidence sensations are required). The whole 'second step' of the B-Deduction is, in light of this, an artificial add-on that can be relinquished once we give up the idea that our conceptual claims must be seen as necessarily grounded in the intuition of spatiotemporal objects and events for them to have objective validity, as it unnecessarily restricts the latter to a particular type of object, namely, objects of empirical perception. This does of course not mean that we are given free rein to let our imagination run riot; cognitive or conceptual claims still need to be assessed as to their objective validity, but this should instead happen wholly inter-conceptually, that is, in terms of how well concepts internally cohere. In the Logic itself, Hegel's version of the Deduction, this is done by showing that objectivity is increasingly determinately articulated in the logic of an array of systematically cohering *pure* conceptual elements, categories.

Hegel's account is not *anti*-reflective, but is rather focused on an internal reflection of reason on the reflective oppositions the absoluteness of which, according to Hegel, Kant, for all his critical discernment, left unchallenged. This suggests that the conceptual oppositions and their resolution—in terms of a relativization or *Verflüssigung*, as it were, of their absoluteness—are something internal to the *Concept*. And the Concept which is this operation of *Verflüssigung* is the synthetic a priori itself, or 'negativity', as Hegel comes to call it, which holds the opposites in check, as it were, that is, binds them but also first enables their differentiation. The Concept or self-consciousness is not a self-standing principle let alone a method but it is that which first shows, almost phenomenologically, in the course of the Logic and immediately from the very start of the Being logic, what it means that form and content or any seemingly contrasting concepts are opposites, but also are necessarily combinable for objectively valid cognition to be possible, and importantly, it shows *how* this dialectic proceeds.

This has nothing to do with a two-way determination between reality and the ideal form of the understanding, or reality itself being such that our forms of cognizing are receptive to those structures of reality that are somehow amenable to being cognized by us. Hegel is *more* of an idealist than Kant is, rather than less so; it is not for nothing that Hegel labels his idealism an 'absolute idealism', there is no deflationary way around it. There is no reality as such, that is, something that would be outside the Concept, outside what is ideal, which somehow determined concepts or our form of thought in the same way that concepts or our forms of thought determine reality. The 'real' is just an element of the conceptual repertoire at our disposal for making intelligible claims about anything, real or imagined, object or event, in virtue of the synthetic a priori, that is, in virtue of 'negativity' that is the relation between the pure concepts in our repertoire. There are no application conditions or schematization requirements for the concepts other than the internal logic of their cohering.

To ask the question 'Yes, but how do such concepts in the end apply to independent real things, for surely concepts do not *generate* reality?' is to misunderstand Hegel's metaphysical logic. Hegel does not make the metaphysically intemperate claim that the Concept generates reality *de re*, or in any existential sense, but nor is it necessary to bridge some sort of gap between concept and reality. What he does argue is that there is nothing about reality that we would be precluded *in principle* from knowing, and any possible object for knowledge is always inside the scope of our conceptual scheme, not *outside* it in the sense of it being absolutely independent requiring a bridging between it and our conceptuality. Much like Kant, in fact, an object for Hegel has its actuality in virtue of the form by way of which it is intelligible; it is not some existing thing on which properties supervene or that in some second step happens to be known by us, and happens to be conceptually determined by us. Its conceptual determinations fully capture the object's actuality, what it concretely means for that object to be *an object* with such and such properties, which should not be conflated with saying that the mind or *Geist* or Reason generates, in an existential sense, material stuff. For both Hegel and Kant, the central thought is the possibility of an object *as* an object and how the possibility of it being known is fundamentally informed by this conception of an object *as* an object. The form of an object is at the same time the form under which it can be known, for its form is nothing but the unity of apperception, or self-consciousness. There is no discrepancy here, a gap between the metaphysical or ontological and the epistemological, that needs bridging.

When Hegel talks about the 'Absolute' or, still in *Glauben und Wissen*, about 'absolute identity' he does not mean that the logic is 'closed' as if *per impossibile* it concerned a 'complete' system of positive factual claims or empirical truths that is not open to revision. Hegel's absolute idealism is as much (and not more than) about *possible* knowledge as Kant's transcendental idealism, but unlike Kant, Hegel does not tie down knowledge to the need for *empirically* evidential grounds (i.e. experience). The point on which Hegel disagrees most with Kant is what he thinks is the unnecessarily restrictive scope of transcendental logic, namely the restriction to sensible intuition for real possibility. This does not mean that for Hegel one does not have an empirical intuition when one experiences a cup in front of one, say. But Hegel denies that empirical intuition can have any cognitively determining role in addition to the apperceptive determination in virtue of our rational capacity. There is much less difference here with Kant than might appear on first reading the two-step argument in the Transcendental Deduction; Kant after all emphasizes, in a pivotal section in the second step of the B-Deduction, that the act of the understanding is the determining act, whilst inner sense is the determinable. The passivity of sensibility does not add anything to what the understanding, in virtue of the synthetic act of apperception, already accomplishes in terms of the conceptual determination of an empirical object.[10] Kant wishes to stress that concepts do not generate the existence of the object out of themselves, hence the need for an intuition of an object as the necessary condition of the object's real possibility. Hegel takes this for granted as far as empirical objects are concerned, but at the same time an empirical intuition should not be taken to be a necessary condition of the real possibility of just *any* object. It cannot be a condition, for example, of God's possibility (regardless of the question whether he exists or not).

What is important is to realize that Hegel did not criticize Kant because he was too much of an idealist and not realist enough, but because he was not *enough* of an idealist, and in some sense still held onto a finite reality outside concepts for the access to which a separate means is required (i.e. pure intuition), for no good general *philosophical* reasons. 'Reality' is not, according to Hegel's logic, what we commonly regard as the finite world of knowable objects. It is in fact the Concept which is reality (or more precisely, 'actuality'), whilst at the same time such common concepts as 'reality' are rather concepts that still belong to the 'uneducated mind' that has not yet grasped the logic of absolute idealism which has no need for exogenous grounding:

> True infinity, thus taken in general as *existence* posited as *affirmative* in contrast to abstract negation, is *reality* in a higher sense than it was earlier as *simply* determined; it has now obtained a concrete content. <u>It is not the finite which is the real, but rather the infinite. Thus reality is further determined as essence, concept, idea, and so forth</u>. In connection with the more concrete, it is however superfluous to repeat such earlier and more abstract categories as reality, and to use them for determinations more concrete than they are by themselves. Such a repetition, as when it is said that essence, or that the concept, is real, has its origin in the fact that to uneducated thought the most abstract categories such as being, existence, reality, finitude, are the most familiar.
> WL, GW 21:136 [Hegel 2010b:119], my underlining

9.5 Concluding Remarks

There are ambiguities in the way that Hegel and Hegelians have traditionally read Kant's argument in the Deduction, some of them having to do with a (partial) misreading of Kant, by Hegel himself, but mostly by Hegelians, and I have tried to clarify some of those assumptions underlying that partial misreading by Hegel himself in Chapter 8 of my earlier book (Schulting 2017a), and by Hegelians in my account of Pippin's reading of the Deduction in Chapter 7, and others in the current chapter, of this volume. On the other hand, there are more affinities between Kant and Hegel than may at first appear and than I made it out to be in earlier work. Here, I have pointed out in which direction one should take this affinity to go. In Chapter 8 and the present chapter of the book you have in hand, I have made an attempt to outline some of those affinities. But the full picture is a complex one, which requires more comprehensive future study.

Notes

Chapter 1

1. For discussion see Schulting (2017a, 2018b).
2. See e.g. Bowman (2013), Kreines (2015), and Martin (2012). Note that Pippin himself does not characterize his interpretation of Hegel's logic as a- or non-metaphysical per se; in fact he argues that Hegel's logic is a metaphysics strictly speaking.
3. Note however that already Descartes used the term *appercevoir* in his Principles: 'Par le mot de penser, j'entends tout ce qui se fait en nous de telle sorte que nous l'appercevons immediatement par nous-mêmes...' (*Principes*, AT IX, 28).
4. This is an element of Kantian apperception that is picked up by Hegel in his account in *Faith and Knowledge*. See Schulting (2017a), ch. 8.
5. This sense of 'derivative' is different from the earlier-mentioned Wolffian sense of 'derivative'. The sense in which it is criticized here is that, on this particular model, self-consciousness is not seen as *sui generis* or original, but must be seen as having a cognitive-functional role, and is 'reflection-theoretical'.

Chapter 2

1. See Miles (2006:2ff., 28) for references.
2. In the *Conflict of the Faculties* Kant also refers to the 'Copernican hypothesis', by way of analogy with 'the standpoint taken from the sun'—which is the standpoint of Reason—that contrasts with our own, empirical 'choice of standpoint' regarding 'the course of human things', that is, as seen from the earth (SF, AA 7:83, trans. mine).
3. For further references, see Miles (2006:1n.3).
4. Miles (2006:1) notes that the term 'revolution' appears no less than six times in the second-edition preface alone.
5. Notice that at A257/B313 Kant speaks of the 'Copernican world system', which is to be associated with a 'contemplative astronomy', leaving aside here the context in which he makes this remark. In a *Reflexion* that is part of a series of reflections on the indispensability in philosophy of hypotheses, Kant explicitly relates the phrasing 'Das Copernicanische Weltsystem' to the hypothesis of earth rotation (Refl 2680, AA 16:468; also Refl 2675, AA 16:463). One should also acknowledge that

Kant was well versed in cosmology and must have been well informed about the implications of the Copernican revolution for astronomy given an early publication in which he argued for an early version of what is now known as the Kant-Laplace nebular hypothesis about the origin of our solar system. See NTH (1755), AA 1:215–368. For a brief account of Kant's version of the nebular hypothesis see Friedman (2006:309ff.). Also PG, §7 ff., AA 9:166ff.; the *Physical Geography* was published by Theodor Rink in 1802 based on Kant's lecture notes (probably without Kant's express authorization), and have recently been published as volume 26 in the *Akademie Ausgabe*. These notes show that Kant was well versed in the mathematics involved in astronomy. Of special interest here is §9, AA 9:170ff.

6 This contradicts, quite clearly, with Miles's remark that 'the heliocentric world picture is not even alluded to in the key passage of the Preface in which the reference to Copernicus occurs' (2006:3).

7 Sometimes more general references to Kant's Copernicanism are made with the perspectival nature of our experience in mind. See e.g. Price (2007). Price refers to Kant's Copernican analogy in the light of his thesis of causal perspectivalism and, strikingly, even suggests that the analogy would consist in the fact that Kant points to an anthropocentric element in *Copernicus's* own alleged cosmological perspectivism. Notice that Allison also speaks of Kant's 'anthropocentric model of cognition' (Allison 2004:37).

8 Cf. Miles (2006:6n.17, 7n.18). Likewise, Miles himself suggests that Kant's reference to Copernicus 'first thoughts' (Bxvi) has to do with a 'reversal of the ontological realism of common sense' (2006:13, 29); cf. Miles (2006:3n.10), where, whilst referring to Hanson, Miles quotes a remark on common sense from the preface of Copernicus (1992:4). According to Miles, the aptness of Kant's analogy with Copernicus lies precisely in the fact that 'as in the case of Copernicus, the key innovations involved in Kant's "veränderte Methode der Denkungsart" constitute a quite deliberate *inversion* of the familiar standpoint of sound common sense' (2006:3). Gardner (1999:42) appears to suggest the same. However, I believe that Copernicus's mention of 'common sense' in the preface to *On the Revolutions* is so incidental to pleading his case that it does not warrant resting one's interpretation of the Copernican turn on it.

9 See e.g. Ameriks (2006:78).

10 This critique is often attributed to Bertrand Russell (see note below). However, Norman Kemp Smith observed already in 1913 that Kant's revolution prima facie resembles more a 'Ptolemaic-anthropocentric metaphysics' (Kemp Smith 1913; this view is repeated in Kemp Smith 1999:22ff.).

11 In his *Human Knowledge, Its Scope and Limits* (1948), Russell writes: 'Kant spoke of himself as having effected a "Copernican revolution", but he would have been more accurate if he had spoken of a "Ptolemaic counter-revolution" since he put Man back

at the centre from which Copernicus had dethroned him' (as quoted by M. Miles 2006:28).
12 Cf. Strawson (1968:22ff.).
13 See also Bird (2006:31).
14 Cf. PG §9, AA 9:177.9–13.
15 Cf. Ameriks (2006:296).
16 Bird's (2006:30) reasoning that the 'alteration in our way of thinking', of which Kant speaks (e.g. Bxix, Bxxii note), is to do simply with 'a change from one point of view to another' is typical of the lack, in the literature, of an account of Kant's motivation to *argue* for changing the point of view, which is precisely what any interested reader of Kant's ostensibly revolutionary philosophy would wish to know. To be fair, Bird does go on to give a more balanced view of the matter than is suggested by his remark. But, notwithstanding an interesting general account of the second edition preface, Bird, like most commentators, fails to exploit the Copernican analogy itself by probing the close systematic similarities between Kant's and Copernicus's methods of reasoning.
17 This explains why in the past commentators have argued that the heliocentric consequences of the Copernican revolution are of no relevance to Kant's analogy, which supposedly is merely concerned with explaining apparently objective phenomena in terms of subjective conditions (cf. Miles 2006:2ff., 28; Miles gives Kemp Smith and Paton as illustrations of this view); but the dissociation of Kant's interest in making the analogy from the postulation of a heliocentric universe is of course dependent on what I contend is the mistaken notion of Kant's main concern as having to do with *perspectivism*. It is clear at any rate that on *perspectivism* the central feature of the Copernican revolution, i.e. the truth of heliocentrism, cannot be accounted for.
18 Cf. J. Van Cleve (1999:5–12). See Ameriks (2006:77–88) for a critique of Van Cleve's phenomenalistic reading of Kant's idealism in the context of a general study of Berkeleyan interpretations of Kant's idealism. I am not sure if Van Cleve's complex interpretation can indeed be qualified as a standard phenomenalistic, let alone Berkeleyan reading of Kant's idealism. See also Schulting (2017a), ch. 4.
19 Cf. the often-maligned passage in the fourth paralogism in Kant's *Critique* at A369, where Kant claims that 'all appearances must be considered mere representations' (see also Chapter 6).
20 See Schulting (2017b).
21 Although ostensible equally unconvinced of what I call AH (cf. Miles 2006:20) as the analogy is, as Miles justly notes, 'far more illuminating than is generally recognized' (2006:4), effectively Miles's recent interpretation of Kant's Copernican turn does not, to my mind, differ significantly from the standard reading. As noted earlier, Miles (2006:25) sees the analogy in Kant's and Copernicus's attack on common sense, but

even if this were the case, pointing this out would not explain both their motivations to launch such an attack. Only insight into the motivation or reasons behind it could establish the aptness of the analogy. Furthermore, although he rightly notes the importance of experiment for Kant's thought, I find Miles's interpretation of central tenets of Kant's thought so off the mark, in particular his talk of the mind *imposing* its conditions or laws on things or nature (2006:4, 7, 10, 13) and of Kant's supposed 'transcendental turn toward ontological idealism' (2006:10), that I am unsure as to whether he can cash out what he claims to be the central motifs behind the Copernican analogy (see for a summary of his account Miles 2006:4–7).

22 See Schulting (2017b).
23 I thank Claudio La Rocca for rightfully insisting on this important point.
24 I have provided a more extensive account of these features, in the context of a reading of Kant's Transcendental Deduction, elsewhere (Schulting 2017a, 2018b).
25 See also A849/B877; cf. Refl 4284, AA 17:495, and Prol §35, AA 4:317.
26 Significantly, Kant labels the 'pure concepts of the understanding', 'e.g., ... substance', 'ontological predicates' in the first introduction to the *Critique of Judgment* (KU, AA 5:181). Cf. ÜE, AA 8:190n. See also in particular V-Met/Mron, AA 29:784–5 [dated ca. 1782–83].
27 See also a letter to L. H. Jakob (Br, AA 10:494).
28 But cf. V-Met/Mron, AA 28:876, V-Met-L2/Pölitz, AA 28:541, V-Met/Dohna, AA 28:679, V-Met/Vigil, AA 29:949, 956, 960, 988.
29 See Schulting (2018b), ch. 3.
30 Cf. the oft-quoted passage at B75: 'Thoughts without content are empty, intuitions without concepts are blind.' For discussion, see Schulting (2017a), ch. 5.
31 I derive this label from Cassam (2007:1–9). See Cassam (2007:51–84) for a précis of transcendental arguments that have some connection to Kant's argument in the Transcendental Deduction. Cassam himself offers a critical account of transcendental arguments, which presents them as different from the epistemological 'how-possible' questions in which Cassam is specifically interested.
32 See Schulting (2018b), ch. 3.
33 See Copernicus (1992:11ff.). The book's full title in Latin is *De revolutionibus orbium caelestium*, published in Nuremberg in 1543. Copernicus espoused the heliocentric theory essentially already in the earlier *Commentariolus*, which he distributed among peers but which remained unpublished. Also just prior to the publication of *On the Revolutions*, Copernicus's supporter G. J. Rheticus summarized the heliocentric theory in his *Narratio prima* (1541). For these works see Copernicus (1990).
34 All sorts of technical detail in Copernicus's complex argumentation have evidently been omitted, not least because, as is well known, the greater part of Copernicus's classic consists of abstruse, now (partially) obsolete, mathematical calculations, which are entirely beyond the grasp of the uninitiated, including yours truly.

Moreover, Copernicus's innovations in mathematical astronomy were just the start of a mathematically simplified 'Copernican' astronomy, for which later Kepler and others, improving on and modifying Copernicus's inventions, were as much responsible as Copernicus himself (this is also noted by Guyer 2006:385n.11). Here, I am merely interested in the general, philosophical, thrust behind Copernicus's 'first thoughts', which must be seen as underpinning his calculations. See for more technical detail Kuhn (1985), a revolutionary classic in its own right in the history and philosophy of science, which predated and ushered in Kuhn (1996).

35 In the passage at Bxvi, where Kant makes the Copernican analogy, Kant speaks of 'celestial host' (*Sternheer*), suggesting that the galaxy is at issue, although the problem for Copernicus specifically concerned planetary cycles, not the fixed stars; so 'celestial host' should be taken in a broader sense here, as including the planets. Schönecker et al. (2011) read this differently.

36 See Copernicus (1992:22ff.). Cf. PG, §9, AA 9:171ff. It appears that Kant only distinguishes two motions, 'one namely around [the earth's] own axis *or its daily* [motion], the other around the sun or its yearly motion' (trans. mine and emphasis added). Kuhn suggests that the reason that Copernicus still required three circular motions for the earth has to do with his traditional (Aristotelian) belief that 'the earth is a planet which is carried about the central sun by a sphere just like the one that used to carry the sun about the central earth' (Kuhn 1985:164).

37 More precisely, it was the Pythagorean Philolaus of Croton (ca. 470 to ca. 385 BC) who already advanced a cosmology in which the earth was removed from the centre, although in Philolaus's system the earth did not orbit the sun but rather the central fire. It is this Philolaus to whom Kant himself refers as Copernicus's precursor in a *Reflexion* (Refl 5064, AA 18:77), where Kant writes: 'Just like when *philolaus* said that the earth moves and *copernick* proved it' (trans. mine). In the preface to *On the Revolutions*, Copernicus too, in a quoted remark from Plutarch, mentions Philolaus as a precursor who floated the idea of the earth's motion (Copernicus 1992:5, 12).

38 The ecliptic is the great circle on the celestial sphere around which the sun appears to be moving annually. See Kuhn (1985:23) for clarification.

39 As quoted by Kuhn (1985:177–81).

40 Cf. Popper (2002:245). See also A125, where Kant writes: 'Thus we ourselves bring into the appearances that order and regularity in them that we call nature, and moreover *we would not be able to find it there if we, or the nature of our mind, had not originally put it there*. For this unity of nature should be a necessary, i.e. *a priori* certain unity of the connection of appearances' (emphasis added). See Schulting (2018b), ch. 11.

41 Evidently, the scientist need not have a firm grasp of the deeper methodological underpinnings of his own practice, let alone of its philosophical groundwork, in order to be able to do what he does. Cf. MAN, AA 4:472.13–35.

42 There is of course also a clear disanalogy with the scientific hypothetico-deductive method: the typical scientist's practice consists in positing falsifiable theses, whereas the philosopher does not posit falsifiable theses but puts forward hypotheses with a view to apodictically proving principles that hold a priori and necessarily, and are not vulnerable to revision.
43 The omitted passage is the one where Kant makes the Copernican analogy.
44 In the passage following this one, Kant argues that, *mutatis mutandis*, the same holds regarding the object's conformity to *conceptual* conditions.
45 Cf. Prol §9, B125, and A128ff.
46 For Kant on truth, see Prauss (1973). See also Schulting (2017a).
47 At Bxvii ff. Kant speaks of a '*rule* [of the understanding] I have to presuppose in myself before any object is given to me', and 'which *rule* is expressed in concepts a priori, to which all objects of experience must therefore necessarily conform, and with which they must agree' (emphasis added).
48 Cf. Axiv: 'I have to do merely with reason itself and its pure thinking; to gain exhaustive acquaintance with them I need not seek far beyond myself, because it is in myself that I encounter them.'
49 Regarding the 'self-knowledge' of reason and the demand of systematicity in metaphysics, which is at issue here, see e.g. Baum (2001:25–40).
50 This limitation is related to Kant's notorious distinction between appearance and thing in itself. In a note in the B-preface of the *Critique* (Bxviii–xix note), Kant suggests that the experiment of pure reason is concerned with this distinction in order to demonstrate that the moral faith of the human being may be kept up, while at the same time a thoroughgoing determinism can be maintained in the realm of material, phenomenal nature. It is this distinction which Kant associates with the touchstone for the justification of transcendental idealism; this might appear to be a different distinction than the distinction between two ways of considering the correspondence relation between thought and object, but this is only seemingly so. Kant's transcendental distinction between appearance and thing in itself is directly proportional to this latter distinction. Put differently, Kant's idealism follows logically from the Copernican turn of the Critical position regarding truth. How the inner connection between these two distinctions must be characterized precisely is a matter for further study.
51 Kant must be taken to distinguish between the negative and positive senses of the notion of hypothesis. For Kant, as here in the A-preface, hypothesis usually connotes mere probability or taking something to be true on subjective grounds, and can therefore never be a ground for apodictic certainty due to its mode of inference, which is to infer from the consequences to their ground (see Refl 2687, AA 16:471; cf. Log, AA 9:84–5; interestingly, Kant points out here in the Jäsche Logic passage that, in contrast to the majority of hypotheses in science, '[t]he Copernican system,

on the other hand, is an hypothesis from which everything can be explained that ought to be explained therefrom' [Log, AA 9:86, (Kant 2004a:586)]). Nevertheless, in the B-preface—when he makes the analogy with Copernicus and speaks of reason's analogue of experiments in science, which he associates with reason's own 'attempt', as he puts it, to alter its way of thinking—Kant clearly values hypothesis positively insofar as it leads to an increase in rationality (cf. again Bxxii). Although they are not grounds for apodictic certainty, hypotheses help us to get to the truth. As he puts it in a *Reflexion*, '[h]ypotheses are indispensable. I. *They are experiments of the understanding*. One must approach many a truth along the path of probability' (Refl 2675, AA 16:463 [Kant 2005:47], emphasis added).

52 Peter Heath's translation in the Cambridge edition (Kant 2001) gives 'matter' for *Sache*. However, almost always when, in conformity with its usage in the *Schulphilosophie*, Kant uses the term *Sache* he means the really existing thing. Cf. A143/B182, A574–5/B602–3.

53 See also Refl 3850 and 3852 (AA 17:312) and OP, AA 21:114.

54 See for a paradigmatic description of the aspect of self-legislation in Kant's moral philosophy in particular GMS, AA 4:431.

55 This project was addressed in great detail in Schulting (2018b).

Chapter 3

1 This is also a reason why Hegel's criticism of Kant's alleged 'bad' subjectivism is misplaced (see Schulting 2017a), ch. 8. Transcendental apperception is precisely designed by Kant to avoid psychological misreadings of self-consciousness.

2 This is an element of Kantian apperception that is picked up by Hegel in his account in *Faith and Knowledge*. I discuss the early Hegel's reading of transcendental apperception in detail in Schulting (2017a). But see also Chapters 7–9, this volume.

3 In the Dutch translation of the *Critique* (Kant 2004b:203) *Radikalvermögen* is aptly rendered *oervermogen*, which translates back into German as *Urvermögen*. See Schulting (2017a:17).

4 Cf. Anth §4 note, AA 7:134n.

5 For a full account, see Schulting (2018b:318–22).

6 Of course, transcendental apperception is not the sufficient condition for the *existence* of objects as things in themselves (although transcendental apperception is the ground of the *determination* of the existence of things). On this topic, see further Schulting (2017a, 2018b).

7 For references to recent literature, see Schulting (2018b), ch. 8. For an account of Reinhold on this score, see Chapter 6, this volume.

8 The Friedländer anthropology (1775–76) reads: 'The cessation of all sensation is unconsciousness. If one cannot get out of this state of sensation, then this is death. Sleep is the cessation of all sensation in a healthy state. It is an insensibility to and unconsciousness of outer objects' (V-Anth/Fried, AA 25:511 [Kant 2012a:80]). Cf. Anth, AA 7:166 (§27), where Kant speaks of unconsciousness as 'a foretaste of death' (Kant 2007:277).

9 Cf. Anth, AA 7:142: 'The cause of these errors is that the terms *inner sense* and *apperception* are normally taken by psychologists to be synonymous, despite the fact that the first alone should indicate a psychological (applied) consciousness, and the second merely a logical (pure) consciousness' (Kant 2007:255). Kant speaks simply of apperception here, but he means of course *transcendental* apperception, not empirical apperception, which is equivalent to inner sense (cf. A107).

10 Dyck (2014:65) believes that in Kant's precritical lecture notes 'inner sense is understood *in much the same way as it would be in the KrV*.' I think this is mistaken. See my critique of Dyck's position in Schulting (2016d).

11 See e.g. the Pölitz notes from the 1770s, V-Met-L1/Pölitz, AA 28:227. However, notice that here Kant might still be considered to be quite close to a Wolffian view of the self in that *conscientia psychologica*, which is a '*subjective* consciousness', 'a forcible state', and not 'discursive, but intuitive' (AA 28:227), is to be taken as consciousness of the self as such, i.e. of 'the soul', 'where we can intuit the substance immediately' (AA 28:226), whereas *conscientia logica* is only directed at objects, i.e. is an '*objective* consciousness', where 'I am conscious of other cognitions [*bin ich mir anderer Erkenntnisse bewußt*]' (AA 28:227, all translations mine). It is this latter logical consciousness, which comes to be associated with transcendental apperception in the Critical period (see Section 3.3). The later Kant of course considers psychological consciousness to concern merely how I appear to myself in inner sense, not how I am as a thing in itself (cf. B152–3, 157ff.). Horstmann (2007:143ff.) provides an illuminating account of why the Pölitz passage could still be seen as compatible with a non-substantialist view of apperception in Kant's silent decade. By contrast, Carl (1989a, b) argues that prior to discovering the paralogisms, Kant still held a problematic ontological view about the self and thus apperception in the mid-1770s (see Schulting 2018b:65–7).

12 In the pre-Critical published works, the term *Bewußtsein* or the cognate *bewußt* occurs, in various contexts, in NTH, AA 1:366; GSE, AA 2:217, 237, 249; NG, AA 2:168, 182, 199; UD, AA 2:284, 286, 290, 299; and, befitting its thematics, most frequently in TG, AA 2:320, 332, 333, 337, 338, 339, 340. The Latin *conscientia* appears in PND, AA 1:401, 403, 406. The term *Selbstbewußtsein* as such does not occur in the pre-Critical corpus, although Kant does speak of 'personal consciousness' (TG, AA 2:338). By comparison, in the early anthropology lectures Kant speaks of 'consciousness of self-activity' (V-Anth/Collins, AA 25:10 [Kant

2012a:17]) or of the 'representation of I' as 'the personality to be conscious of oneself' (V-Anth/Fried, AA 25:473 [Kant 2012a:50]; cf. V-Anth/Pillau, AA 25:736).

13 Cf. V-Anth/Collins, AA 25:10: 'The I is the foundation of the capacity for understanding and reason, and the entire power of cognition, for all these rest on my observing and inspecting myself and what goes on in me' (Kant 2012a:17). See further the references in the note above. Klemme (1996:59–62) makes the interesting claim that Kant was under the influence of Herz's critique of his earlier position in the *Inaugural Dissertation*. Klemme points out that Herz argued that there must be a '"first subject" ... which is numerically simple' in order to be able to conceive of 'the unity that is the result of the comparison of representations'. According to Klemme, Herz positions this 'first subject' as the 'epistemic centre'.

14 See also PND, AA 1:403.

15 I thank Steve Naragon for bringing this to my attention.

16 'Quæ ens aliquod distinguit, illa APPERCIPIT, seu eorum sibi est conscium. Perceptio appercepta est COGITATIO ...' (Baumgarten, *Acroasis logica*, Halle and Magdeburg, second edition 1773, 'Prolegomena', §3, pp. 1–2).

17 'Menti tribuitur *Apperceptio*, quatenus perceptionis suæ sibi conscia est. / Apperceptionis nomine utitur *Leibnitius*: coincidit autem cum conscientia, quem terminum in præsenti negotio *Cartesius* adhibet' (PE §25, p. 17). See also PE §26, where Wolff provides the following example for apperception: 'Dum jam scribo, conscius mihi sum me scribere. Quatenus mihi conscius sum actus scribendi, eundem appercipio ....' According to Warda (1922), Kant had apparently no copy of the *Psychologia empirica* in his possession.

18 This passage has been read in two different ways: either the 'or' is disjunctive or it is conjunctive, suggesting that 'consciousness' has 'that inner state' as direct object. The latter option means that apperception is not to be defined as 'consciousness'.

19 See also a passage where Leibniz writes about a wild boar that has the capacity to 'apperceive', even though it does not have understanding or indeed a capacity for second-order reflection (*New Essays*, G 5:159, II.21, §5).

20 Leibniz writes of this law: 'The *Law of continuity* states that nature leaves no gaps in the orderings which she follows, but not every form or species belongs to each ordering' (*New Essays*, G 5:286).

21 See Wolff, VG §§729–30, pp. 454–6.

22 In his copy of Meier's *Auszug aus der Vernunftlehre*, Kant refers to this Wolffian conception of consciousness already early on in Refl 1679 (1752–56): 'To be conscious of a ~~thing~~ representation [*Sich einer ~~sache~~ Vorstellung bewust seyn*] is: to know that one has this representation, that is, to differentiate this representation from the others' (AA 16:80, trans. mine). See also the later account in the *Logik Blomberg*, §13, V-Lo/Blomberg, AA 24:40. Interestingly, Meier distinguishes between 'simple consciousness' (*einfaches Bewußtseyn*) and 'multiple consciousness'

(*vielfaches Bewußtseyn*), whereby the former relates to the consciousness of a representation or thing whose parts (or manifold) cannot be distinguished, whereas the latter concerns a consciousness that includes consciousness of the inner parts of a thing or the manifold contained in the representation (*Vernunftlehre*, Halle 1752, §28, pp. 28-9).

23 Obscurity is not an absolute value. This is confirmed by Kant in a passage in the *Logik Blomberg* (1770s), §125 (V-Lo/Blomberg, AA 24:119), which says that something can never be 'obscure in itself' but only 'relatively', so that what is obscure 'can become clear under certain circumstances, but not under others' (Kant 2004a:93). However, this appears to concern logical obscurity only; elsewhere, Kant says that *psychological* obscurity *is* absolute. I come back to this point further below and in Section 3.4. Wolff too admits the real possibility of perceptions that are totally obscure (PR §§200-1, pp. 93-4). See also La Rocca (2007:65-87) on obscurity in Kant and his rationalist predecessors.

24 See Wolff, PE §§24-6, p. 17, and VG §729, pp. 454-5.

25 '*Anima sibi sui conscia est, quatenus sibi conscia est suarum mutationum veluti actionum: nec aliter sibi conscia. . . . Dum enim attentionem nostram in hoc convertimus, quod rerum perceptarum nobis conscii sumus; nostri etiam nobis conscii sumus. Sed tum apperceptionem, actionem quandam animæ, percipimus . . ., & nos per eam tanquam subjectum percipiens ab objectis, quæ percipiuntur, distinguimus, agnoscentes utique percipiens subjectum esse quid diversum a re percepta. Anima igitur sibi sui conscia est, quatenus sibi conscia est suarum mutationum*' (Wolff, PR §12, p. 7, my underlining).

26 Cf. V-Met/Mron, AA 29:888-90: 'This is the representation of one's representations and therefore is also called apperception.'

27 For an extensive account see Schulting (2018b), ch. 10.

28 See further Schulting (2018b), ch. 10.

29 Cf. V-Anth/Fried, AA 25:482; see also Anth §7, AA 7:140n.

30 Even in the Critical period, e.g. in *Metaphysik Volckmann* (1784-85), Kant holds that consciousness is unique to the intellect, and is not contained in 'sensus, imaginatio' (V-Met/Volckmann, AA 28:449). However, in the somewhat later *Metaphysik Dohna* (1792-93) Kant says that '[s]ense is the faculty of empirical intuitions for becoming immediately conscious of existence in space or in time' (V-Met/Dohna, AA 28:672 [Kant 2001:374], my underlining).

31 V-Lo/Blomberg, AA 24:41, 119; V-Lo/Philippi, AA 24:410; cf. V-Lo/Pölitz, AA 24:511.

32 V-Anth/Fried, AA 25:479; V-Anth/Mron [1784-85], AA 25:1221; cf. V-Met/Mron, AA 29:879.

33 Cf. V-Lo/Blomberg, AA 24:119, §124, on the notion of 'mediate consciousness'.

34 See also the contemporary *Logik Blomberg*, V-Lo/Blomberg, AA 24:41-2, 118-20, and the later *Logik Dohna-Wundlacken*, V-Lo/Dohna, AA 24:702, 725.

35 Confusingly, in MAN, AA 4:542, of course published just prior to the B-edition of the *Critique*, Kant still maintains that consciousness *as such* consists in the clarity of representations. It should also be noted that in the A-Deduction of 1781 Kant appears to still identify empirical consciousness with clarity (cf. A117n), suggesting that obscure representations are therefore unconscious. But what Kant presumably means here is not dissimilar to what he says in the note to B414, namely that clarity in the sense of consciousness is not restricted to apperceptive consciousness but 'also extends', to put it in the terms of the account in the *Anthropology*, to the obscure representations, of which one is indirectly conscious, and which thus makes them '*distinct representations*' and so *relatively* clear, i.e. conscious to *some* degree (Anth §5, AA 7:135 [Kant 2007:246]). Cf. V-Lo/Dohna, AA 24:725: 'Clarity is consciousness <not> only of representations in the whole but also of their partial representations' (Kant 2004a:461).

36 This view also seems to be found in the later Mrongovius anthropology notes: 'We can divide our consciousness into subjective and objective consciousness. Our consciousness is subjective when we direct our thoughts to our existence and to our understanding itself; it is objective when we turn them to other objects' (V-Anth/Mron, AA 25:1219 [Kant 2012a:351]).

37 'With animal souls everything depends on consciousness, *which however they do not show*: but rather actions in accordance with a determinate plan, which they cannot change by means of a reflection upon their current state' (V-Met/Herder, AA 28:901, trans. mine and emphasis added); 'Livestock ... does not have the inner sense to represent to itself its *statum repræsentationis*' (V-Met/Herder, AA 28:868, trans. mine); see also V-Met/Herder, AA 28:864, 911; '[H]owever much animal souls increase in their sensible faculties, consciousness of their self, inner sense, still cannot be attained thereby' (V-Met-L1/Pölitz, AA 28:276 [Kant 2001:87]); '[W]e ascribe to [animals] a faculty of sensation, [reproductive] imagination, etc., but all only sensible as a lower faculty, and not connected with consciousness. We can explain all phenomena of animals from this outer sensibility and from mechanical grounds of their bodies, without assuming consciousness or inner sense' (V-Met-L1/Pölitz, AA 28:277 [Kant 2001:88]); 'Animals have senses and reproductive imagination. ... The faculty of consciousness cannot be attributed to animals' (V-Met-L2/Pölitz, AA 28:594 [Kant 2001:354]). On animal perception, see further Chapter 5.

38 In a *Reflexion* from around 1771 (Refl 4440, AA 17:548), Kant appears to acknowledge that although they do not have the capacity to judge (*iudicandi*) strictly speaking, animals are capable of making distinctions (*diiudicandi*), meaning that they are capable of making a *iudicium sensitivum*, but not a *iudicium intellectuale*. I thank Steve Naragon for bringing this *Reflexion* to my attention.

39 Also in the later *Metaphysik Mrongovius* (V-Met/Mron, AA 29:888, 906), Kant still denies animals consciousness. See also V-Lo/Dohna, AA 24:689–90, 702.

40 A modified translation would probably be: 'the consciousness of the manifold representations *in* a unity in one consciousness', as it concerns the consciousness that many representations are contained in one unitary representation.
41 On the other hand, in *Metaphysik von Schön* Kant still appears to hold on to the problematic view of judgements of perception, which he had proposed in the *Prolegomena* from 1783 but had abandoned after 1786 (see Pollok 2008, 2013). Nevertheless, it is clear that Graf von Schön matriculated only in October 1788, so that the notes must be of a date later than 1788—although they might of course have been copied from earlier lectures.
42 For a full account of the derivation of the a priori concepts or categories from apperception, see Schulting (2018b).
43 'The first and major representation is that of the I or the consciousness of my self, apperception (as Prof. Kant calls it in his *Critique*)' (V-Met/Mron, AA 29:878 [Kant 2001:248]).
44 The term 'apperception', appearing in the original text either as *apperceptio*, *apperceptio empirica*, *apperceptio pura*, *reine Apperception*, *empirische a/Apperception*, *intellectuelle Apperception*, or just *a/Apperception*, occurs 36 times in the entire corpus of metaphysics lecture notes published in the *Akademie Ausgabe*. The term appears in the following places:
V-Met-L2/Pölitz, AA 28:584 (3x), 590 (1x); V-Met/Dohna, AA 28:654 (2x), 670 (2x), 673 (2x); Dohna *Beilage*, AA 28:704 (1x); V-Met-K2/Heinze, AA 28:712–13 (5x), 735 (1x); V-Met/Mron, AA 29:834 (1x), 878 (3x), 879 (1x), 882 (2x), 884 (2x), 888–9 (8x), 906 (1x); V-Met/Vigil, AA 29:970 (1x).
45 Cf. Anth §24, AA 7:161: 'Inner sense is not pure apperception, a consciousness of what the human being *does*, since this belongs to the faculty of thinking. Rather, it is a consciousness of what he *undergoes*, in so far as he is affected by the play of his own thoughts' (Kant 2007:272); Anth §15, AA 7:153: 'A representation through sense of which one is conscious as such is called *sensation*, especially when the sensation at the same time arouses the subject's attention to his own state' (Kant 2007:265). At Anth, AA 7:141, Kant contrasts a '*discursive*' or 'logical consciousness', which is 'pure apperception of one's mental activity', and 'gives the rule', with '*intuitive* consciousness' (Kant 2007:254). See also Anth §§5, 6, 7. In the note to §4 (Anth, AA 7:134n), empirical apperception is identified with inner sense.
46 For a detailed account of the relation between apperception and judgement, see Schulting (2018b), ch. 10.
47 It also conflicts with another passage in the Mrongovius, where it is pointed out that consciousness is *not* restricted to the understanding (and reason), e.g. when Kant talks about the feeling of pleasure: 'Pleasure is thus the consciousness of the agreement of an object with the productive power of imagination of our soul' (V-Met/Mron, AA 29:891 [Kant 2001:259]).

48 However, note that Jorgensen (2009) makes a plausible case for the view that Leibniz himself espouses a gradual theory of consciousness.
49 On the Law of Continuity, see MAN, AA 4:471, 542–3 and V-Met/Mron, AA 29:921.
50 On the topic of consciousness and the categories of quality, see further Schulting (2018b), ch. 8.

Chapter 4

1 I understand Kant's *Erkenntnis* to be more than what is understood by the English 'cognition' and less than the English term 'knowledge' (for which the German equivalent is *Kenntnis* or *Wissen*). For all its potentially misleading connotations to contemporary readers, I shall in general be using the term 'knowledge' for Kant's *Erkenntnis*, and make no specific distinction from the term 'cognition'. For further discussion on this issue, see Schulting (2018b).
2 For an extensive account of interpretative issues, see Schulting (2018b).
3 Cf. Düsing (2013:111–40).
4 See Fichte, GWL, 14.
5 See Henrich (1967:13).
6 Paradigmatically, Henrich (1967).
7 See Düsing (2013:117–18).
8 Kant himself describes this as follows: 'I cannot cognize as an object itself that which I must presuppose in order to cognize an object at all' (A402).
9 Henrich (1976:64 *et passim*).
10 Tugendhat (1997:52) dismisses Kant's transcendental theory as 'obscure'. But it seems to me that here lies precisely the key to solving the riddle concerning the alleged circularity.
11 See Pippin (1997a:43).
12 Cf. Pippin (2014:155).
13 I have dealt *in extenso* with the grounding function of apperception for knowledge in Schulting (2018b).
14 For a different and more detailed view, see Onof (2010).
15 Like Pluhar, Kemp Smith, and Meiklejohn, I read *zu einem Selbstbewußtsein* as meaning 'to one self-consciousness', for if the indefinite article were meant here, the preposition and the article would normally have been contracted to *zum*.
16 For further references, see Chapter 3.
17 For more discussion, see Schulting (2018b), ch. 8.
18 See further the discussion in Schulting (2017a:161–6) and (2018b), ch. 6.
19 On Kant's misleading use of the verb 'to belong' in relation to his employing the indexical 'my', which invites a possessive interpretation of the 'I think' proposition, see Schulting (2017a:163, 185).

20 For a detailed account of the modality of apperception, see Schulting (2018b), ch. 6.
21 On spontaneity in relation to apperception, see my account in Schulting (2017a:124–31).
22 This addition should not be read as if the synthesis were an *a posteriori* one, which might be suggested by Kant's words here. The act of addition, that is, synthesis, is what happens in the background of any act of apperceiving representations as one's own, and which constitutes self-consciousness. The act of addition or synthesis is not something that I need to do *consciously*, so that I apprehend representation B after representation A, and a subsequent representation C after representation B, which would be tantamount to an a posteriori synthesis.
23 I have extensively argued for what I call the rigorous coextensivity of the analytic and synthetic unities of apperception in Schulting (2018b).
24 I must set aside here issues of modality that are alluded to in the above-quoted passage at B133. For more discussion, see Schulting (2018b), ch. 6.
25 Further on this topic, see Schulting (2016d).
26 See also the account at B68–9 in the *Critique*.
27 This knowledge is more than just the 'knowledge' of merely thinking the subject of judgement, as the highlighted *Anthropology* passage suggests.
28 See also B68. The term self-affection suggests that only *self*-perception is concerned in the affective determination of inner sense, but internal affection is involved in *all* determination of sensible manifolds, for any sort of empirical object, as is made clear in the preceding passages of §24. The difference is that in the cognition of outer objects, we are also *externally* affected.
29 For detailed discussion on the differentiation between mere form of intuition and determinate intuition in relation to space as one of the two pure forms of intuition, see Onof & Schulting (2015) and Schulting (2018b), ch. 11.
30 Compare this with the following passage in the B-Paralogisms: 'Thinking, taken in itself, is merely the logical function and hence the sheer spontaneity of combining the manifold of a merely possible intuition; . . . in the consciousness of myself in mere thinking I am the *being itself*, about which, however, nothing yet is thereby given to me for thinking' (B428–9).
31 See also Schulting (2016d:189–91).
32 Ginsborg (2015) has a different view. She appears to be arguing that the spontaneous 'I' of apperception must be able to identify, by means of the faculty of judgement, herself with the spatiotemporally located empirical person that does the apperceiving ('HG', in her case). In my view, the spontaneous activity of a judger is not dependent on such an identification, nor is such an identification germane to the purport of what the judger does and is aware of doing. The 'I' with which the transcendental subject identifies is just the 'I' of judging *qua* being the judger, whereby the fact of the (obviously necessary) embodiedness or personality of the

judging 'I', or that the 'I' is Dennis Schulting or 'HG', is irrelevant to understanding the purport of the judger's agency.

Chapter 5

1. For a detailed interpretation, see Schulting (2018b), ch. 10.
2. For a full account, see especially Schulting (2017a), ch. 4. Cf. Schulting (2018b), chs 4 and 10.
3. In particular, see Schulting (2018b), but also Schulting (2017a), ch. 4. See also Chapter 4 in the present volume.
4. Golob employs the label objectivity[1] in his longer article (Golob 2020), but here I shall stick to objectivity* as it is used in Golob (2018).
5. Recently, Smit (2019) made the same assumption, but I think Golob is right that Kant does not rigorously distinguish between the two terms. Moreover, *Gegenstand* is the German translation of the Latinate *Objekt*, so there is no real semantic difference.
6. I do not think Thomas Nagel's view of something 'what it is like to be' can be transferred to the Kantian context. I also think it is important to make a distinction between viewpoint in terms of 'what it is for x to be *for y*' and in terms of 'there being something that it is like to be'. Nagel seems to conflate these two senses of 'viewpoint'. Nagel believes that 'fundamentally an organism has conscious mental states if and only if there is something that it is like to be that organism—something it is like *for* the organism. We may call this the subjective character of experience' (1991:166). Obviously, one of Nagel's points is to suggest the fundamental alienness of non-human forms of experience, and that we cannot imagine what it is like to have that form of experience. But the way he defines consciousness conflates intransitive and transitive consciousness. For an organism to have some form of consciousness or awareness does not entail that there is something it is like to be that organism *for* itself, that it has subjective experience and thus consciousness of an inner life. A non-human animal (depending on the species) can be attributed creature consciousness (some lesser or greater degree of sentience, responsiveness to stimuli), but not a higher-order form of consciousness, only the latter of which indicates a consciousness *of* something *for* one, in contrast to merely being sentient or responsive, in whichever intricate ways, to sense stimuli.
7. Sometimes Kant also defines consciousness in this way, e.g. in the *Logik*, namely 'Bewußtsein [ist] eine Vorstellung, daß eine andre Vorstellung in mir ist' (Log, AA 9:33; cf. V-Met-L1/Pölitz, AA 28:227), but here, as so often in Kant, transitive consciousness is meant.
8. Cf. Naragon (1990:13).

9 Kant does not employ the term *intentio*, but the Latin *propositum* is a close analogue, since it denotes 'intention', 'plan', 'aim'.
10 This is the root sense of 'object', which is the noun form of the verb *obiicio*, which denotes 'to put in front of', 'to put before'. 'Object' as antonym of 'subject' is of course of relatively late, medieval origin. Cf. Heidegger's etymology, whatever its merit, of *Gegenstand* as the noun variant of the verb *gegenstehen*, something that stands over against, similarly to *obiicio*, meaning 'to place over against', 'to put before/in front of', or 'to throw before/in front of'.
11 See the references in Schulting (2017a), ch. 1, and Chapter 6, this volume.
12 This is the crucial aspect of Kant that Strawson got right with his interpretation of Kant's argument as a transcendental argument about the possibility of experience, namely, that there exists a reflexive relation between the subject and the object of experience. Golob also notes this, but he does not mention the element of reflexivity that is involved and which Strawson points out too. Experience itself expresses this reflexive relation between a subject of experience and the object that it experiences. It is hard to see how an animal has this reflexive awareness, whereby it self-ascribes the representations that it has of objects to itself.
13 Also, animal awareness is not mutually recognitional: animals do not recognize *each other* as having the type of awareness that would characterize them as self-conscious agents. Self-consciousness depends on the recognition of others as themselves being self-conscious agents.
14 Cf. Longuenesse (2017), who relates Sartre's concept of 'non-thetic (self-)consciousness' to Kant's implicit notion of bodily awareness in the 'feeling' of existence that is implied by Kant's 'I think'-proposition. She also rightly differentiates this consciousness from the consciousness of determinate objects, as well as from the consciousness of self as the agent of thought.
15 See the discussion in Schulting (2017a:103), and Golob's own excellent discussion in Golob (2020).
16 Suppose that we were transported back to an ancestral time t, in which dinosaurs roamed the world. The transcendental perspective would ensure that the empirical objects we cognized at t conformed to our forms of intuition and the understanding so as to enable a recognition of those natural objects and events as such in conformity with both the empirical and transcendental laws of nature. Objects are subject to those forms no matter whether humans are around or not to actually observe them.
17 See Schulting (2018b), ch. 11.
18 See V-Met/Herder, AA 28:117.
19 It is thus in principle possible that there is never any instance of actual experience, while the transcendental principles of experience would still hold sway.

Chapter 6

1 'The existence of the thing that appears is thereby not destroyed, as in genuine idealism, but it is only shown that we cannot possibly know it by the senses as it is in itself' (Prol, AA 4:289 [Kant 1977:33]). Kant's idealism is epistemological, not metaphysical. However, this does not mean that Kant's idealism concerns only the *knowledge* of objects, and not the *objects* of knowledge. In some sense, the objects of knowledge themselves are also ideal, that is, ontologically dependent on our forms of knowledge, hence they are mere appearances, that is, representations, and not things in themselves. See further below.

2 In fact, in the notorious passage at A491/B519 Kant appears to be claiming that 'extended beings ... have outside our thoughts no existence grounded in itself'. See also Prol, AA 4:337, where Kant makes the prima facie confusing claim that it can be denied that 'bodies (as appearances of outer sense) exist *outside my thoughts as bodies in nature*' (Kant 2002:128, my underlining). This last aspect (i.e. what is underlined) provides the clue to why Kant is not an empirical idealist. Bodies of course exist outside of us in space (as Kant affirms in the same passage), but space is merely a form of sensibility, hence bodies do not exist outside my sensibility, hence they do not exist outside my representations or thoughts (cf. A370). This is why Kant identifies appearances and representations. However, Kant also points out that 'body ... refers also to the thing *in itself* that underlies this appearance', as much as it refers to 'outer intuition (in space)' (Prol, AA 4:337 [Kant 2002:128], trans. emended), thus underlining a major difference from empirical idealism, for, in Kant's view, the thing in itself does exist independently of the mind.

3 See further Schulting (2011, 2017b).

4 See Kanterian (2013) for a fine critique of Langton on this point.

5 See further Schulting (2017b).

6 For the distinction between representation and represent*ed*, see the discussion further below, where I compare Reinhold with Sellars.

7 See also more recently Jankowiak (2017).

8 See the account in Schulting (2017a), ch. 4.

9 See Ameriks (2012:115–19) for a fine critique of Wood's interpretation of idealism.

10 See Onof (2019).

11 Kant writes: 'The understanding ..., by assuming appearances, grants also the existence of things in themselves, and to that extent we may say that the representation of such beings as underlie the appearances, consequently of mere beings of the understanding, is not only admissible but unavoidable' (Prol, AA 4:315 [Kant 1977:57], trans. emended; see also Bxxvii and V-Met/Mron, AA 29:857). Notice that the fact that the existence of appearances entails the existence of things in themselves does not imply that the existence of things in themselves entails the

existence of appearances—e.g. God is a thing in itself, whose existence, if he were to exist, does not entail the existence of appearances. However, given a relatively orthodox Christian understanding of God as triune, one could of course explain God's immanent economy in such a way that God the Son, as incarnated as a human being (i.e. an appearance in the phenomenal world), is an appearance of God, who is also the Father, where the appearance is identical to the thing in itself underlying it, and the triune God is the thing in itself, whose existence necessarily entails the appearance of the Son. See also Ameriks (2012:86, 116n.39).

12 Cf. Bxxvii and Ameriks's commentary on this passage (2012:116n.39). The problems with assuming numerical identity across the phenomenal/noumenal boundary have been noted before by Schulting (2011) and Marshall (2013).

13 I follow Langton (1998:50, 55, 57, 60, 63) here in distinguishing between, on the one hand, phenomenal substances, which are substances only comparatively speaking, and, on the other hand, a pure concept of substance as an independent being that exists in itself, i.e. unaccompanied, where appearances are, in one sense, accidents of the latter, and, in another sense, identified with the former, namely, when appearances are determined as objects of experience in accordance with the category of substance. My use of 'substance' here refers to the pure concept of substance.

14 As Imhof (2014) rightly indicates, unlike the later works, the *Versuch* is not yet concerned with advancing a strong foundational programme. The best critical introduction that gives a good insight into Reinhold's ambitious overall philosophical agenda, and the problems facing it, is Ameriks (2000), Part II. See also Beiser (1987) and Frank (1997), Part II, for a more historical analysis, and, for a contextualization of the *Versuch*, especially Onnasch's extensive and invaluable introduction including bibliography—a short book in itself!—to his edition of the *Versuch* (Onnasch 2010). Like Ameriks (2000:104), I very much doubt that, on the whole, Reinhold's presumably 'easier' version of the Critical programme, in particular, a deduction of what in Kant are quite clearly *distinct* and *irreducible* cognitive capacities (sensibility, understanding, reason) from the notion of 'representation', would have met with Kant's approval—notwithstanding Kant's positive comments in general on Reinhold's work in correspondence to him (see Br, AA 11:288 and cf. Onnasch 2010:cxii–cxv)—or is indeed a systematic improvement upon Kant, as Reinhold himself thought. However, in the current essay, rather than emphasizing the differences between Reinhold and Kant, significant though they may be, I wish to focus on the extent to which Reinhold's view on the relation between representation and the thing in itself can be seen as Kantian at least in spirit. I thus also ignore the famous criticisms of Reinhold's views on this score by Schulze in his *Aenesidemus*. For an excellent account of Schulze's (and Jacobi's) criticisms of Kant's notion of the thing in itself, see Rosefeldt (2012).

15 I do not consider the different versions of the so-called *Elementarphilosophie*, including alternative accounts of his view of the thing in itself and his representationalist approach, that Reinhold presented in his *Beyträge zur Berichtigung bisheriger Mißverständnisse der Philosophen* (published in two volumes; Jena, 1790 and 1794) or in *Ueber das Fundament des philosophischen Wissens* (Jena, 1791). For a detailed commentary on the origin and development of the *Elementarphilosophie*, see Bondeli (1995). In particular in connection with the place of the *Versuch* in Reinhold's philosophy, see also especially Onnasch (2010).
16 Fabbianelli (2011:30–1, 49, 70ff., *et passim*) appears to read Reinhold's *Versuch* as a psychological treatise of sorts.
17 My reading of Reinhold diverges from that of Ameriks here (see Ameriks 2000:106).
18 This view harks back to a Wolffian distinction. See Chapter 3.
19 Reinhold subdivides the genus 'representation' into its various species, i.e. sensations, thoughts, intuitions, concepts, and ideas, much in the same way as Kant does in the so-called *Stufenleiter* in the *Critique*, but more extensively and more analytically fine-grained than Kant (*Versuch*, §10ff.). What is at issue here, in Reinhold's emphasis on *Vorstellung in engster Bedeutung*, is the *genus* 'representation' and the *pure* capacity for representation (*Versuch* 2:232). See Beiser (1987:250–1).
20 It should be noted that Reinhold avoids the term 'transcendental', but it is clear from the proceedings in the *Versuch* that he carries out a transcendental analysis of our capacity for representation (cf. Fabbianelli 2011:52–3). It should also be noted that Reinhold at first sight seems to employ the term 'internal' or 'inner' as referring to the mind ambiguously, either referring to the *Gemüt*, as a functioning subject's capacity for representation, or even to the body (*Versuch* 2:217), or referring to the capacity for representation purely *qua* such capacity for representation. It is the latter sense that is centrally at issue, when Reinholds talks about 'inner', or 'essential', 'conditions' of a 'mere representation' (*Versuch* 2:243). Cf. Beiser (1987:250–1).
21 Reinhold himself appears to call this approach the 'short route' to idealism: 'If I should hope to be understood by my readers—a hope that I can base on nothing but the circumstance that *my* problem is easier to solve than *Kant*'s—one will start to understand the impossibility of knowledge of the thing in itself, as *Kant* proved, <u>by a shorter route</u>. The thing in itself cannot be *represented*, so how could it then be *known*?' (*Versuch* 2:264, my underlining). However, this remark should not be read simply on its own, outside of the context of the previous 50-odd pages of analysis of the *grounds* on which Reinhold believes that the thing in itself cannot be represented. Nevertheless, Reinhold's claim about the unrepresentability of the thing in itself does look like a short route to the unknowability thesis, in the sense that, as Ameriks (2000:127–8) writes, Reinhold largely dispenses with Kant's lengthy arguments for transcendental idealism in the *Critique*, specifically the details of the

account of space and time in the Transcendental Aesthetic and the Antinomies. But in and of itself this does not invalidate Reinhold's more general claims about the unrepresentability of the thing in itself (cf. Breazeale 2003:251–2). It is of course not representability as such that keeps certain features from being characteristics of things in themselves. There is something about things in themselves which keeps them from being represented as such, namely certain unconditional features that cannot be represented. But there still is an internal connection between these unconditional characteristics and the fact that we cannot *represent* unconditional characteristics: we cannot represent conditionally, namely represent *to ourselves* as representers, what is by nature unconditional.

22 Cf. by contrast Ameriks (2000:130).
23 *Versuch* 2:227–8; cf. *Versuch* 1:149.
24 Cf. Ameriks (2012:85).
25 Ameriks (2000:130–3) notes that the triviality reading can be escaped by focusing on the element of modification that Reinhold talks about, but then indicates some further potential problems for Reinhold.
26 Reinhold contrasts *ideale Wirklichkeit* with *reale Wirklichkeit*, which might come across as odd-sounding expressions. *Wirklichkeit* is a modal term, not to be confused with *Realität*. What I thus take him to mean by these terms is 'ideal existence in the mind' versus 'real existence outside the mind', respectively.
27 Notice that Kant can however be said to be a direct realist in the sense that we directly perceive the *empirically real objects in space*, which are after all nothing but our representations. But contemporary direct realists, such as Langton (1998) and Allais (2015), take this perception to refer to the thing that exists in itself, even though it is emphasized that we do not thereby perceive its intrinsic or mind-independent properties. There is some ground for this view in e.g. Prol, AA 4:337, but Kant's general view (most clearly in the Refutation of Idealism) is that we only directly perceive objects in space, not things in themselves in whatever manifestation.
28 Cf. the editorial note in *Versuch* 2:529n.176.
29 Reinhold uses the Latinate *repräsentieren* (*Versuch* 2:245), which literally translates into German as *vergegenwärtigen*.
30 Reinhold's assumption that matter is necessarily a manifold, and that only form is able to unite the multiplicity of matter is not properly argued, to say the least. In the later *Beyträge*, he admits that indeed this deduction had failed in the *Versuch*.
31 Reinhold probably means that the concept of the thing in itself in general is the 'mere intellectual concept of an *object* in general', not that the latter is the object of the former, as the grammatical structure of the German suggests. Thanks to Christian Onof for flagging this.
32 On Reinhold's views on affection, see *Versuch* 2:282–5, 300–1, 343–4, 350–4, *et passim*.

33 In the just quoted passage, Reinhold might appear to go beyond Kant. Reinhold's assertion seems to claim that *my* having the representation is definitional for the representation *being* a representation. By contrast, Kant would not say that a representation which I do not represent to myself is *eo ipso* not a representation, since this cannot be concluded on the basis of the analytic principle of apperception; for the principle of apperception is not constitutive of the existence or occurrence of representations in the mind, but rather a principle concerning the conditions of the self-ascribability of representations (cf. B132). There could still be representations going on of which I am not conscious (cf. Ameriks 2000:109, 131). But Reinhold of course means representation in the strict sense, namely, a representation of some object, not just alterations in the mind as a result of affection; or, not all that goes on in the mind are strictly speaking *representations* (cf. *Versuch* 2:321), although he does seem to side with Locke in rejecting the possibility of representations of which I am not conscious.

34 In a sense we must be capable of thinking the thing that has an in itself nature also as that 'to which corresponds the mere matter of our representation alone without its form' (*Versuch* 2:403).

35 I discuss some of these commentators in Schulting (2017a).

36 Notice that, for Reinhold as well as Kant, this does not imply that we cannot have a merely *practically* objectively valid cognition of God, although for Reinhold this is arguably more difficult to sustain, given his rather strict deduction from representability.

37 Cf. A681/B709.

38 See Schulting (2017a), ch. 9.

39 See also Schulting (2017a), ch. 9. Notice that ε-determination is not to be understood along the lines of contemporary epistemological conceptions of 'justified true belief'; it rather concerns the necessary (and formally sufficient) transcendental conditions of both experience and the *object* of experience (A158/B197), in line with the Reinholdian/Kantian definition of what first constitutes an object, namely, the connectedness of determinations in a manifold of representations due to the understanding. Object in this sense is a function of the objective unity in the manifold and nothing outside it.

40 The chapter, in the *Versuch*, comparable to Kant's account of the transcendental ideal (and the regulative use of the ideas of reason) is §81, where Reinhold defines what is an 'idea in the narrowest sense' (*Versuch* 2:464–72). Here, Reinhold speaks of the necessary idea of 'unconditioned unity', whose characteristics are 'unconditioned universality or *totality*', 'unconditioned limitation or exclusion of the limiting condition, i.e. *boundlessness*', 'unconditioned concurrence or the all-*encompassing*', and 'unconditioned *necessity*'. This 'unconditioned unity' is 'a necessary object (*Gegenstand*)', something that must be thought, but it is not a 'characteristic of

knowable objects' (*Versuch* 2:466). The aforementioned characteristics cannot be attributed to 'any knowable thing (*Dinge*), insofar as it is knowable' (*Versuch* 2:466).

41 At first sight, the metaphysical dual-aspect reading of Kantian idealism (see Schulting 2011) is able to provide a more coherent interpretation of the relation between the ε-determinations attributed to a thing (including its spatiotemporal properties) and all of the thing's possible properties (its o-determination), which on this reading includes its ε-determinations, without thereby conflating a thing's intrinsic and extrinsic properties, that is, the properties that the thing has as it is in itself and the properties that it has as an appearance. Spatiotemporal properties are not properties of a thing *qua* having intrinsic properties (an in itself nature) but merely *qua* having extrinsic (or relational, or subject-dependent) properties, but both sets of properties are properties of one and the same thing (notwithstanding, of course, the conceptual problems, flagged earlier in Section 6.1, with seeing spatiotemporal properties as the extrinsic or relational or subject-relativized properties *of* things in themselves). But this dual-aspect reading stands in tension with Kant's argument that the determinations of possible experience (including all of the extrinsic properties attributed to objects of possible experience) are not aggregates *of* reality *an sich*, but are only grounded by it. Moreover, this reading assumes numerical identity between an appearance as an object of experience and an underlying thing in itself, thus problematically presupposing a plurality of things in themselves corresponding to their multiple phenomenal counterparts. Further on Kant's idealism, see Schulting (2017b).

42 See further Schulting (2017a), ch. 9.

Chapter 7

1 This is not the same as saying that no nonconceptual content *could* be brought under concepts.
2 In a planned work on Hegel's *Science of Logic*, I expand on the positive story of Kant's influence on Hegel, and how transcendental logic centrally informs the Greater Logic. A more detailed interpretation of the early Hegel's critique of Kant in *Faith and Knowledge*, in particular, is given in Schulting (2017a), ch. 8. See also Chapters 8 and 9, this volume.
3 Sedgwick (1993) comes very much to the defence of Kant, but in other work (Sedgwick 1992, 1997, 2000, 2001, 2004, 2005, 2012) she defends Hegel's reading of Kant (and also that by Hegelians such as McDowell) (see Schulting 2016a). On Sedgwick's views, see further Chapter 9, this volume.
4 I am not sure if such ahistorical validations are a good start in helping us *understand* Kant's position, as it runs the risk of begging his question or at least missing (some

of) its essential elements. Philosophical evaluation is dependent on faithful interpretative work. In reality, however, Pippin's reading is much more heedful of strictly interpretative issues than his statement suggests.

5 Cf. A19/B33. As Kant says here, the relation that an intuition has to the object is an immediate one, consistent with the definition of an intuition as designating immediacy. But this relation (*Beziehung*) is only 'secured' as a relation proper, a *determined* relation, by the functions of the understanding.

6 Cf. Pippin (1989:85). Hegel in fact accuses Kant himself of subverting his own idea of a productive imagination as an original a priori synthesis by regarding it in the end as just an act of the understanding, which Hegel regards as a derivative, a posteriori, act in comparison to the imagination (for details, see Schulting 2017a, ch. 8). This putatively shows that Kant sees the relation between concept and intuition purely as a 'mechanical relation of a unity of self-consciousness which stands *in antithesis to* the empirical manifold, either determining it or reflecting on it' (GuW, GW 4:343 [Hegel 1977:92], emphasis added), thus seeing the relation not as genuinely a priori and as an organic unity holding opposites together (cf. WL, GW 12:22–3).

7 For more on the *Leitfaden*, Schulting (2018b), ch. 5 and Schulting (ms), which contains my most recent views on how to read the *Leitfaden*. For more on McDowell's position, see Schulting (2017a), ch. 5.

8 Sedgwick (2012) likewise argues that Hegel takes Kant to task for the fixation of the separability of form and content, which in Hegel's view is unsustainable if one is to take seriously the Kantian invention of a truly original-synthetic unity of form and content, spontaneity of the understanding and receptivity of sensibility. I briefly discuss the unresolved contradictions in Sedgwick's Hegelian reading of Kant in Schulting (2016a). See also Chapter 9, this volume.

9 Pippin differentiates distinguishability (or 'notional separability' [2015b:67]) from separability (see also Pippin 2005a and 2015a:162). That is, formally, concept and intuition are of course 'distinguishable', but in actual fact, in experience, they are never separable. Or so Pippin argues. It is important to note, in light of criticism by some nonconceptualists (Allais 2009), that by inseparability Pippin (and also McDowell 1996:9, *et passim*) does not mean that intuition does not have a distinctive and distinct role to play in cognition, but rather that the distinctive role it plays is inseparable from the role concepts play; they play their roles together.

10 This is in direct contrast to how for example Gareth Evans pictures the relation between sense content and conceptualization (see Evans 1982:227); see the discussion in Schulting (2016c:v–xiii).

11 Pippin says that Hegel's critique is concerned with the 'strictness' of the distinction (2005a:30n.19), not with the distinction per se.

12 For a critical assessment of the Fichtean legacy of reading Kant's principle of apperception, see Ameriks (2000), esp. ch. 5.

13 I discuss Sedgwick's own, more recent, take on these issues concerning the relation between Kant and Hegel in Chapter 9.
14 I agree with Pippin's radically literal interpretation here, where most Kantians attempt to explain away any constitutive talk. Kant's account in the Deduction is not about a 'subjective unavoidability' but constitutes a 'strong objectivity claim'. That is, 'Kant will try to establish such objectivity by insisting that the categories *constitute* what any possible relation to an object could be, and so what any object in possible relation to us could be' (2005a:32). This indeed goes beyond, as Pippin says (2005a:32), the mere claim that for objects to be *knowable* to us, they must conform to our forms of knowledge. See my own account, also in relation to Pippin, in Schulting (2018b), ch. 10.
15 I expand on the interpretative details of Hegel's reading in Schulting (2017a), ch. 8. See also Chapters 8 and 9, this volume.
16 And this is in fact what Fichte believes (see again GA, I,4:227–8, quoted earlier).
17 Cf. Schulting (2015:570).
18 I agree with Pippin that reference to animal 'experience' is not going to help here. In Pippin (2013), he explicates what he sees as a fundamental difference between the way human beings and animals perceive. See e.g. Pippin's interesting reference to his non-apperceiving dog Molly in Pippin (2013:101–2). Cf. McDowell (1996:64, 182–3). Further on animal perception, see Chapter 5, this volume.
19 See also Pippin (1989:31): 'We are here shifting from an account of thought's relation to the pure manifold of intuition to thought's "self-determination".... This does not at all eliminate the role of the given in knowledge, but it will radically relativize to "thought" the ways in which the given *can be taken to be given*' (emphasis added).
20 Fichte, it should be noted, quite explicitly conflates epistemological and existential conditions. For Fichte—in his interpretation of Kant—receptivity or sensibility is something we ascribe to ourselves purely through thought: '"The capacity to acquire representations by the way in which we are affected by objects" [Fichte paraphrases A19/B33 here, D.S.]—what is it? Since we only think the affection, we undoubtedly only think the common [*Gemeinsame*] of it; <u>it is a mere thought</u>. When one posits an object while thinking it has affected one, one thinks of oneself as being *affected in this particular case*; and when one thinks that this happens with *all* objects of one's perception, one thinks of oneself as *being capable of being affected in general* [*affizierbar überhaupt*], or in other words: <u>through this thinking [*durch dieses dein Denken*], one ascribes receptivity or sensibility to oneself. Thus the object as given is merely thought</u>.... Naturally, all our knowledge starts with *an affection*; but not through an object' (GA, I,4:241, trans. mine and my underlining).
21 And of course one should note the following 'its unity' in the subordinate clause of that sentence (B145).

22 Of course, Hegelians want to stress that Hegel does not, like the rationalists, want to reduce perceptions to confused ideas or concepts (Pippin 1993:291), and also that we are dependent on a content we do not make—because we are discursive thinkers, rather than noetic or intuitive intellects (cf. Pippin 1993:292, Sedgwick 2012). Pippin says: 'Hegel clearly has no interest in returning to some neo-Leibnizian position as a result of his dissatisfaction with Kant's concept–intuition distinction in the Deduction' (1993:295).
23 See also Sedgwick (2012), in particular chs 2 and 4. Cf. Sedgwick (2004).
24 For more details, see Schulting (2017a), ch. 8.
25 See also Sedgwick's (1993:279–80) critique of Pippin on this point.
26 In the *Stufenleiter* (A320/B376-7), Kant appears to define 'perception' as either a sensation (the modification of a subject's inner state) or a cognition, which can in its turn be either an intuition or a concept. This seems to indicate that by 'perception' any representation in sensibility, subjective or objective, can be meant (see also A115, A120, B207, A192–3/B237–8, B275). Perception as such is not *experience*, since experience is 'perception according to rules' (Refl, 2740, AA 16:494, trans. mine), or 'cognition through *connected* perceptions' (B161, emphasis added; cf. Prol, AA 4:298 [§19], 305, and FM, AA 20:276). Experience is contrasted with 'mere perception—whose validity is merely subjective' (Prol, AA 4:304 [Kant 2002:98]).
27 See Schulting (2018b), ch. 11.
28 Briefly, in our nonconceptualist reading of the unity of space in Onof & Schulting (2015), we argue for a distinction between, on the one hand, the *sui generis* unity of space, which we call the unicity of space, and is as such independent of the unity of apperception (categorial unity) and thus independent of the synthesis of the imagination, and, on the other hand, the unity of a determinate space (or determinate spaces), which *is* due to the unity of apperception, by virtue of the synthesis of the imagination. The *sui generis* unity of space defines the essential characteristics of space as the form of intuition (singularity, infinity, mereological inversion), which cannot be reduced to conceptual unity by virtue of the unity of apperception (and thus neither to the synthesis of imagination). This, we argue, refutes conceptualist interpretations of the unity of space (such as Pippin's). Nevertheless, our reading allows for the conceptual grasp of the *sui generis* unicity of space *as* a unity for the understanding, and thus accommodates Kant's claim in the footnote that the understanding determines the spatial manifold 'inwardly' by means of the synthesis of the imagination.
29 It is also unclear how Pippin can acknowledge that 'orientation in space is in some sense pre-conceptual' (1993:291). How is this possible if he denies that there are pure intuitions? For pre-conceptual orientation in space requires a pre-conceptual form of such orientation, which is the pure form of intuition, space. But if Kant's distinction between form of intuition and formal intuition is blurred, as Hegel and

Pippin argue, then it seems hard to visualise a *pre-conceptual* form for spatial orientation, given that, on the Hegelian reading, its unitary form is provided by the understanding via the synthesis of imagination.

30 For an argument, see Schulting (2017a), ch. 5.
31 I employ Longuenesse's (1998:243) phrasing here (cf. B152).
32 This not only affects Pippin's reading. Ever since Henrich's (1969) proposal of a two-step proof structure for the B-Deduction, also many Kantians believe that the 'second step' is meant to prove that any sense content is subject to the categories. For a different reading, see Schulting (2018b), ch. 11.
33 See Longuenesse (1998:196). Cf. Pippin's reflections on Longuenesse's interpretation in Pippin (1997b:322–3).
34 See the essays on the McDowell–Dreyfus debate in Schear (2013), and Pippin's own essay in that volume (Pippin 2013). See also Onof (2016).

Chapter 8

1 I especially thank Kees Jan Brons for his comments on an earlier draft of this chapter. I am confident we have come ever closer to sharing a similar outlook on Hegel.
2 This is the volume *Die Aktualität des Deutschen Idealismus* (Berlin: Suhrkamp 2016). I shall here be referring to the German version of Pippin's article (Pippin 2016), with the corresponding passages in the English version, where they (more or less) overlap, separated by a forward slash. Pippin's new book on Hegel's *Science of Logic* is, appropriately, also called *Hegel's Realm of Shadows. Logic as Metaphysics in the 'Science of Logic'* (Pippin 2018b). See my review in Schulting (forthcoming c).
3 'Indem Denken als tätig in Beziehung auf Gegenstände genommen wird, das *Nachdenken über* etwas, so enthält das Allgemeine als solches Produkt seiner Tätigkeit den Wert der *Sache*, das *Wesentliche*, das *Innere*, das *Wahre*' (W 8:76).
4 Pippin quotes a passage from the *Science of Logic*, where Hegel compares the Logic to Kant's transcendental logic: 'Die klarste Beschreibung der Weise, wie Hegel zwei Drittel seiner Logik, die objektive Logik, verstanden wissen will, lautet so: 'Das, was hier *objektive Logik* genannt worden, würde zum Teil dem entsprechen, was bei [Kant] die *transzendentale Logik* ist [W 5:61]' (2016:165–6).
5 For a detailed account of the role of figurative synthesis, see Schulting (2018b), ch. 11.
6 See further Schulting (2017a), ch. 8.
7 See Schulting (2017c).
8 See Conant (2016). I discuss Conant's position at length in Schulting (ms).

9 In his new book *Hegel's Realm of Shadows*, Pippin appears to argue somewhat differently with respect to the relation between general and transcendental logic in Kant (Pippin 2018b:40–1). Supposedly, following a lead from Rosenkoetter (2014), in the Metaphysical Deduction itself, Kant already makes a distinction between, on the one hand, a purely general logic and, on the other, a logic that has objective content but is not a transcendental logic. I do not think this interpretation comports with Kant's text (despite the putative evidence that Rosenkoetter presents in favour of it). For one thing, it would pose the significant philosophical problem of how *that* supposedly non-transcendental logic is then seen to be linked to the transcendental logic that putatively is first presented in the *transcendental* deduction, without this leading to regress problems which the very *Leitfaden* in the Deduction is supposed to block. Such a rather formalistic understanding of the distinction between general and transcendental logic saddles Kant with an extremely uncharitable position. I also don't think Pippin needs this recourse for his Hegelian understanding of Kant's central argument. I briefly discuss this further in Schulting (forthcoming c).

10 Thanks to Christian Onof for noting this. Pippin actually appears to latterly have shifted his view on this point from first arguing (1989:38) that we need only the first half of the B-Deduction to arguing (2014:148) that all we need is an updated ('properly conceived') metaphysical deduction (cum apperception theory). Recently, Pippin even writes that 'Hegel rejects the very question that is at the basis of the transcendental deduction' (2018a:56). See the note above.

11 See Chapter 5, this volume.

12 See further Schulting (2017a), ch. 8.

13 As Pippin writes, 'the sensible presence of the world in our immediate, receptive contact with it just *could* not violate the requirements of our mindedness' (2005b:212)

14 See further Schulting (2017a), ch. 8.

Chapter 9

1 See Schulting (2017a), ch. 8, which deals with Hegel's critique of Kant.

2 See Schulting (2017a, b).

3 For the long account, and exegetical details, of Hegel's critique of Kant, see Schulting (2017a), ch. 8. See also Schulting (forthcoming d).

4 The addition of the adverb 'formally' is to indicate that we still need a *material* condition for cognition, which provides it real possibility, this material condition being sensible intuitions. But the need for this additional condition does not detract from the fact that objective determinacy is fully and completely satisfied by the apperception principle.

5 The very terminology of 'thing in itself' indicates something about how some thing exists *in itself*, not *for* us (or any cognitive agent). By contrast, to judge about a thing means *ipso facto* that the thing we judge about is *for* us, as judging agents. This follows from the Copernican hypothesis. (Questions about the numerical identity between the thing as it is in itself and as it is for us, as appearance, are at this point not immediately of concern.)
6 See my review of Sedgwick's book (Schulting 2016a).
7 In a planned paper, I discuss more in detail what is at issue in the Being logic, specifically the very first few paragraphs, which form the basis of Houlgate's claim that there is a strict identity between being and thought. I agree with this claim, and I think Pippin does too, but still there are important differences between our readings that decide on the precise qualification of one's interpretation: either ontological in a pre-Kantian sense or transcendental in some sense and nonetheless ontological, but not in a pre-Kantian sense.
8 For a full account of Hegel's critique, see Schulting (2017a), ch. 8.
9 See further Schulting (2017a:399–416).
10 For an extensive account, see Schulting (2018b), ch. 11.

Bibliography

Allais, L. (2009) 'Kant, Nonconceptual Content and the Representation of Space', *Journal of the History of Philosophy* 47(3): 383–413.
—— (2011) 'Transcendental Idealism and the Transcendental Deduction', in D. Schulting & J. Verburgt (eds) *Kant's Idealism. New Interpretations of a Controversial Doctrine* (Dordrecht: Springer), pp. 91–107.
—— (2015) *Manifest Reality: Kant's Idealism and His Realism* (Oxford: Oxford University Press).
Allison, H. (1983) *Kant's Transcendental Idealism. An Interpretation and Defense* (New Haven: Yale University Press).
—— (2004) *Kant's Transcendental Idealism. An Interpretation and Defense. Revised & Enlarged Edition* (New Haven: Yale University Press).
Ameriks, K. (2000) *Kant and the Fate of Autonomy. Problems in the Appropriation of the Critical Philosophy* (Cambridge: Cambridge University Press).
—— (2006) *Kant and the Historical Turn. Philosophy as Critical Interpretation* (Oxford: Clarendon Press).
—— (2012) *Kant's Elliptical Path* (Oxford: Clarendon Press).
—— (2019) *Kantian Subjects* (Oxford: Oxford University Press).
Baum, M. (2001) 'Systemform und Selbsterkenntnis der Vernunft bei Kant', in H. Fulda & J. Stolzenburg (eds) (2001) *Architektonik und System in der Philosophie Kants* (Hamburg: Meiner), pp. 25–40.
Beiser, F. (1987) *The Fate of Reason. German Philosophy from Kant to Fichte* (Cambridge, MA: Harvard University Press).
Bird, G. (2006) *The Revolutionary Kant. A Commentary on the 'Critique of Pure Reason'* (Chicago/La Salle, IL: Open Court).
Bondeli, M. (1995) *Das Anfangsproblem bei Karl Leonhard Reinhold. Eine systematische und entwicklungsgeschichtliche Untersuchung zur Philosophie Reinholds in der Zeit von 1789 bis 1803* (Frankfurt a.M.: Klostermann).
Bowman, B. (2013) *Hegel and the Metaphysics of Absolute Negativity* (Cambridge: Cambridge University Press).
Brandt, R. (1994) 'Rousseau und Kants "Ich denke"', in R. Brandt & W. Stark (eds) *Autographen, Dokumente und Briefe. Zu Edition, Amtsgeschäften und Werk Immanuel Kants* (Hamburg: Meiner), pp. 1–18.
Brandt, R. & W. Stark (eds) (1987) *Neue Autographen und Dokumente zu Kants Leben, Schriften und Vorlesungen*, Kant-Forschungen, Bd. 1 (Hamburg: Meiner).
Breazeale, D. (2003) 'Two Cheers for Post-Kantianism: A Response to Karl Ameriks', *Inquiry* 46: 239–59.

Carl, W. (1989a) *Der schweigende Kant* (Göttingen: Vandenhoeck & Ruprecht).
—— (1989b) 'Kant's First Drafts of the Deduction of the Categories', in E. Förster (ed.) *Kant's Transcendental Deductions: The Three Critiques and the Opus postumum* (Stanford: Stanford University Press), pp. 3–20.
Cassam, Q. (2007) *The Possibility of Knowledge* (Oxford: Oxford University Press).
Collins, A. (1999) *Possible Experience. Understanding Kant's 'Critique of Pure Reason'* (Berkeley: University of California Press).
Conant, J. (2016) 'Why Kant is not a Kantian', *Philosophical Topics* 44(1): 75–125.
Copernicus N. (1990) *Das Neue Weltbild. Drei Texte: Commentariolus, Brief gegen Werne, De revolutionibus*, ed. H. Zekl (Hamburg: Meiner).
—— (1992) *On the Revolutions*, new edition, trans. and ed. E. Rosen (Baltimore: Johns Hopkins University Press).
Düsing, K. (2013) 'Gibt es einen Zirkel des Selbstbewußtseins? Ein Aufriß von paradigmatischen Positionen und Selbstbewußtseinsmodellen von Kant bis Heidegger', in K. Düsing, *Subjektivität und Freiheit. Untersuchungen zum Idealismus von Kant bis Hegel*, 2nd expanded edition (Stuttgart-Bad Cannstatt: Frommann-Holzboog), pp. 111–40.
Dyck, C. (2011) 'A Wolff in Kant's Clothing: Christian Wolff's Influence on Kant's Accounts of Consciousness, Self-Consciousness, and Psychology', *Philosophy Compass* 6(1): 44–53.
—— (2014) *Kant and Rational Psychology* (Oxford: Oxford University Press).
Evans, G. (1982) *The Varieties of Reference* (Oxford: Clarendon Press).
Fabbianelli, F. (2011) *Coscienza e realtà. Un saggio su Reinhold* (Pisa: Edizione delle Normale).
Frank, M. (1997) *'Unendliche Annäherung': Die Anfänge der philosophischen Frühromantik* (Frankfurt a.M.: Suhrkamp).
Friedman, M. (2006) 'Philosophy of Natural Science', in P. Guyer (ed.) *The Cambridge Companion to Kant and Modern Philosophy* (Cambridge: Cambridge University Press), pp. 303–41.
Gardner, S. (1999) *Kant and the 'Critique of Pure Reason'* (London/New York: Routledge).
Giladi, P. (2017) 'On Schulting on Hegel's Critique of Kant's Subjectivism in the Transcendental Deduction', *Critique* (November issue), https://virtualcritique.wordpress.com/2017/11/10/paul-giladi-on-dennis-schultings-on-hegels-critique-of-kants-subjectivism-in-the-transcendental-deduction/.
Ginsborg, H. (2015) 'The Appearance of Spontaneity: Kant on Judgment and Empirical Self-Knowledge', in H. Ginsborg, *The Normativity of Nature. Essays on Kant's "Critique of Judgement"* (Oxford: Oxford University Press), pp. 202–24.
Golob, S. (2018) 'On Dennis Schulting's *Kant's Radical Subjectivism*', *Critique* (May issue), https://virtualcritique.wordpress.com/2018/05/20/sacha-golob-on-dennis-schultings-kants-radical-subjectivism/.
—— (2020) 'What Do Animals See? Intentionality, Objects and Kantian Nonconceptualism', in L. Allais & J. Callanan (eds) *Kant and Animals* (Oxford: Oxford University Press), pp. 65–87.

Grüne, S. (2009) *Blinde Anschauung. Die Rolle von Begriffen in Kants Theorie sinnlicher Synthesis* (Frankfurt a.M: Klostermann).
Guyer, P. (2006) *Kant* (London/New York: Routledge).
Hanna, R. (2008) 'Kantian Non-Conceptualism', *Philosophical Studies* 137: 41–64.
Hanson, N. (1959) 'Copernicus' Role in Kant's Revolution', *Journal of the History of Ideas* XX(2): 274–81.
Hegel, G.W.F. (1977) *Faith and Knowledge*, trans. and ed. W. Cerf & H.S. Harris (Albany, NY: SUNY Press).
—— (2010a) *Encyclopedia of the Philosophical Sciences in Basic Outline*, trans. and ed. K. Brinkmann & D. Dahlstrom (Cambridge: Cambridge University Press).
—— (2010b) *Science of Logic*, trans. and ed. G. di Giovanni (Cambridge: Cambridge University Press).
Henrich, D. (1967) *Fichtes ursprüngliche Einsicht* (Frankfurt a.M.: Klostermann).
—— (1969) 'The Proof-Structure of Kant's Transcendental Deduction', *Review of Metaphysics* 22(4): 640–59.
—— (1976) *Identität und Objektivität. Eine Untersuchung über Kants transzendentale Deduktion* (Heidelberg: Carl Winter Universitätsverlag).
—— (1988) 'Die Identität des Subjekts in der transzendentalen Deduktion', in H. Oberer & G. Seel (eds) *Kant. Analysen – Probleme – Kritik* (Würzburg: Königshausen & Neumann), pp. 39–70.
—— (2019) *Dies Ich, das viel besagt. Fichtes Einsicht nachdenken* (Frankfurt a.M.: Klostermann).
Horstmann, R.-P. (2007) 'Kant und Carl über Apperzeption', in J. Stolzenberg (ed.) *Kant in der Gegenwart* (Berlin/New York: De Gruyter), pp. 131–47.
Houlgate, S. (2006) *The Opening of Hegel's Logic* (West Lafayette, IN: Purdue University Press).
—— (2015) 'Hegel's Critique of Kant', *Proceedings of the Aristotelian Society*, supplementary vol. LXXXIX: 21–41.
—— (2018) 'Thought and Being in Hegel's Logic. Reflections on Hegel, Kant and Pippin', in L. Illetterati & F. Menegoni (eds) *Wirklichkeit. Beiträge zu einem Schlüsselbegriff der Hegelschen Philosophie* (Frankfurt a.M.: Klostermann), pp. 101–18.
Imhof, S. (2014) *Der Grund der Subjektivität. Motive und Potenzial von Fichtes Ansatz* (Basel: Schwabe).
Jankowiak, T. (2017) 'Kantian Phenomenalism Without Berkeleyan Idealism', *Kantian Review* 22(2): 205–31.
Jorgensen, L. (2009) 'The Principle of Continuity and Leibniz's Theory of Consciousness', *Journal of the History of Philosophy* 47(2): 223–48.
Kant, I. (1977) *Prolegomena to Any Future Metaphysics*, trans. and ed. P. Carus, rev. J. Ellington (Indianapolis: Hackett).
—— (1983) *What Real Progress Has Metaphysics Made in Germany since the Time of Leibniz and Wolff?*, trans. and ed. T. Humphrey (New York: Abaris).

—— (1999) *Correspondence*, trans. and ed. A. Zweig (Cambridge: Cambridge University Press).
—— (2001) *Lectures on Metaphysics*, trans. and ed. K. Ameriks & S. Naragon (Cambridge: Cambridge University Press).
—— (2002) *Theoretical Philosophy After 1781*, trans. and ed. H. Allison & P. Heath (Cambridge: Cambridge University Press).
—— (2003) *Theoretical Philosophy 1755–1770*, trans. and ed. D. Walford (Cambridge. Cambridge University Press).
—— (2004a) *Lectures on Logic*, trans. and ed. J. M. Young, (Cambridge: Cambridge University Press).
—— (2004b) *Kritiek van de zuivere rede*, trans. J. Veenbaas & W. Visser (Amsterdam: Boom).
—— (2005) *Notes and Fragments*, trans. and ed. P. Guyer et al. (Cambridge: Cambridge University Press).
—— (2007) *Anthropology, History, and Education*, trans. and ed. G. Zöller & R. Louden et al. (Cambridge: Cambridge University Press).
—— (2012a) *Lectures on Anthropology*, trans. and ed. A. Wood et al. (Cambridge: Cambridge University Press).
—— (2012b) *Natural Science*, trans. and ed. E. Watkins et al. (Cambridge: Cambridge University Press).
Kanterian, E. (2013) 'Bodies in *Prolegomena* §13: Noumena or Phenomena?', *Hegel Bulletin* 34 (2): 181–202.
Kemp Smith, N. (1913) 'The Meaning of Kant's Copernican Analogy', *Mind* XXII(88): 549–51.
—— (1999) *A Commentary to Kant's Critique of Pure Reason*, 1923 edition (Amherst: Humanity Press).
Klemme, H. (1996) *Kants Philosophie des Subjekts* (Hamburg: Meiner).
Kreines, J. (2015) *Reason in the World. Hegel's Metaphysics and Its Philosophical Appeal* (New York: Oxford University Press).
Kuhn, T. (1985) *The Copernican Revolution. Planetary Astronomy in the Development of Western Thought*, renewed edition (Cambridge MA: Harvard University Press).
—— (1996) *The Structure of Scientific Revolutions* (Chicago: University of Chicago Press).
Land, T. (2014) 'Spatial Representation, Magnitude, and the Two Stems of Cognition', *Canadian Journal of Philosophy* 44(5–6): 524–50.
Langton, R. (1998) *Kantian Humility. Our Ignorance of Things in Themselves* (Oxford: Oxford University Press).
La Rocca, C. (2007) 'L'intelletto oscuro. Inconscio e autocoscienza in Kant', in C. La Rocca (ed.) *Leggere Kant. Dimensioni della filosofia critica* (Pisa: Edizione ETS), pp. 63–116.
Longuenesse, B. (1998) *Kant and the Capacity to Judge* (Princeton: Princeton University Press).
—— (2017) *I, Me, Mine. Back to Kant and Back Again* (Oxford: Oxford University Press).

Marshall, C. (2013) 'Kant's Appearances and Things in Themselves as Qua- Objects', *Philosophical Quarterly* 63 (252): 520–45.

Martin, C. (2012) *Ontologie der Selbstbestimmung. Eine operationale Rekonstruktion von Hegels 'Wissenschaft der Logik'* (Tübingen: Mohr Siebeck).

McDowell, J. (1996) *Mind and World*, 2nd edition (Cambridge, MA: Harvard University Press).

—— (2009) *Having the World in View. Essays on Kant, Hegel, and Sellars* (Cambridge, MA: Harvard University Press).

McLear, C. (2011) 'Kant on Animal Consciousness', *Philosophers' Imprint* 11(15): 1–16.

Miles, M. (2006) 'Kant's "Copernican Revolution": Toward Rehabilitation of a Concept and Provision of a Frame-Work for the Interpretation of the *Critique of Pure Reason*', *Kant-Studien* 97(1): 1–32.

Moore, A. (2012) *The Evolution of Modern Metaphysics: Making Sense of Things* (Cambridge: Cambridge University Press).

Nagel, T. (1991) 'What Is It Like to Be A Bat?', in T. Nagel, *Mortal Questions* (Cambridge: Cambridge University Press), pp. 165–80.

Naragon, S. (1990) 'Kant on Descartes and the Brutes', *Kant-Studien* 81(1): 1–23.

Onnasch, E.-O. (2010) 'Einleitung', in K.L. Reinhold, *Versuch einer neuen Theorie des menschlichen Vorstellungsvermögens*, ed. E.-O. Onnasch (Hamburg: Meiner), pp. xi–clvii.

Onof, C. (2010) 'Kant's Conception of Self as Subject and Its Embodiment', *Kant Yearbook* 2 (May): 147–74.

—— (2016) 'Is There Room for Nonconceptual Content in Kant's Critical Philosophy?', in D. Schulting (ed.) *Kantian Nonconceptualism* (London/New York: Palgrave Macmillan), pp. 199–226.

—— (2019) 'Reality In-Itself and the Ground of Causality', *Kantian Review* 24(2): 197–222.

Onof, C. & D. Schulting (2015) 'Space as Form of Intuition and as Formal Intuition: On the Note to B160 in Kant's *Critique of Pure Reason*', *Philosophical Review* 124(1): 1–58.

Pippin, R. (1989) *Hegel's Idealism. The Satisfactions of Self-Consciousness* (Cambridge: Cambridge University Press).

—— (1993) 'Hegel's Original Insight', *International Philosophical Quarterly* XXXIII(3): 285–95.

—— (1997a) *Idealism as Modernism. Hegelian Variations* (Cambridge: Cambridge University Press).

—— (1997b) Review of Béatrice Longuenesse, *Kant et le pouvoir de juger* (PUF, 1993), *Journal of Philosophy* 94(6): 318–24.

—— (2005a) 'Concept and Intuition. On Distinguishability and Separability', *Hegel-Studien* 39/40: 25–39.

—— (2005b) *The Persistence of Subjectivity. On the Kantian Aftermath* (Cambridge: Cambridge University Press).

—— (2013) 'What is "Conceptual Activity"?', in J. Schear (ed.) *Mind, Reason and Being-in- the-World. The McDowell-Dreyfus Debate* (London: Routledge), pp. 91–109.

—— (2014) 'The Significance of Self-Consciousness in Idealist Theories of Logic', *Proceedings of the Aristotelian Society*, vol. CXIV, issue 2, pt 2: 145–66.

—— (2015a) 'Finite and Absolute Idealism. The Transcendental and the Metaphysical Hegel', in S. Gardner & M. Grist (eds) *The Transcendental Turn* (Oxford: Oxford University Press), pp. 159–72.

—— (2015b) 'John McDowell's Germans', in R. Pippin, *Interanimations. Receiving Modern German Philosophy* (Chicago: University of Chicago Press), pp. 63–90.

—— (2016) 'Logik und Metaphysik: Hegels "Reich der Schatten"', in R. Pippin, *Die Aktualität des Deutschen Idealismus* (Berlin: Suhrkamp), pp. 163–90.

—— (2017) 'Hegel on Logic as Metaphysics', in D. Moyar (ed.) *The Oxford Handbook of Hegel* (Oxford: Oxford University Press), pp. 199–218.

—— (2018a) 'The Many Modalities of *Wirklichkeit* in Hegel's *Wissenschaft der Logik*', in L. Illetterati & F. Menegoni (eds) *Wirklichkeit. Beiträge zu einem Schlüsselbegriff der Hegelschen Philosophie* (Frankfurt a.M.: Klostermann), pp. 43–58.

—— (2018b) *Hegel's Realm of Shadows. Logic as Metaphysics in the 'Science of Logic'* (Chicago: University of Chicago Press).

Pollok, K. (2008) '"An Almost Single Inference"—Kant's Deduction of the Categories Reconsidered', *Archiv für Geschichte der Philosophie* 90(3): 323–45.

—— (2013) 'Wie sind Erfahrungsurteile möglich?', in H. Lyre & O. Schliemann (eds) *Kants Prolegomena. Ein kooperativer Kommentar* (Frankfurt a.M.: Klostermann), pp. 103–25.

Popper, K. (2002) *Conjectures and Refutations* (London/New York: Routledge).

Prauss, G. (1973) 'Zum Wahrheitsproblem bei Kant', G. Prauss (ed.) *Kant. Zur Deutung seiner Theorie von Erkennen und Handeln* (Cologne: Kiepenheuer & Witsch), pp. 73–89.

Price, H. (2007) 'Causal Perspectivalism', in H. Price & R. Corry (eds) *Causation, Physics, and the Constitution of Reality. Russell's Republic Revisited* (Oxford: Oxford University Press), pp. 250–92.

Reinhold, K.L. (2011) *Essay on a New Theory of the Human Capacity for Representation*, trans. T. Mehigan & B. Empson (Berlin/New York: De Gruyter).

Robinson, H. (1994) 'Two Perspectives on Kant's Appearances and Things in Themselves', *Journal of the History of Philosophy* 32(3): 411–41.

Rosefeldt, T. (2012) 'Dinge an sich und der Außenweltskeptizismus. Über ein Missverständnis der frühen Kant-Rezeption', in D. Emundts (ed.) *Self, World, and Art. Metaphysical Topics in Kant and Hegel* (Berlin/New York), pp. 221–59.

—— (ms.) 'Kant on Appearances and Subject-Dependent Properties', unpublished paper.

Rosenkoetter, T. (2014) 'The Logical Home of Kant's Table of Functions', in D. Emundts & S. Sedgwick (eds) *Internationales Jahrbuch des Deutschen Idealismus/International Yearbook of German Idealism: Logik/Logic*, Band 12 (Berlin/Boston: De Gruyter), pp. 29–52.

Russell, B. (1948) *Human Knowledge, Its Scope and Limits* (London: Allen & Unwin).

Schear, J. (ed.) (2013) *Mind, Reason and Being-in-the-World. The McDowell-Dreyfus Debate* (London: Routledge).
Schönecker, D., D. Schulting & N. Strobach (2011) 'Kants kopernikanisch-newtonische Analogie', *Deutsche Zeitschrift für Philosophie* 59(4): 497–518.
Schulting, D. (2011) 'Kant's Idealism: The Current Debate', in D. Schulting & J. Verburgt (eds) *Kant's Idealism. New Interpretations of a Controversial Doctrine* (Dordrecht: Springer Science), pp. 1–25.
—— (2015) 'Probleme des "kantianischen" Nonkonzeptualismus im Hinblick auf die B-Deduktion', *Kant-Studien* 106(4): 561–80.
—— (2016a) Review of Sally Sedgwick, *Hegel's Critique of Kant. From Dichotomy to Identity* (Oxford: Oxford UP, 2012), *Kant-Studien* 107(2): 414–19.
—— (2016b) 'Critical Notice of Robert Pippin's "Logik und Metaphysik. Hegels 'Reich der Schatten'"', *Critique* (October issue), https://virtualcritique.wordpress.com/2016/10/16/critical-notice-of-robert-pippins-logik-und-metaphysik-hegels-reich-der-schatten/.
—— (ed.) (2016c) *Kantian Nonconceptualism* (London/New York: Palgrave Macmillan).
—— (2016d) Review of Corey Dyck, *Kant and Rational Psychology* (Oxford: Oxford UP, 2014), *Studi kantiani* XXIX: 185–91.
—— (2017a) *Kant's Radical Subjectivism. Perspectives on the Transcendental Deduction* (London/New York: Palgrave Macmillan).
—— (2017b) 'Kant's Idealism and Phenomenalism. A Critical Notice of Lucy Allais's *Manifest Reality. Kant's Idealism and His Realism*', *Studi kantiani* XXX: 191–202.
—— (2017c) 'Gap? What Gap?—On the Unity of Apperception and the Necessary Application of the Categories', in G. Motta & U. Thiel (eds), *Immanuel Kant: Die Einheit des Bewusstseins* (Berlin/New York: De Gruyter, 2017), pp. 89–113.
—— (2018a) 'Gaps, Chasms, and Things in Themselves: Reply to My Critics' (book symposium), *Kantian Review* 23(1): 131–43.
—— (2018b) *Kant's Deduction From Apperception. An Essay on the Transcendental Deduction of the Categories*, second and revised edition (Berlin/Boston: De Gruyter).
—— (2018c) 'Zelfbewustzijn, objectiviteit en idealisme. Over *Kant's Radical Subjectivism*' (book symposium), *Tijdschrift voor Filosofie* 80(2): 313–22.
—— (2018d) 'Repliek op de kritiek van De Boer, Blomme, Van den Berg en Spigt' (book symposium), *Tijdschrift voor Filosofie* 80(2): 363–78.
—— (2019) Review of Béatrice Longuenesse, *I, Me, Mine: Back to Kant and Back Again* (Oxford: Oxford UP, 2017), *Philosophical Review* 128(1): 107–11.
—— (forthcoming a) 'Apperception and Object. Comments on Mario Caimi's Reading of the Deduction' (book symposium), *Revista de Estudios Kantianos*.
—— (forthcoming b) 'Apperception, Objectivity, and Idealism', *Proceedings of the 13th International Kant Congress, Oslo 2019*.
—— (forthcoming c) Review of Robert Pippin, *Hegel's Realm of Shadows. Logic as Metaphysics in the 'Science of Logic'* (Chicago: University of Chicago Press, 2018), *Hegel Bulletin*.

—— (forthcoming d) Review of Alfredo Ferrarin, *Thinking and the 'I'. Hegel and the Critique of Kant* (Evanston: Northwestern UP, 2019), *Hegel Bulletin*.
—— (ms.) 'The Unity of Cognition and the Subjectivist *vs.* "Transformative" Approaches to the B-Deduction, Or, How To Read the *Leitfaden* (A79)'.
Sedgwick, S. (1992) 'Hegel's Treatment of Transcendental Apperception in Kant', *Owl of Minerva* 23(2): 151–63.
—— (1993) 'Pippin on Hegel's Critique of Kant', *International Philosophical Quarterly* XXXIII (3): 273–83.
—— (1997) 'McDowell's Hegelianism', *European Journal of Philosophy* 5(1): 21–38.
—— (2000) 'Hegel, McDowell, and Recent Defenses of Kant', *Journal of the British Society for Phenomenology* 31(3): 229–47.
—— (2001) '"Genuine" versus "Subjective" Idealism in Hegel's *Jenaer Schriften*', in R. Schumacher (ed.) *Idealismus als Theorie der Repräsentation?* (Paderborn: mentis), pp. 233–45.
—— (2004) 'Hegel on Kant's Idea of Organic Unity: The Jenaer Schriften', S: Doyé et al. (eds) *Metaphysik und Kritik* (Berlin and New York: De Gruyter), 285–98.
—— (2005) 'The Emptiness of the "I": Kant's Transcendental Deduction in *Glauben und Wissen*', in A. Arndt et al. (eds) *Hegel-Jahrbuch 2005. Glauben und Wissen. Dritter Teil* (Berlin: Akademie Verlag), pp. 171–5.
—— (2012) *Hegel's Critique of Kant. From Dichotomy to Identity* (Oxford: Oxford University Press).
Sellars, W. (1992) *Science and Metaphysics. Variations on Kantian Themes*, reprint [orig. 1968] (Atascadero: Ridgeview).
Smit, H. (2019) 'Kant's "I think" and the Agential Approach to Self-Knowledge', *Canadian Journal of Philosophy* 49(7): 980–1011.
Strawson, P.F. (1968) *The Bounds of Sense. An Essay on Kant's 'Critique of Pure Reason'*, 2nd printing (London: Methuen).
Thiel, U. (2011) *The Early Modern Subject. Self-Consciousness and Personal Identity from Descartes to Hume* (Oxford: Oxford University Press).
Tugendhat, E. (1997) *Selbstbewußtsein und Selbstbestimmung: Sprachanalytische Interpretationen*, 6th edition (Frankfurt a.M.: Suhrkamp).
Van Cleve, J. (1999) *Problems from Kant* (New York: Oxford University Press).
Warda, A. (1922) *Immanuel Kants Bücher* (Berlin: Breslauer).
Wolff, M. (1995) *Die Vollständigkeit der kantischen Urteilstafel* (Frankfurt a/M: Klostermann).
Wolff, R. (1973) *Kant's Theory of Mental Activity*, 2nd printing (Gloucester, MA: Peter Smith).
Wood, A. (2005) *Kant* (Oxford: Blackwell).
Wunderlich, F. (2005) *Kant und die Bewußtseinstheorien des 18. Jahrhunderts* (Berlin/New York: De Gruyter).

Index

absolute (idea), the, 166, 185, 190, 194, 199
absolute idealism, 5–6, 13–14, 142, 194, 198–9
absolute identity, 5, 152, 182–3, 185, 199
activity (*Tätigkeit*), 5, 7, 13, 48, 53, 56, 67, 70, 79, 109, 123, 130, 135, 139, 144, 148, 166, 181, 193, 208, 212, 214, 226
affection, 10, 40, 74, 88, 90–2, 97, 101, 111, 115–18, 127, 129–30, 132, 134–6, 138, 160, 173, 191, 212, 214, 220–1, 224
Allais, L., 104–5, 116, 144, 220, 223
Allison, H., 17, 24, 51, 120, 202
'altered way of thinking', 6, 17, 22, 24, 26, 31–2, 36–8, 42–3, 202–3, 207
Ameriks, K., 202–3, 217–21, 223
Analogies, the, 103, 106, 109
animal(s), 10, 52, 63, 68, 94, 96–113, 182, 211, 215–16, 224
animal awareness/consciousness/ perception, 10, 63, 96–105, 108–13, 211, 215–16, 224
anthropocentric fallacy, 19
anthropocentrism, 24, 202
anthropomorphic, 98, 103, 112
appearance, 4–5, 7, 11–12, 21, 23, 49, 51, 77, 79, 87–9, 91, 105, 115–22, 126–7, 135, 137, 139, 146, 149, 151, 157, 159, 191, 203, 205–6, 217–18, 222, 228
apperception, *passim*
Aristarchus of Samos, 34
Aristotelian, 179, 186, 195, 205
astronomy, 6, 16–17, 19–20, 22, 24, 33–7, 42, 44, 201–2, 205

Baum, M., 206
Baumgarten, A., 27, 47, 52, 54, 63, 66, 87, 209
Beiser, F., 129–30, 218–19
Berkeley, G., 4, 23, 25, 191, 203
Bird, G., 203
Bondeli, M., 219
Bowman, B., 201

Brandt, R., 52
Breazeale, D., 220

capacity to judge, the, 63, 67, 102, 191, 197, 211
Carl, W., 208
Cassam, Q., 204
categories, the, *passim*
causal, causality, 27, 31, 40, 97, 102, 104, 109, 117–18, 123, 188, 202
circularity, 9, 75–6, 213
clarity, clear, 53, 55–6, 58–61, 68–70, 137, 210–11
Collins, A., 51
complex, complexity, 10, 53, 101, 103, 105, 110, 122
Conant, J., 105, 226
Concept, the, 181, 197–8
conceptualism, conceptualist, 12, 103, 108, 141–3, 147, 149, 153–4, 161–2, 167, 194, 225
consciousness, *passim*
Copernican analogy, 6, 15–25, 37, 39, 42, 202–7
Copernican hypothesis, 4, 6, 14–19, 33, 35–6, 41–3, 45, 189, 192, 201–2, 228
Copernican revolution, 6, 15–20, 22, 24, 26, 33–7, 42, 93, 189, 201–5
Copernicus, N., 6, 15–25, 33–7, 39, 41–2, 44, 202–5, 207
correlationist, 167
cosmology, 19–22, 34–5, 202, 205
creature consciousness, 10, 96, 100–1, 103, 215

death, 51, 208
deduction, the (Transcendental) Deduction, viii, 1, 7–9, 11–13, 29, 43, 45, 49–50, 64, 66, 73, 75, 78, 81, 87, 89, 93–4, 96–7, 103–7, 109–10, 117, 121, 130, 142–3, 145–7, 149–51, 155–8, 160–2, 170–4, 176, 179–80, 184–6,

191–2, 195–7, 199–200, 204, 211, 218, 220–1, 224–7
Descartes, R., 3, 22, 72, 201
dialectic, 183, 185–6, 193, 198
distinct, distinctness, 55–8, 69–70, 104, 106, 108–9, 113, 127, 132–4, 136, 147–8, 157, 161, 167, 211, 218
Düsing, K., 213
Dyck, C., 57–8, 208

earth rotation, 16, 33–6, 42, 44, 201
empirical apperception, 48, 51, 66, 68, 73, 81, 87–8, 91, 208, 212
empirical psychology, 47, 51, 66, 88, 92
empiricism, 40, 94, 111, 126
Evans, G., 223
experience, *passim*

Fabbianelli, F., 219
Fichte, J.G., viii, 5, 7, 9, 11–12, 48, 74–80, 86, 90–1, 122, 150–3, 155, 161, 213, 223–4
forma dat esse rei, 42–4
formal intuition, 107, 159–60, 225
form(s) of intuition, 45, 90, 97, 131, 138, 158–60, 180–1, 184, 192, 214, 225
Friedman, M., 202

Gardner, S., 202
general logic, 13, 169–71, 174–9, 227
geocentric, geocentrism, 17, 23, 33–5, 42
Giladi, P., 187–9, 192–3, 195
Ginsborg, H., 214
God (divine), 5, 40, 137, 166, 199, 218, 221
Golob, S., 96–8, 100–2, 104–6, 108–11, 113, 215–16
Grüne, S., 110
Guyer, P., 17, 19, 205

Hanna, R., 176
Hanson, N., 15–18, 202
Hegel, G.W.F., viii–ix, 5, 7, 11–14, 48, 94, 112, 132, 141–4, 146, 150–3, 155–9, 161–2, 165–71, 173, 176–7, 179–90, 192–201, 207, 222–8
heliocentric, heliocentrism, 15, 17, 23–4, 33–4, 36, 42, 202–4
Henrich, D., 58, 71, 76–7, 213, 226
Horstmann, R.-P., 208

Houlgate, S., 13, 194, 228
Hume, D., 3
hypothesis, hypothetical method, 38, 42–3, 45, 82, 201, 206–7

idealism, 4–6, 11, 13–14, 23, 25–6, 50, 107, 115–17, 119, 122, 124–7, 131, 142, 150, 166, 168, 187–9, 191–2, 194, 196, 198–9, 203–4, 206, 217, 219, 222
identity, 5, 7–10, 13, 49, 58, 67, 73–81, 84–7, 112–13, 118, 127, 132, 151–2, 167–70, 172–3, 178, 180, 182–3, 185, 194, 199, 218, 222, 228
imagination, 89–90, 99–100, 102, 105, 107, 110, 156–7, 159, 162, 172–3, 175, 195, 197, 211–12, 223, 225, 226
Imhof, S., 218
immediacy, immediate, 53, 59, 69–70, 72–4, 78–9, 84, 87, 90–1, 93, 97, 103, 105, 110, 112–13, 134, 144, 146, 152, 157, 161, 183, 201, 208, 210, 223, 227
infants, 82, 97, 100, 104, 182
inner sense, 8, 10, 48, 51–2, 55, 62–3, 65–8, 73–4, 78, 81, 87–8, 90–2, 96, 99–100, 199, 208, 211–12, 214
intellectual intuition, 78–9, 86–7, 90, 95, 194
intentionality, 10, 97–9, 102, 108, 110–11, 113, 117, 147, 160–1, 170, 216
intransitive consciousness, 51, 101, 215
intuition, *passim*
intuitive intellect, 86, 225
'I think', the, 1, 9, 12, 49, 72–4, 76, 78, 80–4, 91, 94, 96, 151, 213, 216

Jankowiak, T., 217
Jorgensen, L., 55, 213
judgement, 58, 63–4, 96, 102–3, 111–12, 141, 144–5, 160–1, 167, 170–1, 174–6, 178–81, 184–6, 191, 197, 212, 214

Kanterian, E., 217
Kant-Laplace nebular hypothesis, 202
Kemp Smith, N., 24, 202–3
Klemme, H., 52, 209
knowledge, *passim*
Kreines, J., 13, 201
Kuhn, T., 34–6, 205

Land, T., 108
Langton, R., 116, 127, 217–18, 220
La Rocca, C., 204, 210
law of continuity, 8, 55, 61, 68–9, 209, 213
Leibniz, G.W., Leibnizian, viii, 3, 6, 8, 29, 47–8, 52–6, 61, 69, 87, 154, 161, 209, 213, 225
Leitfaden (guiding thread), 145, 160, 170, 176, 179, 223, 227
Locke, J., 3, 54, 221
Longuenesse, B., 104, 161, 216, 226

McDowell, J., 146, 167, 189, 196, 222–4, 226
Marshall, C., 218
Martin, C., 13, 201
mathematics, 3, 22, 24, 34–5, 38–9, 44, 168, 177, 184, 202, 204–5
Meier, G., 66, 209
Metaphysical Deduction, the, 170–1, 179, 227
metaphysical logic, 12–13, 165–6, 198, 201
metaphysical space, 107
metaphysics, 3–4, 6, 12–18, 20, 22–3, 25–31, 35–7, 39–41, 43–5, 53, 123, 165–9, 185–6, 189, 193–4, 201–2, 206
method, 22, 24–5, 31–3, 37–8, 42, 44–5, 53, 184, 186, 189, 197, 202–3, 205–6
Miles, M., 16–17, 24–5, 201–4
Moore, A., 169

Nagel, T., 215
Naragon, S., 209, 211, 215
natural science (physics), 24, 38, 53
Newton, I., 53
nonconceptual, nonconceptualism, 12, 96, 103–4, 107, 113, 142–9, 153, 158, 160, 174, 176, 180, 222–3, 225
noumenal, 76, 137, 139, 192, 218

object, *passim*
object-directedness, 102, 108, 113
objective validity, 3–4, 12, 20, 31, 104, 149–50, 171–2, 178, 180, 197
objectivity, 4, 10, 14, 27, 50, 63, 93–4, 96–7, 100, 111, 113, 117, 131–2, 146, 181, 186–91, 197, 215, 224
obscure, obscurity, 8, 52, 56, 59–62, 67–70, 210–11

Onnasch, E.-O., 218–19
Onof, C., 107, 159, 213–14, 217, 220, 225–7
ontology, 4, 6, 13, 17, 27–8, 30, 107, 122, 124, 138–9, 141, 166, 168, 189, 194, 199, 202, 204, 208, 217, 228

paradigm shift, 6, 18–19, 22, 24, 33–4, 42, 44
Paralogisms, the, 59, 61–2, 72–3, 76, 208, 214
perception, *passim*
perspective, 14, 17–19, 21–5, 30, 34, 40–2, 72, 97–8, 100, 103, 106–7, 113, 149–50, 153, 156, 161–2, 168–9, 171, 178–80, 182–4, 186–7, 189, 193, 197, 216
perspectivism, 18–25, 42, 202–3
petites perceptions, 55–6
phenomenal, phenomenalism, 10, 23–5, 50, 78, 96, 103, 106–7, 110, 113, 116–17, 119, 126, 139, 189, 203, 206, 218, 222
Philolaus of Croton, 205
Pippin, R., 3, 6, 7, 12–14, 48, 141–62, 165–84, 186, 194, 200–1, 213, 223–8
Pollok, K., 212
Popper, K., 25, 205
Prauss, G., 206
Price, H., 202
psychological, 2, 7, 23, 47–8, 51–2, 55, 61, 66, 69–70, 78, 86, 90, 92, 95, 122, 187, 207–8, 210, 219
psychological darkness, 61
Ptolemaic astronomy/system, 19–20, 24, 33–5, 202
Ptolemaic counter-revolution, 202

rational psychology, 51, 87
rationalism, rationalist, viii, 10, 26, 28–9, 34–5, 48, 50–1, 63, 65, 73, 87, 93, 96, 123, 135, 166, 194, 210, 225
realism, 4, 6, 14, 17, 93, 106, 116, 127, 131, 166, 168, 174, 187, 202, 220
reality, 13–14, 21–2, 26, 28–30, 35, 62, 128, 139, 167–8, 181, 185, 187–8, 190, 191–2, 197–200, 222
receptivity, 66, 89, 123, 128, 143–4, 146, 156, 159, 166, 223–4

reflection, 3, 9, 26–7, 29–30, 37, 54–5, 59, 73–4, 80, 82, 93–4, 186, 197, 209, 211
reflection philosophy, 94
reflection-theoretical, 73, 201
reflexivity, self-reflexivity, 3, 6–8, 10, 13, 26, 29, 31–2, 48–9, 54–7, 60, 67, 70, 79–80, 93–4, 98, 101–2, 108, 124, 166, 216
Refutation of Idealism, the, 89, 220
Reinhold, K.L., viii, 5, 10–11, 51, 115, 121–39, 207, 217–21
relation to (an) object, 21, 30, 41–2, 48, 63, 65, 67, 94, 104, 108, 110–11, 119, 134, 144, 149, 151, 156, 169, 171, 175–8, 206, 216, 223–4
representation, *passim*
representation of my representations, 57, 98
representationalism, representationalist, 5, 11, 23, 75, 121–2, 124, 129, 139, 195, 219
represent*ed*, a, 5, 11, 27, 40, 57, 112, 116–17, 123–32, 217
representing, a, 123–6, 128, 130
Robinson, H., 120
Rosefeldt, T., 116–17, 119, 218
Rosenkoetter, T., 227
Russell, B., 19, 24, 202

Sartre, J.-P., 216
Schear, J., 226
Schönecker, D., 205
science(s), 3, 10, 15–16, 21, 24–6, 28–9, 33, 36–9, 43–4, 53, 96, 110, 166, 184, 205–7
Sedgwick. S., 142–3, 150–2, 190, 192–3, 195, 222–5, 228
self-affection, 90–1, 214
self-consciousness, *passim*
self-intuition (*Selbstanschauung*), 78, 89–91
self-knowledge (of reason), 3, 9–10, 29, 31, 37, 41, 44, 71, 73–4, 86–7, 89–92, 98, 188, 206–7
Sellars, W., 11, 123, 126, 217
sensibility, *passim*
Smit, H., 215
solipsism, 188–9
soul, 5, 52–3, 55, 60, 62–3, 68, 79, 87, 123, 125–6, 208, 211–12

space, 21, 45, 65, 80, 95, 102, 104–11, 120–1, 128, 131, 137, 139, 147, 159, 162, 184, 186, 189, 192, 196, 210, 214, 217, 220, 225
spatial determination, 102, 107–10
speculative realism, 106, 168
Spinoza, B. de, 119
spontaneity, 66, 78–9, 84, 90, 143, 146, 156, 159, 176, 214, 223
Strawson, P. F., 30, 203, 216
subjectivism, 13–14, 18, 22, 100, 166, 187–9, 191, 207
substance, 3, 63, 73, 75–9, 87, 104, 119, 121, 123, 166, 168, 178, 204, 208, 218
synthesis, 7–8, 49, 58, 64, 76–8, 84–6, 89–92, 102, 104–5, 107–13, 145–6, 151, 157–8, 162, 172–3, 175, 177, 183, 195, 214, 223, 225–6

table of categories, the, 171
table of judgement, the, 171
Thiel, U., 7, 48, 53, 55, 57, 98
thing in itself, things in themselves, 4–5, 11–12, 14, 26, 28, 89, 91, 100, 115–22, 124–39, 150, 187–8, 190–2, 196, 206–8, 217–22, 228
transcendental, *passim*
transcendental apperception, *passim*
transcendental arguments, 30–1, 204, 216
transcendental content, 145, 173–7, 179
transcendental idealism, 4–6, 14, 119, 187, 196, 199
transcendental logic, 13–14, 28, 111, 169–72, 174–9, 196, 199, 222, 226–7
transcendental object, 110–11, 113, 133, 182
transcendental reflection, 26, 29–30
transcendental (Copernican) turn, the, 5–6, 19, 21, 24, 26, 30, 40, 52, 97–8, 100, 107, 120, 123, 202–4, 206
transitive consciousness, 99–101, 103, 215
'treatise of method', 32
truth, 4, 21, 31, 33, 39, 40–2, 45, 126, 138, 153–4, 166, 176–7, 199, 203, 206
Tugendhat, E., 74–5, 79–80, 85, 213

unconscious, unconsciousness, 51, 55, 59–61, 68–70, 94, 208, 211

Van Cleve, J., 24, 117, 203

Warda, A., 54, 209

Wolff, C., Wolffian, viii, 3, 6–8, 47–62, 67, 69, 87, 98, 201, 208–10, 219
Wolff, M., 170
Wolff, R., 51
Wood, A., 117, 217
Wunderlich, F., 60

www.ingramcontent.com/pod-product-compliance
Lightning Source LLC
Chambersburg PA
CBHW072141290426
44111CB00012B/1945